MONOGRAPHS OF THE
SOCIETY FOR RESEARCH IN
CHILD DEVELOPMENT

Serial No. 234, Vol. 58, Nos. 5–6, 1993

THE ARCHITECTURE AND DYNAMICS OF DEVELOPING MIND: EXPERIENTIAL STRUCTURALISM AS A FRAME FOR UNIFYING COGNITIVE DEVELOPMENTAL THEORIES

Andreas Demetriou
Anastasia Efklides
Maria Platsidou

WITH COMMENTARY BY
Robert L. Campbell

AND A REPLY BY THE AUTHORS

MONOGRAPHS OF THE SOCIETY FOR RESEARCH IN CHILD DEVELOPMENT
Serial No. 234, Vol. 58, Nos. 5–6, 1993

CONTENTS

ABSTRACT

DEMETRIOU, ANDREAS; EFKLIDES, ANASTASIA; and PLATSIDOU, MARIA. The Architecture and Dynamics of Developing Mind: Experiential Structuralism as a Frame for Unifying Cognitive Developmental Theories. With Commentary by ROBERT L. CAMPBELL; and a Reply by ANDREAS DEMETRIOU, ANASTASIA EFKLIDES, and MARIA PLATSIDOU. *Monographs of the Society for Research in Child Development*, 1993, **58**(5–6, Serial No. 234).

This *Monograph* presents a theory of cognitive development. The theory argues that the mind develops across three fronts. The first refers to a general processing system that defines the general potentials of mind to develop cognitive strategies and skills. The second refers to a hypercognitive system that governs self-understanding and self-regulation. The third involves a set of specialized structural systems (SSSs) that are responsible for the representation and processing of different reality domains. There are specific forces that are responsible for this organization of mind. These are expressed in the *Monograph* in terms of a set of five organizational principles. The developmental course of the major systems is outlined. Developmental change is ascribed by the theory to the interaction between the various systems. Different types of development require different change mechanisms.

Five studies are presented that provide empirical support for these postulates. Study 1 demonstrated the organizational power of principles and SSSs. Study 2 showed that the SSSs constrain the effect of learning. Study 3 established that the hypercognitive system does function as the interface between tasks and SSS-specific processes or between SSSs and general cognitive functions such as attention and memory. Study 4 investigated the relations between one of the components of the processing system, storage, and two different SSSs expressed via two different symbolic systems, namely, the numeric and the imaginal. Finally, Study 5 examined the interaction between the components of the processing system and the relations between each of these components and one SSS, namely, the quantitative-relational SSS. The theoretical implications of these studies with regard to general issues, such as the nature of representation, the causation of cognitive change, and individual differences in cognitive development, are discussed in the concluding chapter.

I. INTRODUCTION

Since Piaget, the study of cognitive development has focused on four major aspects of the growth and organization of cognitive abilities: their *structure*, their *timing*, their *mechanisms*, and their *causes*. These have been reflected in the four major questions that have directed research:

1. Into what kind of functional systems are cognitive abilities organized?
2. When do changes occur, and how long do they take to complete?
3. How are these changes effected and consolidated?
4. What causes changes in the abilities themselves as well as in their organizational systems?

The massive empirical evidence that had been collected by the 1970s has made it clear that the Piagetian answers to each of these four questions are not completely satisfactory (Brainerd, 1978; Elkind & Flavell, 1969; Flavell, 1985). As a result, several alternative theories have appeared in recent years, each motivated by the ambition to be more successful than classic Piagetian theory. Some of these theories have been called "neo-Piagetian" because they attempted to resolve the anomalies of Piagetian theory without rejecting its basic epistemological assumptions regarding the constructive and self-regulated nature of cognitive development. Such theories have also adopted some basic Piagetian notions that seemed either to stand up well to the test of time or to possess heuristic power, such as the notions of "stage" and "structure." The theory that we have been developing over the last 14 years belongs to this class (Demetriou, 1983, 1989, 1990; Demetriou & Charitides, 1986; Demetriou & Efklides, 1979, 1981, 1985, 1987, 1989, in press; Demetriou, Efklides, Papadaki, Papantoniou, & Economou, in press; Demetriou, Gustafsson, Efklides, & Platsidou, 1992; Demetriou, Platsidou, Efklides, Metallidou, & Shayer, 1991; Efklides & Demetriou, in press; Efklides, Demetriou, & Gustafsson, 1992; Shayer, Demetriou, & Pervez, 1988). To avoid confusion, however, we must stress that our theory is by no means tied to the classic Piagetian paradigm insofar as basic theoretical concepts or empirical methods are concerned; in fact, in some respects it is closer to differential and modern cognitive psychology than to Piagetian thinking. Consequently, before presenting the theory itself, we spell out how it relates to some of the dominant epistemological traditions of modern psychology.

The theory we propose remains close to classic Piagetian theory in at least two respects. First, our system fully endorses the Piagetian assumption that human intelligence is both the means and the product of self-regulated and constructive interaction between the individual and his or her environment (see Piaget, 1971). Second, the cognitive phenomena we investigate are the same as those originally brought into focus by Piaget, such as thought that is classificatory, quantitative, causal, etc. In fact, our theory originated in an attempt to cope with the problem of inconsistency of performance attained on Piagetian tasks that are presumed to tap the same underlying operational structure (Demetriou & Efklides, 1979, 1981). Thus, even in its present formulation, the theory may be viewed as seeking to model the same categories of reason that attracted the interest of the young Piaget.

Insofar as method is concerned, our theory is closer to the developmental tradition in some respects and to the psychometric tradition in others. We usually work with relatively large numbers of subjects on group tests that involve many different aspects of thought activity. The construction of these tests is inspired by epistemological-developmental rather than psychometric concerns in that they address different cognitive operations (e.g., isolation of variables, proportionality, etc.) and not traditionally defined dimensions of ability (e.g., fluid or crystallized intelligence). Moreover, the structuring of item difficulty is referenced by criterion rather than by norm; that is, it is set by assumptions regarding the developmental status of the cognitive process represented by an item rather than by success rates of a given population on the item.

It should be noted that, by its very nature, group testing is based on the assumption that thought activity is organized along a number of specifiable dimensions of ability on which individuals can be differentiated. That is, the fact that some individuals may be better, for example, on spatial tasks and others on verbal tasks is taken to imply that the processing of spatial tasks is based on different processes than those underlying the processing of the verbal tasks. In other words, it is assumed that reliable patterns of individual differences may be used as signs indicating the boundaries among cognitive structures. We accept this assumption.

The data that we obtain are usually analyzed by a multiplicity of methods in which factorial approaches, especially modern confirmatory factor analysis and structural equation modeling, always play a major role. Traditional developmental methods, such as clinical interviews and longitudinal examinations, and/or experimental methods, such as training experiments, are also used in order to cross-validate hypotheses about structure and development (Demetriou & Efklides, in press; Demetriou et al., 1992; Efklides et al., 1992; Shayer et al., 1988).

As regards the interpretative constructs, the system is again eclectic. Depending on the specific theoretical needs, it draws on developmental and psychometric traditions or on modern cognitive science in general and information-processing theories in particular. The link between our system and modern theoretical approaches has often been provided by other neo-Piagetian theories of cognitive development, especially those of Case (1985) and Pascual-Leone (1988). The componential analysis of intelligence structures pioneered by Sternberg (1977) has motivated our search for families of component abilities, even though the components that Sternberg proposes differ from those specified in our theory. In sum, our theory is inspired by the assumption that the developing mind can be understood only if the strong points of the developmental, the psychometric, and the cognitivist traditions are allowed to converge and inform each other.

The primary aim of this *Monograph* is to elaborate the theory we propose so that the answers it has provided over the years and under different experimental conditions may be integrated into a comprehensive system. Evidently, it is neither possible nor legitimate to ignore answers proposed by other theorists; hence, a second aim of this *Monograph* is to integrate our theory with the other neo-Piagetian theories of cognitive development wherever this is conceptually possible or empirically sound. In particular, the relations between our theory and those of Bickhard (Campbell & Bickhard, 1986), Case (1985), Fischer (1980), Flavell (1988), Halford (1982), and Pascual-Leone (1970; Pascual-Leone & Goodman, 1979) will be discussed in some detail. We shall also attempt to relate our proposed model to current literature that is concerned with the architecture and functioning of the cognitive system in problem-solving situations.

The strategy of presentation is as follows. First, in Chapter I, we outline our general model of the developing intellect, basing our account on the research conducted in our laboratory between 1977 and 1987. The following chapters describe a series of five studies that we conducted in the last 5 years whose aim was to test the original model and extend it so as to accommodate phenomena with which we had not dealt at the beginning. In the final chapter, we propose some general conclusions regarding the nature of cognitive structures and development; these are based on the studies presented in this *Monograph* and may be taken as our present answers to the four basic questions we posed above.

II. THE ARCHITECTURE OF DEVELOPING INTELLECT

THE THREE DIMENSIONS OF DEVELOPING INTELLECT

Developing intellect may be construed as a three-dimensional concept. In its broadest definition, its vertical dimension represents the commonalities and differences that may exist between the variants $x_1, \ldots, x_n$ of a given ability X and that are acquired at times $t_1, \ldots, t_n$, respectively. Defined more strictly, these variants may be regarded as levels $l_1, \ldots, l_n$ of a necessary developmental sequence that are always acquired in the order $(l - 1) \rightarrow (l) \rightarrow (l + 1)$. In such cases, it is assumed that subsequent levels evolve from (or are constructed on) the preceding levels through a transformation mechanism that renders the system more efficient vis-à-vis whatever aspect of the environment requires the use of ability X. When this stricter condition is met, theorists ascribe vertical structure to development (cf. Wohlwill, 1973).

The horizontal dimension represents "the relationship between vertically structured sequences. Specifically, horizontal structure is said to exist under two conditions. First, a *set of abilities X . . . Z* advance concurrently along their level sequence so that a given level l_i of each is acquired within the same time interval. Second, all abilities at the given level l_i share a minimum set of common functional properties which makes them equivalent to each other. Horizontal structure is ascribed to this common background" (Demetriou & Efklides, 1988, p. 204). The term "ability" refers here to any organized set of mental schemes, rules, or operations that are brought to bear on a relatively broad conceptual domain; one may refer, for example, to "numerical," "classification," or "hypothesis formation" ability.

The third dimension basically represents the content $c_1, \ldots, c_n$ to which level l_i of an ability X may be applied at time t_i. Thus, for example, numerical ability may be applied to understanding the value of money, mailing addresses, bus numbers, and, of course, standard arithmetic problems. This dimension may also represent the symbolic means $sm_1, \ldots, sm_n$ through which an ability is expressed or implemented: a person may represent to herself, or convey to others, her understanding of number in numbers, words, pictures, or even gestures. Consequently, the third dimension may be used to indicate the conceptual and/or symbolic depth characterizing a given ability X at a given level l_i (see Demetriou & Efklides, 1981, 1988).

THEORIES OF INTERDIMENSIONAL RELATIONS

Theoretically, the relations among the three dimensions may range from complete interdependence to complete orthogonality. Thus, implicitly or explicitly, the specification of these relations has always been the central problem of cognitive developmental research. Notwithstanding the risk of oversimplification, three kinds of models have been proposed to account for these relations: vertical dimension dominance models (V-models); horizontal dimension dominance models (H-models); and equidimensional models (E-models).

V-Models

Piagetian theory exemplifies this type of model. In brief, the main Piagetian postulate (see Piaget, 1973; Piaget & Inhelder, 1967) is that the self-regulated transformation of a tightly organized set of mental operations that occurs with increasing age (the vertical dimension) controls the nature and transformation of many different abilities (such as classification, seriation, causality, social understanding—i.e., the horizontal dimension) and content domains as well as of symbolic faculties (such as language, imagery, and drawing—i.e., the depth dimension). In other words, the Piagetian solution almost completely reduces the horizontal and the depth dimensions to the vertical one; the concept of horizontal décalage was proposed ad hoc and never actually integrated into the theory (see Pinard & Laurendau, 1969; Wohlwill, 1973).

One might argue that Piaget did in fact do justice to the dimensionality of thought by organizing his empirical research around such different conceptual domains as the development of mathematical (Piaget, 1952), categorical (Inhelder & Piaget, 1964), spatial (Piaget, Inhelder, & Sheminska, 1960), and causal-experimental thinking (Inhelder & Piaget, 1958). This is indeed true. However, Piaget (1973) always regarded himself as the theorist of the epistemic subject. According to his definition, the "epistemic subject" refers to the general mechanisms of understanding that are common to all humans of the same age. Thus, individual differences or domain variations in understanding are noise factors hindering the specification of the epistemic state of a given age rather than integral factors of developing mind that need to be studied and explained in their own right. As a result, he always strove to specify the common operational core underlying different domains. Even when faced with evidence that cognitive performance is much less consistent than would be expected on the basis of the notion of *structure d'ensemble* (Flavell & Wohlwill, 1969), Piaget did not abandon his conviction that there should be a system of general rules governing the organization of different domains of knowledge and even of such dynamic functions as understanding (Piaget, 1978) or the grasp of consciousness (Piaget, 1974). Instead, he argued that a different, more basic system than that of symbolic logic, which he used originally, may be needed, proposing category theory as a better candidate (Piaget, 1979).

In our view, it is precisely this conviction that empirical evidence has shown to be untenable. A number of "neo-Piagetian" theorists, however, sought to resolve the anomalies of the Piagetian model by redefining the vertical dimension and abandoning the strict logical/operational definition of successive developmental stages in favor of a procedural/functional one. According to these theorists, the successive stages are constrained by a specifiable upper limit of mental power (Pascual-Leone, 1970), or of short-term storage space (Case, 1985), or of primary memory (Halford, 1988). In other words, these theorists argued that the limitations of information-processing capacity determine both the kind and the complexity of concepts that an individual can comprehend or invent at any level l_i. In fact, Pascual-Leone has recently gone so far as to argue, like Piaget, that mental power constrains the construction of such diverse aspects of behavior as motor skills (Pascual-Leone, 1988) and linguistic performance (Johnson, Fabian, & Pascual-Leone, 1989).

These theories ascribe the undeniable variability between abilities and concepts to one or more of the following reasons. First, while the abilities or concepts appear to tap the same capacity level, they actually do not. Second, even when they do tap the same capacity level, the individual associates them with different levels either for idiosyncratic reasons such as cognitive style (Pascual-Leone & Goodman, 1979) or because of differential learning opportunities, support, and familiarity. Fischer (Fischer & Farrar, 1988) in particular has elaborated extensively on how environmental support and practice may make an individual oscillate within a zone of proximal development. This zone is defined with reference to a single hierarchy of skill levels to which all abilities and concepts may, in principle, be reduced. Therefore, the functional levels that define a person's zone of proximal development are actually nothing more than a performance array corresponding to the supposedly "real levels" of a grand hierarchy. In sum, the neo-Piagetian models, like the Piagetian one, reduce the horizontal and depth dimensions of development to the vertical one, albeit in a more elegant way.

H-Models

Disenchantment with Piagetian theory, together with the rise of modern cognitive science (Gardner, 1985), has led many developmental researchers to what we have called "the subject-matter science" (Demetriou & Efklides, 1988, p. 205). The common assumption of models belonging to this "science" is that the peculiarities of different knowledge domains or symbolic systems matter more than any possible underlying domain-free structural characteristics. In effect, theory and research are directed to specifying the "mental models" that best capture different conceptual systems at both the macro- and the microdevelopmental levels (cf. Gentner & Stevens, 1983). As developmental constructs, H-models provide elaborate descriptions of the processes through which a "novice" is transformed into an "expert" in particular knowledge domains (cf. Carey, 1985; Chi, 1978). These processes are considered to be practically domain specific, although they are believed to be theoretically transferable across domains. Clearly, these models devalue the vertical dimension in favor of the other two. In so doing, they provide a wealth of findings and descriptions regarding the microstructure of the horizontal and the depth dimensions; however, they fall short of concepts that would help pinpoint and understand interdimensional relations.

E-Models

These models stand between the two dominance models discussed above; their assumption is that, in principle, the three dimensions are equally important as organizational pivots of developing intellect. Thus, instead of being reductionist, E-models attempt to specify the three dimensions vis-à-vis each other. In contrast to V-models, E-models are not directed at delineating a series of formal levels along a single developmental hierarchy. Instead, they aim at tracing the developmental trajectories of different cognitive structures and specifying in what respects the levels of different sequences that are acquired at the same age phase may be similar and in what respects they may be different. In contrast to H-models, E-models are directed at delineating structural boundaries and specifying integral components rather than task-specific representations. In contrast to both of the other types, E-models are therefore more sensitive to both interdimensional commonalities and intradimensional variations. The models proposed by Feldman (1980) and by Turiel and Davidson (1985) as well as our own model fall into this category. This is the model that we present in what follows.

7

THE CONSTITUENTS OF EXPERIENTIAL STRUCTURALISM

By definition, an E-model should be able to do justice to all three dimensions of developing intellect. Using Lakatos's (1978) terms, experiential structuralism is best described as a research program that involves several families of theories rather than a single theory. Specifically, it involves three distinct families of theories, each having as its chief concern the phenomena of cognitive organization and change that are related to one of the three dimensions (i.e., vertical, horizontal, and depth development).

The first family of theories is concerned with the principles of cognitive organization. These principles aim to explain why human cognition is multi- instead of unidimensional and to specify why it tends to construct the particular structures it does out of its interactions with the environment. The principles of cognitive organization may thus be regarded as the hard core of experiential structuralism: they underlie the assumption that multiple dimensions and structures do exist, and they show how one has to go about pinpointing the boundaries between different structural systems. Consequently, these principles specify the entries to be placed along the three dimensions.

The second family of theories is concerned with describing the cognitive structures and substructures as well as with the ways in which they can be used by the thinker. In other words, this family of theories aims to describe the composition and functioning of each cognitive structure over different contents and symbolic media as a smoothly running unit. Therefore, they are mostly concerned with the specification of the second (horizontal) and the third (depth) dimensions of developing intellect.

The third family of theories aims to describe each structure and substructure along the time dimension and to explain why and how they change. Two kinds of theories are contained in this family. One consists of descriptive theories that chart the nature and functioning of different structures and components at successive phases of the life cycle. The second involves explanatory theories that aim to specify the causes that activate change in one or more structures and the mechanisms used to implement the transformation of a structure from a given level l to a subsequent level $l + 1$. Hence, this third family of theories is mainly related to the vertical dimension.

To return to the four questions raised at the beginning of this *Monograph*, theory building with regard to the principles of cognitive organization (the first family of theories) and with regard to the composition of mental structures (the second family of theories) would generate answers primarily related to the first question, which asks about the kinds of systems into which cognitive abilities are organized. Therefore, these two families of theories provide the framework for understanding the architecture of mind. The third family of theories is mostly concerned with the last three questions and therefore with the description and the causation of change (i.e., the when, how, and why of development). Therefore, this family of theories would aim to highlight the dynamics of developing mind.

THE PRINCIPLES OF COGNITIVE ORGANIZATION

The five general principles that we discuss below are those of (1) domain specificity, (2) formal-procedural (or operating-computational) specificity, (3) symbolic bias, (4) subjective equivalence-distinctness, and (5) functional-developmental specificity of cognitive components, skills, or processes. We view these principles as the organizational pivots of developing cognition in that they refer to the conditions under which particular cognitive components, skills, or processes are fused together into broader and more efficient *specialized structural systems* (SSSs).

These systems are called *experiential* "because (a) they reflect the way the person has organized the facts or events he/she has observed or interacted with, (b) they are more or less so felt, and (c) possibly so cognized by the person" (Demetriou & Efklides, 1988, p. 175). These structures can also be demonstrated experimentally because they constrain the ways in which persons encode, represent, process, and solve problems. Epistemologically speaking, the five principles indicate that we define psychology itself as being at the same time the science of behavior, of experience, and of the experience of experience.

The Principle of Domain Specificity

This principle is based on three fundamental assumptions. The first is that reality is variable and multifaceted. It consists of elements—be they objects, persons, or events—that bear properties differing in physical identity and functioning. The particular nature of the properties that define these elements constrains the type and range of relations by which they can be interconnected. "Therefore, a set of elements bearing on the same properties and being connected by the same type of relations constitute a reality domain which is psychologically different from other domains involving elements with different properties and relations" (Demetriou & Efklides, 1988, p. 195).

The second assumption is that the individual and reality are structurally tuned. This implies that the person tends to organize his interactions with reality into structural systems that preserve the dynamic and figural peculiarities of different reality domains. It is in this sense that the structural

9

systems are regarded as *specialized*—they originate from and direct the person's interactions with special reality domains.

The third assumption is that any reality element may be characterized by sets of different properties. This implies that any element may be part of several reality domains at the same time. The conclusion is straightforward. Reality domains are to be defined with reference to the properties to which the individual attends rather than with reference to the elements themselves. The person's intentions and/or interpretations are consequently of paramount importance in determining which "reality domain" is attended to and, therefore, which specialized structural system is activated. Evidently, this third assumption has crucial implications concerning issues such as the preservation of the structural and functional autonomy of the SSSs, their possible coordination, and the role of the individual as well as of the cultural/social context of knowledge in this regard. These issues are discussed in the concluding chapter of the *Monograph*.

The Principle of Formal-Procedural Specificity

This principle follows directly from the principle of domain specificity: if the different specialized structural systems represent different kinds of subject-object interaction networks, one may assume that they constitute different operating/processing systems. In other words, the mental manipulations and/or transformations associated with a given SSS must be such that their application to the relevant reality domain can recover and/or preserve this and only this domain's elements and relations. Otherwise, confusion between reality domains, and all the ensuing negative consequences, would follow.

Consequently, different specialized structural systems are characterized by different formal properties regarding all four important aspects of the problem-solving process: the representation of the problem space (e.g., binary-propositional vs. holistic-imaginal); the definition of the information units relevant to the problem (e.g., alphanumeric digits vs. spatial coordinates); the definition of the operations to be performed on the units (e.g., negation or conjunction of propositions vs. mental rotation or enlargement of an image); and the evaluation of the outcome obtained (e.g., the truth value of an argument vs. the veridicality of an image). An attempt to specify the formal properties of different SSSs has been made elsewhere (see Demetriou & Efklides, 1988).

The Principle of Symbolic Bias

Symbolic systems and subsystems are tools of representation and communication; that is, they are used to encode reality elements and relations so that these can be accurately recalled and efficiently operated on, independently of time and space limitations. Symbol systems are also used to convey one's interpretation of elements and relations to other persons. To be able to preserve this double role, symbol systems must preserve the peculiarities of different reality domains and, in effect, of different subject-object interaction networks. Therefore, to the extent that the principles of domain and formal-procedural specificity hold true, the principle of symbolic bias of the specialized structural systems also follows. That is, each SSS is biased toward the symbolic system or subsystem that is more conducive to the representation of the properties and relations of its own reality domain, thus allowing the efficient application of its own operating processes to the elements of the reality domain concerned.

Three points need to be underscored with regard to symbolic bias. First, the objects of symbolism are the properties of elements and the relations among these properties rather than the elements themselves. Therefore, the same reality element may be encoded in several symbol systems, depending on which of its properties are being considered. For example, an element may be taken as just a digit to be placed along a numerical dimension, a property to be classified into a class hierarchy, or a cause to explain a given result. Second, the same property or relation may be encoded in several symbol systems. For example, numerosity may be expressed in gestures, images, words, or numbers. Third, different properties or relations may be encoded in the same symbol system. For example, a causal relation and a plain covariation may both be verbally encoded; however, one of the possible alternatives would always be closer than the other to capturing all the characteristics of the relevant properties or relations, and the SSS concerned would be biased toward that alternative. This possibility of alternating between symbol systems appears conducive to enabling the person both to discriminate the boundaries between different SSSs and to discover when and how they may be interrelated and intercoordinated.

The Principle of Subjective Equivalence-Distinctness of Abilities

This principle is cumulatively derived from the first three. Specifically, a structurally (first principle), computationally (second principle), and symbolically (third principle) variable and multifaceted intellect will usually operate under conditions of uncertainty, provided that no overlearned response has already been fabricated. This is usually the case with problem-solving situations. Under these conditions, efficient cognitive functioning raises the question of how the person comes to make reasonably correct decisions about the structure, computational procedure, etc. that she is required to bring to bear on the problem. In other words, how does the individual manage to navigate in the ocean of conflicting mental states that ambiguous situations tend to create?

Piaget's (1971, 1974) answer to the question of self-management in problem-solving situations was built around the notion of logical necessity. According to Bickhard (1988), this approach reduces all knowledge to logicomathematical structures and essentially disregards adaptable knowledge as being a flexible system that enables the thinker to construct differentiable representations of potential environments. Furthermore, it minimizes the active role of the thinker as a meaning-making system (Kuhn, 1983). Even the "grasp of consciousness" (Piaget, 1974) is never there when needed because each stage can become the object of consciousness only at subsequent stages. Thus, from the point of view of the utility of consciousness, in Piagetian theory the developing person is condemned to chasing his tail forever.

In fact, this criticism applies equally to all neo-Piagetian V-models that do not provide for what Kuhn (1983) has termed the "higher-order executive-2" (see also Campbell & Bickhard, 1986), namely, a mechanism that would enable the person to understand what a problem is about and hence decide what strategies to activate and how to apply them. It has to be emphasized, however, that this problem is endemic to V-models because of their very nature. Such models do not face the problem of "mental self-government"—to use Sternberg's (1988) terms—because the dominating strategies and the ensuing solutions to problems are always derivatives of the sole and omnipotent cognitive structure—be it logically (Piaget), functionally (Fischer), or quantitatively (Pascual-Leone) defined—that is available at a given point in time (Demetriou & Efklides, 1990). One of the issues at stake for all these theories is to specify the factors that either hinder or facilitate the structural organization or capacity available for processing the input and producing an outcome at the respective level of complexity.

The problem does not actually arise in the H-models because these relegate strategy selection to domain guidance. At the extreme, these models, which are today dominated by information-processing approaches, would resort to associationist interpretations regarding strategy selection (e.g., Siegler, 1988). Thus, even when elaborating on metacognition, they refer to it as "just a label on another box in the information processing boxology" (Campbell & Bickhard, 1986, p. 88).

The analysis presented above implies that the developing person is programmed to experience her cognitive encounters accurately enough to make the differentiations required for decisions concerning the most appropriate course of mental or overt action vis-à-vis the particular characteristics and demands of the problem at hand. In practice, this principle implies that cognitive experiences that differ from each other according to the three principles listed above are subjectively distinct: the greater the number of dimensions on which two mental states differ from each other (reality domain, computational specificity, symbolic bias), the more different will they be felt to be and/or cognized about by the subject. In the absence of such differences, mental states become subjectively equivalent. We regard this principle to be one of the sine qua non conditions of an adaptable relation among mental life, behavior, and reality—that is, of a relation that satisfies the "best interests" of the person in both the short and the long run. Evidently, a relation of this kind is both a cause and an effect of development. The principle that aims to capture the general characteristics of development is examined next.

The Principle of Developmental Variation

The four principles listed above conjointly determine the general characteristics of development, namely, that development is bound to produce intra- and interindividual variation concurrently with commonalities owing to the very nature of subject-object relations as well as the within-subject organization.

By definition, advancing time covaries with increasing experience. However, the time t devoted to interaction with a given reality domain Dm_i is necessarily withheld from possible interactions with other reality domains Dm_{N-i}. Therefore, with respect to time t, the knowledge of and interaction facility with Dm_i would be privileged relative to the domains Dm_{N-i}. However, there will also always be experience of experience: the organism gets to know how it is connected to reality, how it can attribute reality elements to its representations, how it can mobilize different mental functions for the sake of particular mental goals, and, at the least, how it feels to have a processing system activated and running. This implies that any organism-reality interaction concurrently generates both domain-specific and organism-specific knowledge and skills. The latter type of knowledge and skills can, at least indirectly, be transferred over different domains because it permits the individual to become more knowledgeable and efficient in self-understanding and -management.

It is highly improbable that an individual would either distribute his time evenly across different reality domains or never come across a given domain Dm_i. If this assumption is true, then two implications follow: while intra- and interindividual variation would be the rule in development, it is also probable that there would exist a certain range to this variation. This range would be increasingly limited as a function of the growth of the importance of self-understanding and -management, together with that of the possible operation of a central capacity construct (see Case, 1985; Fischer, 1980; Halford, 1988; Pascual-Leone, 1988).

13

The term "range of variation" may be reminiscent of Vygotsky's (1978) concept of "zone of proximal development" as it has been integrated in Fischer's theory (Fischer & Silvern, 1985). However, it should be underscored that the two terms are not identical. In our theory, "variation" refers to the condition of being at nonequivalent levels of two or more developmental sequences whose levels correspond to the same age but are not the same either structurally or functionally. In Fischer's theory, however, it refers to the condition of having attained different levels of the *same* hierarchy over different contents.

SPECIALIZED STRUCTURAL SYSTEMS

The following description of five specialized structural systems aims to demonstrate how they differ from each other with reference to the organizational principles discussed above. It must be stressed that these particular five systems (as well as the two domain-free systems to be described later) were empirically identified in a number of cross-sectional as well as longitudinal, and experimental as well as psychometric, studies that were analyzed by a number of different methods, such as factor analysis (exploratory or confirmatory), prediction analysis, and analysis of discrimination levels (see Demetriou, 1990; Demetriou & Efklides, 1985, 1989; Demetriou et al., in press; Efklides & Demetriou, in press; Efklides et al., 1992; Shayer et al., 1988). The description of the five specialized structural systems gives substance to the first two families of theories mentioned above. This is so because it exemplifies how the different characteristics and demands of different aspects of the environment interact with the developing mind to produce structures that specialize in the representation and processing of each aspect. Table 1 summarizes the modal characteristics established for the different systems in relation to the organizational principles presented above as well as the traditional tasks representative of each system.

1. The Qualitative-Analytic Specialized Structural System

This SSS involves those abilities that enable an individual to decipher and/or operate on categorical, matrix, and serial structures. As an operating system, this SSS is analytic in that it attempts to disentangle "real objects" from "pure properties." For example, the property of being "green" or "red," "square" or "triangular," "tiny" or "huge," always coexists with other properties. In fact, class inclusion research (Inhelder & Piaget, 1964; Markman & Callanan, 1984) has shown that construction of a versatile analytic system able to overcome the strong gestalt effects exerted by the inevitable

TABLE 1

The Modal Characteristics of the Five Specialized Structural Systems (SSSs)

Characteristics of Each Specialized Structural System

SSSs	Application Domain	Component Abilities	Task Loadings	Modal Inquiring Systems	Symbolic Bias
Quantitative-relational	Quantifiable reality	Quantitative specification and representation. Dimensional-directional construction. Dimensional-directional coordination	Measurement, number, conservation, physical equilibrium (e.g., balance), and proportionality tasks	Leibnizian: strict deductive systems operating on well-defined problems	Mathematical symbolism
Qualitative-analytic	Categorical, matrix, and serial structures	Analysis of qualitative structures in their properties. Disembedding of properties and restructuring according to one or more criteria	Classification, seriation, class inclusion, matrices, analogical reasoning tasks	Leibnizian (e.g., class inclusion) and Lockean: inductive systems generalizing from sense data (e.g., concept formation, matrices)	The static/declarative components of language (e.g., nouns)
Imaginal-spatial	Reality that can be projected onto the mental buffer holistically	Addition and subtraction of details; integration; reformation and/or transformation; rotation; referential coordination	Piagetian mental imagery tasks, coordination of perspectives, spatial reasoning tasks	Any	Mental images
Causal-experimental	Interactive and causal structures	Binary combinations; hypothesis formation; experimentation (i.e., isolation of variables); model construction	Combinatorial, permutation, isolation of variables, interpretation of ready-made experiments; design of complex experiments, theory formation tasks	Leibnizian (e.g., combinations); Lockean (e.g., hypothesis formation); Kantian: multimodal, synthetic systems integrating the other systems into internally consistent holistic perspectives (e.g., model construction)	The dynamic procedural components of language (e.g., verbs)
Verbal-propositional	Formal/mental relations among logically constructed entities	Selective repression of semantic networks unrelated to the argument processed and assembly of the related semantic elements	Syllogistic and propositional reasoning tasks	Any. Also Hegellian: it recognizes, defines, and accepts logical contradiction	The logical/syntactic components of language (e.g., "if . . . then," "either . . . then," "either . . . or," etc.)

coexistence of properties in the real world is a long and cumbersome process.

As a representational system, the qualitative-analytic SSS ignores the quantitative aspects of the properties it processes and focuses on their qualitative aspects. In so doing, it produces the networks of declarative and categorical knowledge that we construct about the world we live in. The system of "natural kind" terms seems particularly accurate in this regard (e.g., terms such as "cat" vs. "animal" are more apt to reveal their class inclusion relations than terms denoting classes defined by convention such as "red things" vs. "square things"). This is possibly the reason why inductive reasoning with natural kind terms is efficient from as early as 3–4 years of age (Gelman & Markman, 1987).

2. The Quantitative-Relational Specialized Structural System

This SSS is concerned with the quantifiable aspects of reality. As such, it is relational in nature because any quantity Q consists of other quantities $q_i, \ldots, q_n$, and it exists as a quantity Q only in relation to other quantities $Q \pm 1$. As an operating system, the quantitative-relational SSS involves abilities that enable the thinker to (re)construct the quantitative relations between elements varying along one or more dimensions as well as the relations between the dimensions themselves. This system is considered to involve the following three components.

Abilities of quantitative specification and representation.—These enable the person to see reality as composed of aggregate systems whose basic property is simply the *increase, decrease,* or *redistribution* of elements independently of the particular properties characterizing the elements. The cornerstone of this component is the four basic arithmetic operations. The formation of these operations is based on the subject's "quantifying" actions on reality (e.g., bringing in and removing, sharing, counting, measuring, etc.). The basic characteristic of these actions is that they transform different reality elements into equivalent enumerable units by purifying them of their particular characteristics; for example, the specific properties of objects are largely irrelevant to the action of bringing them together or distributing them among three children. The more advanced abilities to be described below are based on the intercoordination of the basic quantification abilities.

Abilities of dimensional-directional construction.—These enable the individual to reduce the first-level quantitative constructs that emerge from the functioning of the first component into dimensions and to grasp the direction (increase or decrease), scaling (e.g., arithmetic, geometric, logarithmic, etc.), or form (e.g., linear or curvilinear) of their variation. Thus, they may be regarded as the foundation of mathematical thinking. The construction of metric systems with reference to concepts such as weight, height, distance, etc. is evidently closely tied to the development of these abilities.

Abilities of dimensional-directional coordination.—These are applied on the dimensions generated by the second component with the aim of enabling the thinker to specify their possible covariations. It is these abilities that make it possible to engage in complex mathematical thinking, such as proportional and probabilistic reasoning.

The domain of application of the quantitative-relational SSS biases that SSS to a symbolic system that would be conducive to fixing and preserving the mentally constructed dimensions as elements of further thought activity independently of their original external referents. Thus, mathematical symbolism becomes necessary as a means for the representation and manipulation of elements whose particular properties are irrelevant to processing.

3. The Causal-Experimental Specialized Structural System

This specialized structural system "is directed to the processing of those causal reality structures which have a minimum degree of complexity, so that a minimally disciplined search is required if the relations between elements are to be located and specified. So defined, the [causal-experimental SSS] enables the person to disembody the sought-after causal structure from a broader coexistence structure in which it is embedded" (Demetriou & Efklides, 1988, p. 185). In other words, this system enables the individual to dissociate causal relations from the more general structures of coexistence in which they are embedded. In the service of this general function, the causal-experimental SSS involves combinatorial, hypothesis-formation, experimentation, and model-construction abilities.

Combinatorial abilities function as the means used exhaustively to define the broader coexistence structure that one would have to operate on in order to generate all possible relations among the elements of which the causal ones are a subset.

Hypothesis-formation abilities enable the person provisionally to differentiate the conceived combinations into categories of possible causal relations. At a general level, the relations between a possible causal factor and a given result fall in one of the following five categories: necessary and sufficient; necessary and not sufficient; not necessary and sufficient; not necessary and not sufficient; or negative or incompatible. Hypothesis-formation abilities enable the person to deduce testable predictions about possible causal connections between the elements involved in a coexistence structure on the basis of the information available.

Experimentation or hypothesis-testing abilities enable the person to "materialize" hypotheses in the form of complementary experiments. The ability to isolate variables is probably the cornerstone of this set of abilities. This is equivalent to applying the scheme "all other things but the factor tested should be kept equal" in order to see whether varying this factor produces the hypothesized effect.

Model-construction abilities enable the individual properly to map the results of experimentation onto the original hypothesis so as to arrive at an acceptable interpretative framework or theory. A model should involve statements about causes, effects, and irrelevant variables; in other words, it should differentiate the sought-after causal structure from the broader coexistence structure in which the former is embedded.

As a representational system, the causal-experimental SSS involves interpretative models aimed at capturing the network of dynamic interactions of which the individual is aware. Thus, it has to be biased toward a kind of symbolism that is able to preserve the dynamic character of the interactive structures represented, that is, the cause-effect relations that, by definition, consist of agents and recipients of action having direction, intensity, duration, etc. The dynamic-procedural component of language (e.g., prepositions, adverbs, and verbs) as opposed to the static-declarative one (e.g., nouns) seems suited to encoding the models that this SSS comprises or works with.

4. The Imaginal-Spatial Specialized Structural System

This SSS is directed to those aspects of reality that can and need to be preserved on a mental screen or buffer as integral wholes that can be visualized by the "mind's eye" (Kosslyn, 1978). As an operating system, it is *dynamic* in the sense that it enables the person mentally to visualize elements, or parts and/or states of elements, in relation to each other. It is to be noted here that, according to Freyd (1987), mental images are characterized by representational momentum; that is, they preserve the dimension of time at the level of representation as an intrinsic property of the elements represented. The dimension of time is known to be a crucial component of perception. The dynamic nature of imaginal-spatial thought has also been stressed by Piaget (Piaget & Inhelder, 1971). Therefore, this is the system par excellence for the representation and processing of forms and spatial relations, both dynamic and static.

More specifically, this SSS involves abilities that enable the person to execute on the level of imagery whatever actions she can execute on real objects—in fact, one is much freer to manipulate objects mentally than physically. Thus, the individual can add or subtract characteristics from the image of an object, she can integrate different images into one, just as she can put objects together, and she can displace, reshape, or rotate the objects in an image in the same way as she does in reality. However, images do not necessarily preserve the real scale of objects or physical layouts, and the alternative images of an object or layout are usually not equally well focused, accurate, or coordinated vis-à-vis their real counterparts. Thus, the execution of actions on the level of imagery may result in distortions that are gradually removed by re-presenting, reworking, and reorganizing on the mental level the corresponding real actions in light of their real results. The component abilities of the spatial-imaginal SSS are those that enable the person to manipulate elements and relations on the level of imagery without grossly distorting the appearance of these elements and their relations as they exist in reality.

As a representational system, the imaginal-spatial SSS seems biased to imaginal/figural symbolism that is able to preserve the apparent properties of elements and layouts as well as their relations in three-dimensional space. An inner kinesthetic language able to preserve representational momentum may also be involved. It is interesting to note in this regard that, under some conditions, movement information is more important for infants' recognition of objects than information about shape and color (Spelke, 1982).

5. The Verbal-Propositional Specialized Structural System

It would be trivial to assert that any reality domain may be encoded in a set of verbal predicates and processed through propositional reasoning. To avoid such triviality, the distinguishing characteristics of this SSS are conceived to lie in that it "is directed more to the formal or mental relations between entities logically constructed by the subject himself than to relations among entities existent in the observable reality" (Demetriou & Efklides, 1987, p. 43). As an operating system, the verbal-propositional SSS seems to function as an agent charged with two main duties: "First, to selectively cut down those semantic networks which, being unrelated to the formally determined goal of the task at hand, will divert processing to probably sensible but logically irrelevant conclusions. Second, to assemble the defended elements of the argument so as to produce a logically valid conclusion. In other words, the propositional processor functions in both ways: it suppresses and creates meaning at the same time" (Demetriou & Efklides, 1988, p. 188).

As a representational system, the verbal-propositional SSS must have recourse to a "code of logical validity." This code might be conceived as a rule system that implicitly or explicitly prescribes, first, how to separate the logically relevant from the irrelevant components of the premises involved in an argument (e.g., "focus on the connectives, and ignore the terms following") and, second, how to separate the alternative valid relations ensuing from a given sequence of connectives (e.g., in an "if . . . then" argument, any of the instances p.q, $-$p.q, and $-$p.$-$q can, and instance p.$-$q cannot, be true). Consequently, the propositional SSS seems to be biased to that aspect of the verbal mode (e.g., connectives and quantifiers) or any of its substitutes (e.g., notation of logic) that would help the person both reject the logically irrelevant and process the relevant elements of an argument (Demetriou & Efklides, 1988). In sum, this specialized structural system may be differentiated from the others more by reference to the principles of computational specificity and symbolic bias than by reference to the other principles.

THE HYPERCOGNITIVE-REFLECTING STRUCTURAL SYSTEM

According to the last two of the principles of cognitive organization and functioning that we discussed earlier, the way in which we understand our understanding of the world and of other people determines how we represent real objects and how we process their relations. This postulate implies that there must be a system of declarative as well as procedural knowledge that stems from and guides the interaction between the person and reality as well as among the various SSSs we described.

Many different terms have been used to denote this system. "Metacognition" (Flavell, 1979), "personal theory of mind" (Flavell, 1988; Wellman, 1990), "implicit theories of intelligence" (Sternberg, 1985), "meaning-making executive" (Kuhn, 1983), "reflection" (Campbell & Bickhard, 1986; Piaget, 1974), and "mental self-government" (Sternberg, 1988) are among them. As will be seen, whatever is denoted by each of these terms constitutes part of our definition of the *hypercognitive-reflecting system*. We opted to coin a new term, not to increase confusion, but to emphasize that this is not a "plain" system to be conceived as being at the same level as the domain-specific SSSs (as many, ourselves included [Demetriou & Efklides, 1985], have done in the past). Rather, it is a *supersystem*, from the perspective of the functioning both of the other systems and of itself. First, the functioning of all other SSSs contributes to its formation and continuously shapes its functioning. Second, its functioning is applied to all other systems—both domain specific, like the five SSSs noted above, and domain general, like the hardware system to be discussed below—and, by its application, it causes permanent changes in their functioning. Consequently, it surpasses all other systems in terms of both its origin and its jurisdiction.

Because of its nature as the individual-environment or the SSS-SSS interface, the hypercognitive system is related to all three families of theories mentioned before. Specifically, as a description of the individual's active involvement (compare this to the principle of subjective equivalence-distinctness of abilities) in the construction of his own mental structures (the five SSSs and their components), the hypercognitive system must be a part of any theory that aims to describe what structures exist (the second family of theories) and to explain why and how they are formed, developed, and refined (the first and the third family of theories). In other words, the hypercognitive system is a higher-order construct to be used for the understanding of the functioning and development of other, lower-order structures. At the same time, the hypercognitive system is a structural complex to be described and understood as such. From this point of view, the discussion of this system enriches the second family of theories, which is concerned with the cognitive structures themselves.

A final word is in order here regarding the superiority of the term "hypercognition" over the term "metacognition," which has dominated the literature in recent years. The latter implies the assumption that self-understanding and -management come after cognition (*meta* in Greek means "after" or "beyond" in time or space). Being neutral in this regard, the former permits assumptions that self-understanding and -management come before, or concurrently with, cognition as well.

What is involved in hypercognition? From the point of view of the present theory, the regulatory role of hypercognition is to be seen at two levels of generality: one controlling functioning at the macrodevelopmental level, the other controlling functioning at the microdevelopmental level.

General Self-Representation and -Management

The first level of generality is the person's general representation of herself as a cognitive system vis-à-vis a world conceived as a system that poses problems and raises questions. This general representation can be analyzed into three relatively distinct types of models that, taken together, constitute what might be called the "personal theory of mind" (see Wellman, 1990).

a) A model of cognitive functioning.—This model organizes knowledge and beliefs regarding the structural and dynamic characteristics of the human cognitive system. It posits, for instance, that there are different mental functions like perception, attention, or memory and that different types of mental work—such as memorizing a poem versus a shopping list—require different strategies and pose different degrees of mental strain. This model should involve descriptions and prescriptions about how problems are to be approached and processed so as to render processing effective.

b) A model of intelligence.—This model organizes knowledge and beliefs regarding what is considered to be intelligent behavior in a given environment. It involves descriptions and prescriptions about how cognitive functioning is to be used in order to meet objectives and standards set by the person himself, his social group, and his culture. The study of implicit theories of intelligence has shown that lay representations of the nature of intelligence are notably close to standard scientific models, emphasizing self-control and self-management, the ability to learn, verbal fluency, and social flexibility as important components of intelligence (Sternberg, Conway, Ketron, & Bernstein, 1981).

   c) *Image of cognitive self.*—At the intersection of these two models there should be the model—or, more accurately, the image—that the person has about herself as an intelligent and cognitive being. This model should involve answers to such questions as, What kind of cognitive processor am I? What problems do I like to work on? How flexible, or efficient, or intelligent, or wise, am I? Do I always manage to stick to my short- or long-term problem-solving plans? How efficient am I in the use of different psychological functions such as memory, imagination, and problem solving, given the demands of different types of problems? (see Efklides & Demetriou, in press).

   It should be mentioned here that modern self-efficacy theory also postulates that the image of the cognitive self is an important component of cognitive functioning. According to Bandura (1989, p. 730), "It is partly on the basis of self-beliefs of efficacy that people choose what challenges to undertake, how much effort to expend in the endeavor, and how long to persevere in the face of difficulties. . . . When they achieve substandard performances, people who have self-doubts about their capabilities slacken their efforts or abort their attempts prematurely, whereas those who have a strong belief in their capabilities exert greater effort to master the challenge."

On-Line Self-Understanding and -Management

   The second level of generality is the self-monitoring, self-regulation, and planning that operate during on-line processing. Thus, it involves processes activated from the very first moment of a person-task encounter until the production of a solution to the task is achieved. These processes have to be connected via a two-way channel with all three models described in the previous section. The strongest connection, however, must be with the model of general cognitive organization and functioning since that is the one that involves propositions about intra- and inter-SSS connections as well as about connections between the cognitive system and the environment. Thus, it is assumed that a person-task encounter activates the following sequence of estimation processes.

   a) The *acquaintance estimators* are the first to be activated, and they underlie decisions as to whether anything similar to the task at hand has been encountered by the individual in the past. Thus, these estimators contribute to the determination of what kind of experience the thinker may have, if he has any, with the problem at hand. In practice, the acquaintance estimators shape the person's decision either to carry on or to interrupt processing at the outset on the basis of a few salient task characteristics and the feelings that these generate in the person. In other words, these estimators operate on the basis of a sketch representation of what the problem is about, so as to determine whether involvement would be worth the effort to be invested. Thus, up to this point, evaluatory acts should be intermingled with field and associative effects generated by the stimulus composition of the problem as well as by the overt or covert responses that they may have elicited in the past.

b) The decision to carry on processing activates the *task-SSS affiliation estimators.* "Once activated, they alternate scanning between, on the one hand, the salient content characteristics of the tasks, their interrelationships, and the problem goal, and, on the other, the stored knowledge, rules, and mechanisms" (Demetriou & Efklides, 1988, pp. 189–190), with the aim of selecting whichever network seems most conducive to the attainment of the problem goal as represented by the thinker. The selection of a network is tantamount to handing subsequent processing to the dynamics of the selected network and the deactivation of the other candidate networks. In our theory, these networks are the specialized structural systems. Therefore, these estimators underlie how the thinker represents the problem situation *to herself.*

Evidently, this representation may not always coincide with the representation of the problem as construed by other thinkers, the problem setter included. This, of course, is a developmental question to be dealt with later. It should be underscored, however, that the nature and efficiency of subsequent processing depend entirely on the decisions prompted by the task-SSS affiliation estimators.

c) Important decisions remain to be made even after an SSS has dominated. Specifically, the thinker has to decide which of the constituent components of the selected specialized structural system is most appropriately brought to bear on the problem. For instance, in a case where the causal-experimental SSS has dominated, are hypothesis-formation or hypothesis-testing abilities required? If both are judged to be needed, how are they to be ordered in time so as to meet the problem goal as fully as possible? Such decisions are regulated by the *goal-task-specific procedures affiliation estimators* that regulate what declarative and procedural schemes are brought onto the assembly line and combined so as to produce a solution that would satisfy the goal as fashioned by the previous estimators.

d) A special kind of evaluation is conducted by *processing load estimators,* which "enable the cognitive system to formulate a conception of the task demands mainly in regard to the mental strain or effort the selected procedures will impose on the cognitive system" (Demetriou & Efklides, 1989, p. 417). These estimators are assumed to be activated at nodal points in the problem evaluation process when a selection between competing processes is to be made; the need for selection imposes a strain on the system because consideration of alternatives is by definition more effortful than is execution of a single process. These estimators are important in regulating processing in both the short and the long run. In the short run, they influence the person's decisions as to whether it is worthwhile to attempt solving the problem at hand. In the long run, they may influence the person's attitudes to categories of problems by dictating what should be avoided and what can be processed.

e) Once a solution has been produced, the *success estimators* are activated; these enable the individual to judge whether the solution is relevant, adequate, and errorless. The functioning and the decisions produced by success estimators will be affected to a large extent by previous decisions made under the guidance of the other estimators. For example, relevance estimation would tell the subject whether the solution he produced belongs to the same specialized structural system that had been selected under the guidance of the task-SSS affiliation estimators. If the person thinks that the selected SSS was relevant, and if he produced a solution that does belong to this SSS, then he will judge the solution to be relevant, even if the original SSS selection had been wrong. Likewise, estimations of adequacy and errorlessness will depend on exactly how the problem goal had been represented and on what specific processes had been brought to bear on it.

From the point of view of our theory, the principle of subjective distinctness-equivalence of abilities leads to the assumption that an individual's representation of her cognitive structures and functions would be a more or less veridical reflection of structures and functions that can be identified empirically. In other words, the subjective structure of cognition must correspond to its objective structure. It is only under this condition that the estimators described above would be able to direct the individual to make correct decisions as to what specialized structural system and what specific processes must be activated at a given person-task encounter. Also, the repeated ascription of a task to an SSS would result in strengthening the task-SSS relations. That is, each task-SSS affiliation decision increases the likelihood that the same decision will be made in the future. Therefore, the functioning of these estimators contributes to the formation of the different SSSs. The study described in Demetriou and Efklides (1989) provides strong support for these assumptions.

THE PROCESSING SYSTEM

To understand what a problem is about, one must be able to represent for oneself the minimum connections between the elements that define its identity. For example, in grasping the relation between two terms in regard to any criterion (bigger, heavier, etc.), one needs to keep at least two elements together for the minimum amount of time that is required by the "mind's eye" to "see" their relation. In Halford's (in press) terms, this constitutes the dimensionality of a problem. Keeping any of these elements active for less time than is necessary would cause the processing enterprise to collapse because no connection can be constructed between vanishing representational entities. Since information units tend to vanish from memory anyway owing to the decay of trace strength and interference from other stimuli (Baddeley, 1991), this means that the faster a person is capable of building the necessary connections, the more probable it is that she would meet the problem demands.

Problem solving is normally a decision-making process that occurs in a stepwise fashion (Simon, 1981). This implies that, to solve a problem, one needs to have control of the information that should, and should not, be represented and/or responded to at each decision-making point. This is necessary for the system to remain directed toward whatever aspect of the problem and component of the plan are the most appropriate at the given moment. This may be conceived as a control mechanism whose main function is to enable the thinker to decide which of the pieces of incoming (and frequently competing) information should be responded to. These decisions have to be made within the time limits defining the flow of information in the system as well as the limits defining the minimum coactivation requirements of the dimensions of a concept, if the concept is to be grasped as such. In practice, this mechanism functions like a multiswitch, suppressing responses to some stimuli in favor of responses to others. The faster and more accurate this control mechanism is, the more probable it is that the right connections (as determined by the demands of the given moment) will be grasped and that the right actions will be assembled at the right time, resulting in the achievement of the final goal with the minimum cost of effort, response, and time.

In sum, the processing system is defined by our theory as a dynamic field where information is represented (i.e., encoded and kept active), protected (i.e., refined, dissociated, or disassociated from interfering information), and processed (i.e., connected, compared, transformed, or combined) over an as yet undefined time interval that is required by the thinker to make sense of the information and, if required, go beyond it. As such, it involves three interdependent but distinct components: *speed of processing, control of processing,* and *storage.*

Many other authors have attempted to integrate these components into a comprehensive theory of cognitive development. For Pascual-Leone (1970, 1988; Johnson et al., 1989), general capacity is equivalent to the mental energy required actively to boost the problem goal and the goal-relevant schemes and to inhibit whatever irrelevant schemes invade central computing space. Pascual-Leone has defined precisely only one aspect of these three parameters; this is the k parameter in his well-known equation that defines mental power (Mp) as equal to the energy spent to boost the task goal or the executive e plus the goal-relevant schemes k:

$$Mp = e + k. \tag{1}$$

The energy required to boost the executive (i.e., e) is considered constant and was never actually defined. The energy required to inhibit irrelevant competing schemes does not even appear in the equation.

Case's (1985) definition of capacity is partly similar to Pascual-Leone's definition of Mp. In Case's terms, *total processing space* is the sum of *operating space* (OP) and *short-term storage space* (STSS). OP is the space in which the task-related schemes are really assembled, and it is actually occupied by the processing operations themselves. STSS is the space where the problem solver stores the pointers required to keep track of the sequence of objectives and strategies ensuing from the problem representation. Thus, Case's OP and STSS seem to correspond roughly to Pascual-Leone's e and k components, respectively.

However, there is an important difference between these two theories: in Case's theory, total operating space does not increase with development, as it does in Pascual-Leone's theory. According to Case, OP decreases systematically with advancing age because of increasing operational or processing efficiency. As a result, STSS increases. Case has operationalized processing efficiency in terms of the speed with which a given operation (such as counting) is executed and presented evidence showing that the relation between storage space and efficiency defined in this manner is almost perfectly linear. Thus, Case has studied only two of the components of the processing system since the notion of a control function as we defined it here has never been included among the stated concerns of his theory.

Halford (in press, chap. 3) has distinguished between short-term memory and active memory: "Short term memory stores must be used to retain results of earlier processing steps, ready for use in subsequent processing. It probably also serves other functions, such as retention of a solution plan, place-keeping, pointers to relevant information, and so on. However, the active processing that is responsible for the manipulative aspects of reasoning seems to be at least partially independent of short term storage systems." He has also argued that the manipulative aspects of reasoning are more related to active memory.

"Active memory" is defined as the system in which a given set of information units can remain active above a minimum level of trace strength, permitting the thinker to be aware of them and to process them. According to Halford, the capacity of active memory is limited. It is assumed that, to remain active in memory, information items must be represented at a minimum level of trace strength. However, the trace strength of individual items varies inversely with the total number of items to be represented. Thus, when the number of items exceeds a certain limit, the trace strength of the individual items falls short of the minimum required strength. The practical implication is that some of the items in a set that overloads the system will be displaced to passive memory (Halford, Maybery, & Bain, 1988).

As defined by Halford, the processing system seems to be a vector of the three components we specified above. As in our theory, it involves a storage space. Moreover, active memory can fulfill its function to the extent that it can circumvent the fading of the trace strength of activated items. This can be achieved either if processing is sufficiently fast to result in the attainment of the goal set within a given period of time (at the end of which the items fade away) or if the items that have to be processed within this time period are well protected from interfering but unrelated items. Thus, the efficiency of active memory seems to be a function of speed and control of processing. However, Halford has not viewed active memory in this way, so he has not explicitly studied either the development of each of the components or their interrelations.

The assumption that cognitive constructions are constrained by the limited capacity of a central processing system has also been entertained by many cognitive and psychometric theories of intelligence. For example, Anderson (1992), Eysenck (1986), and Jensen (1982) have forcefully maintained that variation in general intelligence is a linear function of processing speed, this latter being considered an index of the quality of the functioning of neurons in the brain and neuronal communication. Kyllonen and Christal (1990) emphasized the role of working memory in the development of intelligence. Just and Carpenter (1992) have recently shown that the larger working memory capacity of some individuals makes them more efficient language processors, especially when more complex and/or ambiguous language structures are to be processed. It is to be noted, however, that speed of processing and working memory have been considered by these scholars to be alternative indexes of the same underlying construct rather than integral components of a more general processing system.

THE TIMING OF COGNITIVE DEVELOPMENT

The discussion thus far has focused on specifying how the three general dimensions of developing intellect (i.e., its vertical, horizontal, and depth aspects) interact to create specialized and domain-free structural systems. The present section will focus on the development of these systems; the aim is to show what kinds of problems each system can solve at successive ages, in the hope that the similarities and differences in how these systems function will become more apparent to the reader. A further aim is to set the stage for the discussion of the dynamic interplay between the processing system, general strategies, SSS-specific inquiring rules, and task-specific practices that we present in the concluding chapter.

MAJOR CHANGES IN THE STRATEGIC ORIENTATIONS OF SSS DEVELOPMENT

There is abundant evidence that every domain of cognitive functioning undergoes noticeable changes almost every 2 years from infancy to early adulthood. Taking into account the considerable intraindividual variation in the age points at which different systems change, a rather strong conclusion seems justified—namely, that the cognitive system as a whole is in a process of incessant change in at least some of its parts during approximately the first 25 years of life (Demetriou & Efklides, 1987, in press).

There is also no doubt that increasing age is associated with more than one type of change. Although there is no general agreement as to what type of change occurs at what age, all theorists would agree that cognitive development brings about at least four different types of change, namely, *representational, structural, expansional,* and *refinement* changes (see Biggs, 1992; Case, 1985; Fischer, 1980; Flavell, 1985; Kuhn, Amsel, & O'Loughlin, 1988). Codifying the different types of change could become the starting point for illuminating some of the more obscure aspects of cognitive development.

Representational Changes

Insofar as the specialized structural systems are concerned, there is general agreement that the changes between the ages of 1 and 2 years are of the representational kind: the cognitive system shifts from sensorimotor to symbolic representations in all SSSs. There is also reasonable agreement that the 11–13-year-old change is of a similar nature in that it makes the system shift from what might be called "referential" or "denotational" representation ("concrete," in Piagetian terms) to what we have called "suppositional" (Demetriou & Efklides, 1987) or "implicational" representation (the closest equivalents to our terms are "formal" [Inhelder & Piaget, 1958], "abstract" [Fischer, 1980], "disembedded" [Donaldson, 1978], or "vectorial" [Case, 1985] representation). This shift is indicated by the fact that the cognitive system becomes able, for the first time, to conceive of the implicit—that is, of the existence of properties and connections that lie behind overt reality and that can be brought to light through various inquiring processes.

This change in orientation can be seen in the kind of problems that become soluble in the context of all SSSs. Thus, the preadolescent can coordinate algebraic statements in order to define a quantity (e.g., $x = 4$ if $x = u + 1$ and $u = 3$; Demetriou et al., 1991). Or, to test the effect of light on the growth of plants, she may grow lentils under the sun and beans in a shadowy place because "the plants have to be the same and these are not actually different as they are both pulses" (Demetriou & Efklides, in press): the need to control variables as a means of uncovering the unknown is now understood. Similarly, at this age, the propositional SSS becomes capable of inverting (falsifying) simple logical statements and of grasping unstated but logically implied possibilities (Demetriou & Efklides, in press; Efklides & Demetriou, in preparation). The qualitative-analytic SSS can operate on very complex patterns of properties even when these need to be first disentangled from irrelevant properties (Demetriou & Efklides, in preparation). Finally, the imaginal-spatial SSS can now follow variously rotating stimuli (clockwise and counterclockwise) from both the perspective of the subject and the perspective of other possible observers (Demetriou, Loizos, & Efklides, in preparation).

Structural Changes

Structural changes may be defined as bringing about the ability to make full use of the representational mode with which the individual is operating. A good way to achieve this is to bridge at least two representations and build representational complexes, implying an ability to withhold a response to one representation until the response to another one is computed. There is reasonable agreement that the change during the period from 5 to 7 years of age is of this type. It enables the child to structure and build referential representational complexes; in consequence, reasoning becomes self-guided.

Prior to this shift, during the period from 3 to 5 years of age, the cognitive system operates in the case of all SSSs on the basis of some salient, usually single, dimension or property. This dimension functions as a perceptual or representational marker that is directly linked to the right solution. Once processing is focused on it, the marker functions like a trigger that yields the right answer. Thus, taking the quantitative-relational SSS, where two sets clearly differing in number have to be compared, a global concept of numerosity can yield solutions to simplified one-to-one correspondence tasks (see Gelman & Gallistel, 1978) or balance tasks (Case, 1985). In the qualitative-analytic SSS, seriation reasoning is based on gestalt complexes (e.g., there are "many things," "big things," etc.) rather than on transitive relations. In a similar vein, the spatial-imaginal SSS is quite precise in the formation of static, global, and inflexible images, but dynamic images that can be freely redescribed and merged to represent the unknown cannot be formed (see Ackerman, in press; Demetriou, 1983; Karmiloff-Smith, 1990). With regard to causality, thinking at most permits one to differentiate random from determinate phenomena and to effect "cataloging explorations" (see Kuzmak & Gelman, 1986). Finally, the verbal-propositional SSS is limited to an automatic or logically undifferentiated use of propositions.

By contrast, during the period from 5 to 7 years of age, simple markers are superceded by integral models, and "inferential triggering" gives way to inferences based on systematic integration. Thus, for instance, the child becomes able to operate on one representation from the perspective of another by referring to the identity of elements so as to resist perceptual misguidance due to the varying appearances of reality elements or to coordinate concepts so that comparisons with regard to a given dimension become possible (e.g., bigger, smaller, etc.).

The transition that occurs between 14 and 16 years of age seems to be of a similar nature. Of course, it has to be borne in mind that operating with suppositional representations is by definition a multifaceted enterprise because an idea can be supposed but not accepted only if it can be perceived, at least implicitly, from the perspective of another idea. However, the suppositions that are possible at an earlier age seem to be undifferentiated. For instance, the idea of relations between relations is present at the age of 12 or 13 years, but it is only intuitive—that is, it cannot be quantified through a process of analyzing all component values and relations involved. The subject can isolate variables in order to test a hypothesis with which she is presented, but she cannot integrate alternative data patterns so as to formulate her own hypotheses and map them on a series of experimental manipulations. At about the age of 14 years, however, the adolescent becomes able to build suppositional or implicational representational complexes. As a result, she now can combine combinations of data so as to form valid working hypotheses about all the possible causal effects that may lead to a specific outcome. The quantitative-relational SSS becomes capable of estimating inversely varying complex proportional relations and even of matching their components with abstract strings of algebraic expressions. Likewise, the propositional SSS becomes creative, self-aware, and directed by the sensed need for logical consistency. New propositional networks that are formally and materially sound are first formed on the basis of the premises provided, and their logically necessary implications are subsequently determined.

Expansional and Refinement Changes

The remaining types of change refer to less pervasive transformations of the cognitive system. These intervene between the change from representational shift to representational bridging as well as its obverse. *Expansional* changes affect the number of single or bridged representations that can be dealt with. For example, in the period between ages 7 and 10, the problem space of the task at hand may be painstakingly analyzed into its component elements (e.g., the properties or dimensions that define a Raven-like matrix). Once these component elements can be identified, they can then be operated on at a subsequent stage of processing, provided the operations needed were already functional at the previous level (Shayer et al., 1988). Karmiloff-Smith (1990) would say that the child becomes able to analyze a procedure that could run until then only as a gross entity into its components and use the components as data structures in other parts of the system. Therefore, she is able to build new concepts or representations out of units already available. This is indexed by the child's ability to define quantities in terms of their interdependent dimensions (hence conservation), define classes in terms of "pure properties" such as "greenness" and "redness" or "squareness" and "circularness" (hence multiple classification), and formulate dynamic images of objects that do not exist by combining parts of available images into new ones (e.g., a human with wings). Besides, theories in action now appear to guide the operation of causal systems (Karmiloff-Smith & Inhelder, 1974). This indicates an emerging differentiation between the apparent and the real cause of a given result.

Similar changes occur during the period from 16 to 20 years of age as the individual becomes able to interrelate the abstract networks that he has been able to construct since the previous level; for example, he is able to integrate a series of experiments into a comprehensive model with regard to a phenomenon and accept at the same time that that model may still be incomplete and falsifiable. This is equivalent to saying that thought becomes an instrument of epistemological inquiry and can result in the formation of general causal theories, formal systems, or systems of forms, such as those produced by science, logic, and the arts, respectively. That is, thought acquires properties characterized by many as postformal (Commons, Richards, & Kuhn, 1982; Demetriou, 1990; Demetriou & Efklides, 1985).

Finally, *refinement* changes may be defined with reference to the old notion of discrimination learning. That is, refinement changes are changes that focus the application of a given operation or skill on those problems that are more relevant to this operation or skill. Thus, these kinds of changes may result in the narrowing of the application domain of an operation; at the same time, however, they make the functioning of the affected operation more accurate and efficient. It is more than likely that refinement changes occur at every phase of development in relation to all kinds of mental operations. In fact, some kind of refinement in the functioning of the operations that are acquired at a given phase may be necessary if the other, more pervasive changes described above are going to take place.

MAJOR CHANGES IN SELF-UNDERSTANDING AND -MANAGEMENT

We proposed earlier that the hypercognitive-reflecting system involves general self-representation and -management, which control cognitive functioning at the macrodevelopmental level, and on-line self-understanding and -management, which control processing at each person-task encounter. In this section, we try to pinpoint the general developmental tendencies that characterize the evolution of each of these two components.

General Self-Representation and -Management

We have argued in previous sections that the general personal theory of mind comprises a model of cognitive organization and functioning, a model of intelligence or ability, and a model of oneself as an intelligent and cognitive being. Our concern in this *Monograph* is limited to only the first of these models, which is discussed here from a developmental perspective and addressed empirically in the study reported in Chapter V.

Changes in the Understanding of Cognitive Organization and Functioning

It is well documented that, by about age 2 years, infants understand that they are connected to reality through their senses and that they may intentionally disconnect from it by ceasing to look, listen, etc. They also appear to understand that such channels of cognitive connections vary with circumstances and are largely independent of one another and that different people may connect with the same things through different channels (Flavell, 1988). There is also abundant evidence that children are able clearly to distinguish between internal mental phenomena and external physical and behavioral phenomena by the age of 3 years. By this age, children understand that processes such as thinking, knowing, remembering, and imaging take place in the mind, are not public, and possess unique properties. For instance, they understand that an object can be transformed in imagery in ways that are impossible in reality (Wellman, 1990). From the age of 4 or 5 years, children also effect a rudimentary differentiation among mental functions, such as memory, attention, comprehension, and perception (see Miller & Aloise, 1989; Moore, Bryant, & Furrow, 1989; Wellman, 1985).

Having acquired an awareness of mental representations, children older than 5 or 6 years "become increasingly attuned to the possibility of multiple representations in situations where this possibility is hard to notice or credit, and also increasingly able to determine exactly what these different representations might be. In addition, they probably arrive at some important new insights concerning mental representations. One likely candidate is the awareness that mental representations are potentially *recursive*—for example, the recognition that I can think about your thoughts, about my thoughts and so on" (Flavell, 1988, p. 250). However, they still believe that there must exist some single "correct" representation of the given thing that is acceptable to everyone. It is only in adolescence that the realization that knowledge may be inherently subjective and relative begins to emerge. That is, adolescents seem to move from the belief that there are mental representations of reality to the belief that there may be no reality beyond mental representations. This is obviously a radical change in the development of theory of mind and mental representation (Flavell, 1988).

Our own studies (Demetriou, 1990; Demetriou & Efklides, 1985, 1989, 1990) have also shown that children can differentiate mind from reality and that they can also differentiate among general mental functions. However, they do not understand that tasks addressed to different SSSs—such as an isolation-of-variables versus a proportional task—require different mental operations if they are to be solved properly. This understanding first appears at about the age of 12–13 years, when it appears that the child becomes sensitive to the differences in experiences evoked by different kinds of tasks. As a result, children become able to evaluate with impressive accuracy the mental load of tasks addressed to different developmental levels, their success on these tasks, and the procedural-operational similarities and differences among tasks belonging to several SSSs. However, sensitivity to one's own cognitive functioning is not identical to self-awareness. It is only in late adolescence (i.e., after the age of 16–18 years) that an accurate sense of differences and similarities between different mental processes turns into a refined theory of mental processing. Individuals of this age appear able to analyze what they feel in terms of the operations they employ while processing tasks in the context of different SSSs. Thus, it is only quite late in development that they can formulate a map of different cognitive systems, subsystems, and skills.

The On-Line System

We consider the structure of the on-line evaluation/regulation system to be developmentally invariable. Specifically, we argue that the acquaintance → task-SSS → subgoals-specific components → success evaluation sequence of control actions is present at every level of development. The way the system functions, however, should undergo considerable change with increasing age because the relative weight of the processes dominating each of the four phases of the control sequence should vary with increasing experience. For example, it is plausible to assume that the importance of the acquaintance estimators should be less during the very early or the very late stages of acquiring a concept (either macro- or microdevelopmentally) than during the intermediate ones: the less expertise or familiarity one has with a problem, the more probable it is that one will respond randomly or in a trial-and-error fashion. Similarly, it seems very likely that development or increasing expertise brings about automated approaches to problems that render acquaintance estimation unnecessary. It is also more than likely that changes in the relative importance of the on-line regulation components will be directly affected by changes in the individual's theory of mind and the general processing capacity as well as in the SSSs themselves. To our knowledge, no empirical studies have to date investigated the development of these components of hypercognition; one of the studies that we undertook for this *Monograph* was designed to provide evidence related to this issue.

THE DEVELOPMENT OF PROCESSING CAPACITY

In a theory such as ours, two issues are of primary importance. The first concerns the development of each of the three components of processing capacity—that is, speed of processing, control of processing, and working memory—and their dynamic interrelations with increasing age. How do speed of processing, control of processing, and storage change with age, and how do changes in any one affect changes in the others? The second issue centers on the relations between developments of any of these three components and that of the hypercognitive system and/or the specialized structural systems identified by the theory.

There is no generally accepted answer to either of these questions. Case (1985), Halford (in press), and Pascual-Leone (1970) have taken considerable pains to show that the expansion in processing capacity is the driving force behind cognitive development. However, they disagree as to the identity of what develops and the nature of its development.

According to Pascual-Leone, the portion of mental power required to boost the executive (i.e., the problem goal and the general schemes prescribing its attainment) levels off at the age of 2–3 years and remains constant thereafter. From this age on, further development in mental power can be spent in the representation and processing of task-related figurative (i.e., declarative) and operative (i.e., procedural) schemes. According to the evidence presented by Pascual-Leone and his colleagues (Burtis, 1982; de Ribaupierre & Pascual-Leone, 1979; Johnson et al., 1989; Pascual-Leone, 1970), the M-power available at age 3 enables the child to represent 1 unit of information in addition to the executive. This is the k factor in Pascual-Leone's formula referred to previously (see eq. [1] above). This factor increases by 1 unit every second year until it reaches its maximum value of 7 units at the age of 15 years. Thus, every second increase in the value of k is associated by Pascual-Leone with a shift to the next major stage of the Piagetian system (preoperational, concrete, and formal operational). In fact, Pascual-Leone has attempted to show that the typical Piagetian tasks that can be solved at each of the major Piagetian stages do have an M-demand that is equivalent to the Mp available at the age corresponding to these stages (see de Ribaupierre & Pascual-Leone, 1979; Pascual-Leone & Goodman, 1979).

In sum, three points need to be stressed with regard to Pascual-Leone's definition of the processing system. First, capacity itself is thought to increase with increasing age. Second, this increase is additive; the system can handle an increasing number of units until it reaches its maximum potential at a predetermined age level. Third, although complex structures may appear qualitatively different from simpler structures, the units that can be boosted by the system as such are thought to be quantitatively the same.

Case's position is opposite to Pascual-Leone's in regard to all three points. According to Case (1985), the increase in processing capacity is apparent rather than real; that is, storage space increases because operating space decreases within a constant total operating space. With regard to the second issue, Case believes that the development of short-term storage space is not additive but a process of recycling and defines it in terms of his "common-ceiling" model. According to this model, "basic capacity never exceeds about 4 units. What happens is that successive levels of operation become progressively more efficient until they reach this asymptotic value. And, as they do so, some higher level operation begins its development and the entire process recycles" (Case, 1985, p. 427). Case argues that the recycling sequence involves four levels: operational consolidation, unifocal coordination, bifocal coordination, and elaborated coordination. Structures involving one, two, three, and four elements can be constructed at these four levels, respectively. This four-level sequence recycles four times in such a way that the last level of a given cycle is the first level of the next cycle. The cycles that are equivalent to major developmental stages are as follows: sensorimotor (1–18 months of age), interrelational (1½–5 years), dimensional (5–11 years), and vectorial (11–19 years). Therefore, one, two, three, or four sensorimotor, interrelational, dimensional, or vectorial units can be held in short-term storage space at the respective level of the recycling sequence. This implies that, according to Case, the relation between short-term storage space and the development of cognitive structures is linear only within stages. Case (1985; Case, Kurland, & Goldberg, 1982) has presented extensive empirical evidence in support of this model.

Evidence obtained by other investigators supports some of Case's views and fails to support others. Specifically, in a series of experiments involving subjects aged 8–22 years, Kail (1986, 1988) has shown that the developmental functions of speed of processing of such diverse abilities as mental rotation, name retrieval, visual search, memory search, and mental addition are identical in shape. These functions were exponential in form and characterized by a similar rate of developmental change, namely, a large decrease in the execution rate of these processes from age 8 to about age 12 years, when speed of performance approached asymptote. Although the other two components of the processing system were not represented in Kail's studies, this evidence is in line with the claim that processing efficiency increases systematically with age and that this increase may have a role in the development of the other components of the processing system or of the other SSSs. However, the form of the functions obtained by Kail suggests that changes occurring before the age of 8–12 years may not be the same as later changes. This is in disagreement with both Case's and Fischer's (1980) view that there is a single cycle of levels that is reiterated over the different major stages (or tiers) of development. It also needs to be emphasized that, although similar in shape, the functions were not identical in absolute values. For instance, memory search was faster than mental rotation, and this in turn was faster than mental arithmetic. This finding suggests that, even if there is only a single pool of processing potential, it may be used differently by different computational systems.

In another set of studies, Bjorklund and Harnishfeger (1987, p. 122) showed that "comparable expenditure of mental effort produced different levels of memory performance for subjects of different age. Equivalent changes in the use of mental effort (relative to baseline) resulted in greater performance for older relative to younger subjects." In practice, these results showed that the execution of memory strategies, such as organization according to category membership, may require so much mental effort in young children that no capacity is left free for storage. Therefore, the better performance of older subjects seems to result from the extra resources available to them relative to the younger children, resources that can be spent for storage rather than only for increased processing efficiency. Contrary to Case's claims, these findings suggest that the storage component of the processing system may also increase with age.

Anderson (1992) has recently incorporated the notion of speed of processing into his theory of cognitive development in a heretical fashion. Specifically, he accepts the view that general intelligence depends on the speed of processing. However, contrary to all other theories of cognitive development discussed above, he argues that speed of processing does not change with development. Therefore, cognitive development cannot be ascribed to changes in speed of processing. This claim is intended to account for the fact that individual differences in intelligence are stable despite the systematic increase of cognitive abilities with development. According to Anderson, cognitive development is due to maturationally determined changes in domain-specific modules, such as the spatial and the phonological modules.

To conclude, the work summarized above only partly answers the questions raised at the beginning of this section concerning the development of the three components of the processing system. It suggests—although this suggestion is now disputed—that speed of processing and storage do change systematically with age and that such changes are interrelated and may even be related to the change in various cognitive skills represented by our SSSs. The processing system does seem to undergo major changes at the ages that have been associated with changes in cognitive or hypercognitive structures. However, the evidence regarding the nature of these changes is entirely inconclusive. As it stands, it is impossible to determine whether the development of any of the components is additive or a process of recycling. Moreover, there is no evidence whatsoever concerning the development of the control-of-processing component. Finally, there is a complete lack of evidence with regard to the possibly differential relations between the components of the processing system and the different SSSs.

QUESTIONS TO BE INVESTIGATED

Two major conclusions are suggested by the theoretical exposition attempted above. On the one hand, the assumption of our theory with regard to the basic architecture of developing mind is supported by empirical evidence. That is, it does seem to be the case that cognitive development takes place on three fronts, namely, the processing system, the hypercognitive system, and the specialized structural systems. There is also evidence to suggest that each of the systems on each front is a multistructural complex. We hope that it has also become obvious that each structure may be seen as a vector of three dimensions: the vertical (i.e., What level of complexity has a given structure or component attained at a given point in time?), the horizontal (i.e., What is the domain of application of the structure or component?), and the depth dimension (i.e., What is the particular content structured by the structure or component, and what is the symbolic medium in which it is represented?). Finally, the empirical evidence is congruent with the assumptions of the theory about the dynamics of developing mind—

specifically, that development in any structure or system may result from changes that have occurred in other structures or systems.

On the other hand, however, we hope that our theoretical exposition has also made it clear that many important questions about cognitive development still remain to be answered. Some of these questions follow:

1. How do the organizational principles interact to produce specialized structural systems during development?

2. How is change in a given component carried over to other components both within and across domain-free or specialized structural systems?

3. How does learning affect the development of different specialized structural systems at different developmental and/or age levels?

4. What, precisely, is the role of the domain-free systems in the organization and development of the specialized structural systems?

Primarily the first, but also the second, of these four questions is concerned with the structure of developing mind. The last two questions in particular, but also the second, are concerned with the mechanisms and causes of cognitive development. Obtaining an answer to the last three questions will necessarily provide evidence about the timing of the development of different systems as well. Therefore, the four questions outlined above may be seen as a better-focused restatement of the four questions posed at the beginning of the *Monograph*.

The studies that we present in this *Monograph* aim to generate answers to these questions. Specifically, Study 1 attempts to demonstrate the organizational power of the principles that we listed and the SSSs that we described (question 1). This study also provides evidence about the intra- and inter-SSS interactions during development (question 2). Study 2 aims to show that the SSSs constrain the effect of learning. That is, it presents a training experiment that was designed to investigate (*a*) the trainability of two SSSs and the transfer of learning between them and (*b*) if and how the trainability of the two SSSs depends on general intelligence (question 3). Study 3 focuses on the hypercognitive system, aiming to show that this system functions as the interface between tasks and SSS-specific processes or between SSS and general cognitive functions such as attention and memory (question 4). Finally, Studies 4 and 5 focus on the processing system. Study 4 investigates the relations between one of the components of the processing system, storage, and two different SSSs expressed via two different symbolic systems, namely, the numeric and the imaginal. Study 5 investigates the interaction between the components of the processing system and the relations between each of these components and one SSS, namely, the quantitative-relational SSS (questions 2 and 4).

III. STUDY 1:
THE EMPIRICAL STATUS OF DIMENSIONS,
PRINCIPLES, AND SPECIALIZED STRUCTURAL SYSTEMS

The primary aim of this study was to demonstrate empirically that the organizational principles listed in the preceding chapter function as forces that interact to produce the specialized structural systems (SSSs) described by the theory. This is equivalent to saying that the study aimed to show that developing intellect can be defined by the three dimensions (vertical, horizontal, and depth) specified in Chapter II; as noted in the context of that discussion, it is these principles that specify the actual psychological entities to be placed along each dimension.

A study directed toward this goal must involve tasks that represent different cognitive domains, symbol systems, and developmental levels. Consequently, a second aim of the study was to examine how different components both within and across SSSs are interwoven during development in expectation that the pattern of interactions obtained might throw some light on the dynamic aspects of cognitive growth by showing how changes in one part of the cognitive system influence those occurring in other parts.

OPERATIONALIZATION OF CONSTRUCTS

Reference has been made to the evolutionary (the vertical dimension), the computational (the horizontal dimension), and the content/symbolic (the depth dimension) aspects of developing intellect. Each of these aspects can be treated at least as a nominal dimension because each involves a minimum of two variants that bear a meaningful relation to each other—such as, for instance, a sequence of developmental levels (vertical), different domains (horizontal), and different symbol systems (depth). To specify the relations among all three dimensions, the study's design must involve a set of tasks each of which should represent, to the degree that this is possible, one and only one of the possible vertical × horizontal × depth interactions.

To design tasks that address different symbol systems or reality domains but that are equivalent in developmental level requires using a standard developmental metric to direct task construction across symbol systems and domains; this metric would thus represent the vertical dimension. We used Fischer's (1980) system of skill levels as a guide for designing the various batteries developed for the current study. Specifically, the tasks were constructed to model the level of single sets, mappings, systems, and systems of systems, which constitute the abstract tier according to the skill theory proposed by Fischer (1980). The various tasks and their assumed affiliation to Fischer's skill levels are shown in Table 2.

According to Fischer (1980), cognitive development takes place in four major cycles, or tiers, as follows: reflex (0–4 months), sensorimotor (4–20 months), representational (20 months–10 years), and abstract (10–24 years). Each of these tiers evolves along a four-level sequence in such a way that the last level of a given tier is equivalent to the first level of the subsequent tier. The levels within this sequence are defined by the number of cognitive skills that the individual can integrate in a single cognitive structure. Thus, at each of the four successive levels of each tier, structures composed of one (single sets), two (mappings), four (systems), and eight (systems of systems) cognitive skills, respectively, can be conceived or invented by the person.

Fischer (personal communication, 1989) has analyzed the quantitative-relational-numeric and the causal-experimental-numeric tasks listed in Table 2. He suggested that the tasks scale lower than proposed above. According to his analysis, the first of the four quantitative-relational-numeric tasks is addressed to the level of representational systems instead of the level of single abstractions. The second was considered to be an extension of the skill required by the first task rather than an abstract mappings task. The third was ascribed to the level of mappings rather than to the level of abstract systems. The fourth task was regarded either as a generalization of the third task or, possibly, as "something more." With regard to the causal-experimental-numeric tasks, Fischer proposed that the first might be an abstraction and that the second might be a generalization of the first. He regarded the third task as again possibly addressed to the level of abstract mappings. The fourth was characterized either as an extension of the third or as a system. The two imaginal batteries were not analyzed by Fischer.

The divergence between Fischer's and our ascription of tasks to levels clearly raises problems; it also highlights the fact that the "state of the art" in this field is still a long way from the point at which independent researchers can agree in translating a given theoretical construct into the same measurement device or experimental manipulation, an issue to be discussed later on. Nevertheless, note that, whether by Fischer's or our ascriptions, the tasks do span different developmental levels: testing the study's hypotheses remains possible independently of which interpretation is valid.

The horizontal dimension was represented by two domains: that of quantifiable reality and that of causal reality. The third (depth) dimension was represented by two symbol systems: the numerical and the imaginal. The task was presented either numerically or pictorially, and the subjects had to process information accordingly. Thus, each of Fischer's four levels (at least by our ascription) was represented in each of the four task batteries listed in Table 2: the quantitative-relational-numerical (QR-N); the quantitative-relational-imaginal (QR-I); the causal-experimental-numerical (CE-N); and the causal-experimental-imaginal (CE-I).

The data collected on these batteries were intended to answer two crucial questions. First, are all three dimensions necessary to account for performance on the 16 tasks? Modern confirmatory factor analysis is the method par excellence to use in answering this question: a structural model consistent with the model of developing intellect that we propose here has to involve factors that would clearly map the dimensions described by the theory (see below).

The second question concerns the developmental structuring of the tasks—specifically, whether structural equivalence at different ages necessarily implies developmental equivalence. Methods designed to scale performance on large numbers of items and to test for the reliability of ensuing scales, such as rating scale analysis (Rasch, 1980; Wright & Masters, 1982), are appropriate here. If structural equivalence does imply developmental equivalence, then tasks constructed to represent the same structural level will stand at the same point on a common scale generated by the resulting rating scales, regardless of their SSS or symbolic classification. In any event, the interpatterning of tasks that this method would reveal might throw some light on whatever interactions may exist between mental units or processes both within and across SSSs. These interactions, in turn, may highlight the causes and mechanisms underlying cognitive change.

METHOD

Subjects

In all, 163 subjects were tested: these were about evenly distributed between the ages of 11 (M = 10.9 years), 13 (M = 13.2), 15 (M = 15.2), and 20 years (M = 20.5). The sexes were about equally represented in the first three groups, which consisted of students of an experimental school attached to the University of Thessaloniki. All the 20-year-old subjects were

TABLE 2

TASKS USED TO IMPLEMENT FISCHER'S ABSTRACT LEVELS ACROSS TWO SSSs AND TWO MODES OF SYMBOLIC REPRESENTATION

LEVEL, ATTAINMENT, AGE, AND STRUCTURAL REPRESENTATION	QUANTITATIVE-RELATIONAL SSS		CAUSAL-EXPERIMENTAL SSS	
	Numerical QR-N	Imaginal QR-I	Numerical CE-N	Imaginal CE-I
Systems of representational systems or single abstract sets (10–12 years): $$\begin{bmatrix} M \leftrightarrow N \\ \quad \updownarrow \\ O \leftrightarrow P \end{bmatrix} \equiv S$$	The table below is presumed to correspond to a single abstract set as it shows how watering frequency (times/month) affects the productivity (kg/ha) of plants A and B: Watering 2 4 A .... 2 6 B .... 3 6 The subject has to find out which plant is affected more by watering and explain why. Thus, two variations have to be coordinated into a single set	Two half-full beakers A and B, identical in shape, are presented. The subject is asked to imagine that the width of beaker A will double and the width of beaker B will halve. Which of the two beakers will be the fullest? Thus, two variations have to be coordinated into a single set	A simple hypothesis is given ("The increase in watering frequency increases the productivity of plants"), and the subject is asked to use plants A and/or B and the two watering frequencies (two and/or four times/month) in order to design an experiment meant to test the hypothesis. The experiment is to be presented in a table like the one shown below: Plant Watering 1 .... 2	Two pairs of beakers like those used in the QR-I battery are presented. The one beaker of each pair corresponds to the antecedent condition on which an agent operates. The other corresponds to the consequent. Thus, the two pairs represent two trials of an experiment. The subject is asked to specify the effect of the agent (e.g., neutral, necessary not sufficient, necessary and sufficient) by integrating the two trials of the experiment

42

Abstract mappings (14–16 years): [S — T]	A double table (two tables like the one above) is presented to the subject showing the effects of watering on A and B in two areas I and II. Thus, two single data have to be combined if the question is to be answered	The width of beaker A will double, and the water in it will halve. The width of beaker B will halve, and the quantity in it will double. Which of the two beakers will be the fullest? Thus, two sets have to be mapped onto each other	An experiment had to be designed to test a "double hypothesis" ("Watering increases the productivity of plant A but does not affect the productivity of plant B"). Thus, two experiments had to be integrated into one two-way experiment (plant × watering)	Two trials (one experiment) with liquid A and two trials (one experiment) with liquid B. Thus, the subject has to interpret the imaginal presentation of a two-way experiment
Abstract systems (18–20 years): [$S_{w,x} \leftrightarrow T_{w,x}$]	Two double tables are presented showing the effects of watering on A and B in areas I and II when fungi *are* and *are not* present. Thus, four single or two double sets of data have to be combined	*Beaker A*: water doubles, then halves; height and width of beaker B double. *Beaker B*: water doubles; height of beaker doubles, then halves; width of beaker doubles. Which of the two beakers will be the fullest? Thus, two double mappings have to be coordinated into a system	An experiment had to be designed to test two "double hypotheses" regarding the effects of watering on A in areas I and II and on B in areas I and II. Thus, four single or two two-way experiments had to be integrated into one three-way experiment (plant × area × watering)	Four trials with each of liquids A and B because a second agent was introduced. Thus, the subject had to interpret the imaginal presentation of a three-way experiment
Systems of abstract systems that are single principles (24–26 years): $\left[\begin{array}{c} S \leftrightarrow T \\ \updownarrow \quad \updownarrow \\ U \leftrightarrow V \end{array}\right]$	Four double tables are presented showing the effects of watering on A and B in areas I and II when fungi *are* and *are not* present and fungicide *is not* used and when fungi *are* and *are not* present and fungicide *is* used. Thus, four double single sets or eight single sets of data have to be combined	Two twin beakers. Each part of each beaker was identical to beaker A and B. Each part of each twin beaker was independently transformed by two transformations like the above. Thus, a system of systems of transformations has to be constituted	An experiment had to be designed to test two "fourfold hypotheses" regarding the effects of watering on A and B in areas I and II when *fertilized* and *not fertilized*. Thus, eight single, four two-way, or two three-way experiments had to be integrated into a single four-way experiment (plant × area × watering × fertilizer)	Eight trials with each of liquids A and B because a third agent was introduced. Thus, the subject has to interpret a four-way experiment

43

female college students studying at the University of Thessaloniki. All subjects came from upper-middle-class families and were Greeks living in Thessaloniki, the second largest city in Greece.

Tasks

All batteries used in this study were paper-and-pencil tests. The simplest task in the QR-N battery involved a 2 × 2 table (see Table 2). Specifically, it was stated in the protocol that each of two plants, A and B, is watered two and four times per month, respectively, and produces, respectively, 2 and 6 kg/ha and 3 and 6 kg/ha under the two watering frequencies. Subjects were required to decide which plant is more affected by watering; thus, they had to define the relation between the variables represented in the table. The second, third, and fourth tasks presented three-, four-, and five-way tables, respectively, and required subjects to define the relations accordingly.

The simplest task in the CE-N battery presented a simple hypothesis ("The increase in watering frequency increases the productivity of plants") and asked subjects to use plants A and B and two watering frequencies (two or four times a month) in designing an experiment to test the hypothesis. Thus, this task provides for a 2 × 2 experiment, and it is equivalent in complexity to the simplest QR-N task described above. The other three tasks presented systematically more complex hypotheses so that experiments equivalent in complexity to the second, third, and fourth QR-N battery levels had to be designed by the subjects.

In the QR-I battery, subjects were first taught how a series of "quantitative operators" affects the dimensions that define a quantity of liquid (i.e., height and width of the beaker and quantity of liquid); for example, the application of the operator symbolized by a closed square would double the quantity of liquid, whereas an open square symbol would halve the quantity, a closed circle would double only the height of the beaker, etc. Two half-full beakers were presented to the subjects, with one or more operators depicted above each. The subjects' task was to imagine how the joint application of the given symbols would affect the liquid in each beaker and to specify which one would be "fuller" after these operators were applied. The items in this battery were structured into four difficulty levels, involving, respectively, one, two, three, and four operators. These four levels were presumed to correspond to the four represented in the two batteries described earlier. Two additional levels of greater difficulty were also involved. The tasks at the first of these were similar in structure to those already described and involved five operators. At the second level, two twin beakers were presented, each of which could be independently affected by two operators;

thus, items at this highest level required coordination of operator effects within beakers before the two beakers could be compared.

The first level of difficulty was represented by eight items and the other five by three items each. Within each level, these items tapped understanding of three different types of proportional relations: cross-half comparisons (application of the operators made one of the two beakers one-quarter or two-eighths full and the other completely full); within-half comparisons (both beakers would become less than half full—either one-quarter or two-eighths); and half-half comparisons. This manipulation aimed at differentiating the effect that the type of relations involved might have on development from the effect of the sheer number of operations needed to generate these relations.

The CE-I battery consisted of two parts. The first presented four tasks similar to those of the QR-I battery in all respects except the fact that subjects were required to process the causal rather than the quantitative aspects of the effects exerted by the operators. Specifically, the number of operators and the type of liquid in the beakers were manipulated so that the tasks at levels I, II, III, and IV required interpretation of causal relations in one-, two-, three-, and four-way experiments, respectively.

The second part of this battery directly addressed the basic types of causal relations that can connect a causal agent with an effect. The operators' effects on the liquid in the beaker and their relations to each other were defined so as to simulate the following types of relations in the various tasks: necessary and sufficient; not necessary and sufficient; necessary and not sufficient; not necessary and not sufficient; and negative or incompatible. As in the case of the QR-I battery, these relations were tested within the context of simple (three combinations) and complex (seven combinations) structures.

Scoring

Responses on the QR-N, the CE-N, and the first part of the CE-I battery were scored as 0 (no, irrelevant, or entirely wrong responses), 1 (some elements correct), or 2 (fully correct and sufficiently explained responses). Responses on the QR-I items and on items involved in the second part of the CE-I battery were scored on a pass (1) or fail (0) basis.

Procedure

The subjects were tested in groups during school hours. Two sessions were required to complete testing. The presentation order of the four batteries was counterbalanced across subjects; however, the tasks within a battery were always ordered from the easier to the more difficult ones.

RESULTS AND DISCUSSION

Structure

Confirmatory factor analysis was applied to the 16 scores generated by subjects' performance on the tasks modeling the four Fischer levels across the two SSSs and the two symbol systems. A model consistent with the structural assumptions about the mind that we proposed in the introductory section of this chapter would involve five factors. First, there should be a general factor (G) accounting for a portion of the variance in performance on each of the 16 tasks. This factor would represent the vertical dimension: it would capture the effects of task difficulty since, by design, the only characteristic common to all four batteries was the ascending level of skill required to complete the tasks. There should also be four specialized factors that, in pairs, would represent the other two dimensions. The four QR-N and the four QR-I tasks would all load on the QR factor, while the four CE-N and the four CE-I tasks would all load on the CE factor. Thus, the QR and the CE factors may be taken as the two poles of a dimension representing the principle of domain specificity. The four QR-N and the four CE-N tasks would all load on a factor representing operation through numerical symbolism (N), and the four QR-I and the four CE-I tasks would load on the imaginal symbolism factor (I); these two factors may be taken as the two poles of the depth dimension, representing the principle of symbolic bias.

This model was tested by the latest version of the EQS program (Bentler, 1989), following the nested-factor method pioneered by Gustafsson (1988a, 1988b). Mathematically, this method is based on the assumption that the variance of a variable is a linear function of the set of factors that, according to theory, determine the dimensions of performance represented by this variable. In the present case, it was assumed that the variance in performance on each task may be partitioned into parts related to their developmental level or difficulty, their doman affiliation, and their symbolic bias.

In order to test whether the contribution of each individual factor is significant, one proceeds in a stepwise fashion: progressing from the most general to the most specific factor, only one factor is added to the model at each step. Thus, it is possible to test whether the factor added at a given step accounts for a significant portion of the variance not accounted for by the factors already introduced in the model (i.e., the residual variance). If it does, then introduction of the additional factor into the model will result in a significant reduction of the chi-square statistic, given the difference in the corresponding degrees of freedom. Table 3 presents the statistics on the models that were tested in five successive runs, starting with only the

TABLE 3

RESULTS OF TESTS OF FIT OF NESTED-FACTOR MODELS
OF THE 16 QUANTITATIVE-RELATIONAL (QR) AND CAUSAL-EXPERIMENTAL (CE) TASKS
USED IN STUDY 1

	MODEL STATISTICS				CHANGE		
FACTORS	χ^2	df	CFI	p	$\Delta\chi^2$	Δdf	Δp
G	216.425	104	.843	.00			
+QR	194.363	96	.862	.00	22.062	8	.005
+CE	125.988	88	.947	.00	68.375	8	.001
+N	89.233	80	.987	.22	36.755	8	.005
+I	72.690	72	.999	.44	16.543	8	.050

NOTE.—Each entry for the model statistics shows the fit statistics of the models tested. The model in a given row involves the factor shown in that row and all previous rows. Entries indicating change show the difference between the statistics of the model shown in a given row and the statistics of the model shown in the previous row. The probability that the difference between the two models is significant is also shown (although the fit of the last two models was good, the inclusion of all factors resulted in significant improvement of model fit). The p for a model should be > .05 to indicate that the model is not significantly different from the data. The p for the difference between two models must be < .05 to indicate that the second model is significantly better than the first.

general factor and ending with all the five factors specified above.[1] It can be seen that the introduction of all factors but the I factor resulted in a highly significant improvement in model fit. The introduction of the I factor resulted in only a marginal improvement. It can also be seen in Table 3 that the fit of the complete model, which involved all five factors, was excellent, $\chi^2(72) = 72.690$, $p = .455$, comparative fit index (CFI) = .999. This is the model shown in Figure 1. According to the figural conventions of structural modeling, the three arrows going from a factor (i.e., the constructs symbolized by circles) to a task (i.e., the constructs symbolized by squares) indicate on which factor each of the tasks was prescribed to load. Therefore, it is clearly suggested that performance on each task is conjointly determined by forces peculiar to the principles and the structures described by the theory.

Inspection of Figure 1 suggests some interesting conclusions regarding the relative strength of the various factors. It can be seen that the general factor was the most powerful; this is indicated by the fact that this factor accounted for more variance than the other two factors in all but five of the 16 tasks. The QR factor is also quite strong and, unpredictably, more closely related to the QR-I rather than the QR-N tasks. As has always been the case (see Demetriou et al., 1992; Efklides et al., 1992), the CE factor was rather weak. Interestingly enough, it was positively related only to the two lowest-level CE-N tasks, but it was not related to any of the CE-I tasks. Taken

[1] The correlation matrix, means, and standard deviations of the 16 variables involved in the models tested in Study 1 are shown in Appendix Table A1.

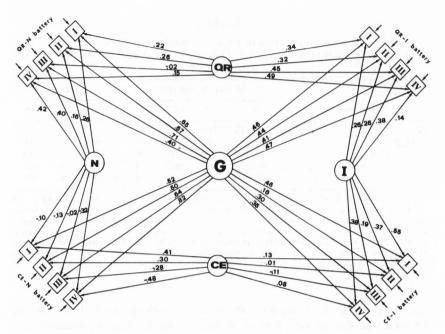

FIG. 1.—The model of mind showing the status of specialized systems, general systems, and organizational principles.

The symbols G, QR, CE, N, and I refer to the general, the quantitative-relational, the causal-experimental, the numerical, and the imaginal factor, respectively. Roman numerals refer to the developmental level of tasks. Depending on the particular combination of characteristics, each task loads on three factors: the general factor, an SSS-specific (i.e., the QR or the CE) factor, and a symbol system–specific (i.e., the N or the I) factor. In the conventions of structural modeling, squares denote observed variables and circles latent variables or factors.

literally, this finding suggests that imaginal symbolism does not facilitate the processing of causal relations. However, such an interpretation is not justified; rather, this finding conforms with the assumption that images often highlight phenomenal relations that may not coincide with true causal relations. Predictably, the N factor is positively, and satisfactorily, related to all QR-N tasks. However, the relations between this factor and the CE-N tasks, although low, were negative. This indicates that the quantitative relations in a task may not be attended to once this task is represented as a causal and not as a quantitative task. Finally, the I factor was about equally, and moderately, related to the QR-I and the CE-I tasks.

Overall, these results indicate that processing of QR-N tasks is based primarily on the general and the quantitative-relational specialized structural systems; these seem to dominate over numerical symbolism as such.

The processing of the QR-I tasks is primarily based on the general and the imaginal systems, suggesting that, in the case of these tasks, forces peculiar to imaginal symbolism dominate over those peculiar to computational specificity. The processing of the easy CE-N tasks is primarily based on the general and the numerical systems, whereas the difficult CE-N tasks are based on the general and the causal-experimental systems. CE-I task processing is almost entirely based on the general system, as the presence of images seems to impede the deciphering of complex causal relations.

Development

Developmental Sequences

Rating scale analysis was used to specify the sequencing of tasks within and across SSSs; as a first approximation, all 54 items were fed into a common analysis. This analysis aimed to align the tasks along the same scale in order directly to show the position of each task relative to all others. This common scale can then be used to guide the construction of the SSS-specific scales that are needed to examine how each of the two systems is related to age independently of the other.

Figure 2 shows the scale along which all 54 items were calibrated. It should be underscored that this scale was very reliable. As indicated by the very high person- and item-separation reliability indexes (.90 and .95, respectively), individuals occupying a given position on the scale succeeded on items below this position and failed on those above; correspondingly, items occupying a given position were solved by persons located at this or a higher position but failed to be solved by those located lower.

Four features of this scale need to be emphasized. First, with the exception of its lower end, the scale is almost perfectly continuous. Second, the two SSSs are inextricably interwoven; neighboring items may be affiliated with either SSS or symbol system. Thus, the transition from the one item to the next as one moves along the scale is very smooth, despite the fact that these items may be affiliated with different SSSs and/or have different symbolic biases. Third, theoretically higher-level items did scale higher within sequences than lower-level items. However, items representing theoretically identical levels across different SSSs, or different symbol systems within an SSS, do not generally occupy the same points on the scale. In fact, close examination of the scale shows that there is a systematic tendency for the causal-experimental items, or those imaginally biased, to scale lower than their corresponding quantitative-relational or numerically biased items. Therefore, structural equivalence does not necessarily imply that the tasks are equivalent in difficulty. The analyses that we consider next focus directly on development, by bringing age onto the stage.

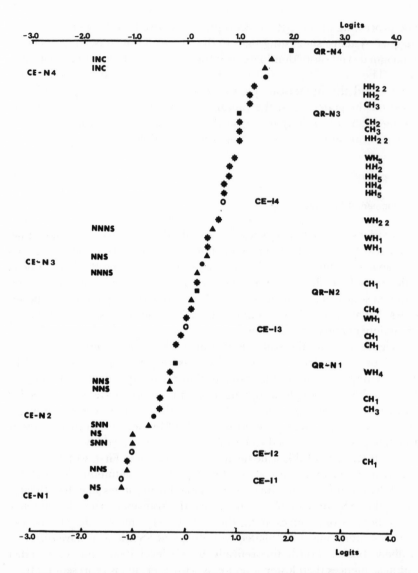

FIG. 2.—The common dimension on which all items used in Study 1 were calibrated by rating scale analysis.

The symbols QR, CE, N, and I refer to the quantitative-relational SSS, the causal-experimental SSS, the numerical symbol system, and the imaginal symbol system, respectively. The symbols CH, WH, and HH refer to cross-half, within-half, and half-half QR-I comparison items, respectively. The numerical index associated with these symbols denotes the number of operators involved. The symbols NS, NNS, SNN, NNNS, and INC stand for, respectively, necessary and sufficient, necessary and not sufficient, sufficient and not necessary, not necessary and not sufficient, and incompatible causal relations tapped by items used in the second part of the CE-I battery. The symbols ■, ●, *, ○, and ▲ stand for the QR-N, the CE-N, the QR-I, and the first and the second parts of the CE-I battery. (The interchange of difficulty from one battery to the other is apparent.)

SSS-Specific Sequences and Growth Functions

In order to obtain a refined picture of development, items addressed to each of the two SSSs were scaled separately. To be comparable, the two scales would have to be equivalent from a measurement point of view—that is, items known to be equivalent in difficulty from our previous analysis would also have to be assigned the same index of difficulty on each scale. In the terminology of rating scale analysis, items equivalent in difficulty would have to have the same logit score when calibrated on different scales. To achieve such equivalence, the two scales were calibrated in reference to the same logit score (i.e., −1.16), which, in each of the two analyses, was anchored to an item shown by the earlier common analysis to be associated with this logit score.

Rating scale analysis provides a logit score for each person that indicates the individual's position on the scale along which the items were calibrated. Practically, this position indicates the cutoff point that demarcates the items that the individual can solve (i.e., items with an equal or lower logit score) from those that he cannot solve (i.e., items with a higher logit score). In order to specify the growth function of each SSS, the average logit attainment of each age group was estimated for each SSS-specific scale. The two functions are shown in Figure 3; the item-to-logit correspondence for each of the batteries is also shown, thus indicating which items could be solved at each of the four ages represented in the study.[2] The shape of the two functions imposes a clear general conclusion: both SSSs are almost linearly and identically related to age. In fact, a 4 (age group) × 2 (SSS) ANOVA indicated a strong age effect, $F(3, 159) = 30.04$, $p = .000$, but no SSS, $F(1, 159) = .14$, $p = .710$, or age × SSS interaction, $F(3, 159) = 2.25$, $p = .085$, showing that the rate of improvement in performance was the same across the two SSSs and the age span represented in the study.[3] At what age, then, can the various tasks representing each of the two SSSs be solved?

With respect to the *quantitative-relational SSS*, it is clear that ascent along the hierarchy of difficulty defined by the QR-I battery is a function of three factors. The first of those is the number of operations to be applied; that is, tasks involving more operations are generally solved later than tasks involving fewer operations.

The intuitiveness of the relations that are involved is a second factor. For instance, Spinillo and Bryant (1991) found that "cross-half" comparison

---

[2] The mean logits and standard deviations involved in the analysis directed to specifying the growth functions of the SSSs used in Study 1 are shown in Appendix Table A2.

[3] It should be mentioned here that preliminary analyses applied to the results of this study and the studies to be described below did not reveal reliable differences between genders. Therefore, the genders were pooled.

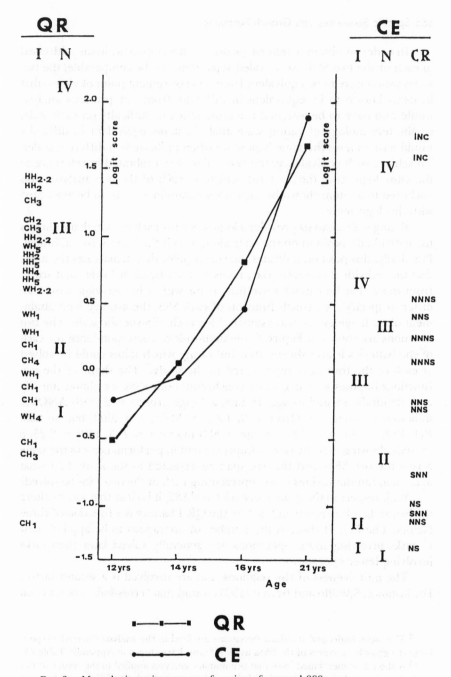

FIG. 3.—Mean logit attainment as a function of age and SSS.
The symbols are the same as those used in Fig. 2. The symbol CR stands for causal relations.

problems (i.e., when one of the beakers to be compared is less and the other is more than half full) are much easier than "within-half" (both beakers are either less than or more than half full) or "half" (both beakers are half full) comparison problems. It seems that the half boundary functions as an *intuitor*, that is, as a readily available mental model against which the "which is more full" proportionality problems are evaluated. Once the conditions of the model (i.e., almost entirely full vs. almost entirely empty) are located in the data (either perceived or mentally constructed), then a comparison can be induced without any further processing that would fully quantify the relations involved. Of course, the concept of an intuitor is broader than the half-boundary conditions. In more general terms, an intuitor can be defined as a readily available conceptual block that functions as an organizer of information coming into the processing space via either a bottom-up or a top-down channel and that generates solutions to problems once some minimum conditions are identified in the problem representation.

The third factor consists of the number of concept dimensions that are affected by the operations applied. One may contrast here operators affecting the height of the beakers with those affecting their width: the first type of operators does not directly affect the liquid in the beaker, whereas the second automatically changes the dimensions defining the volume of the liquid.

It can be seen that, at age 12 years, subjects were able to solve all single-operator problems that involved cross-half comparisons. At this age, subjects were also able to solve a few problems involving more than one operation if the result of applying these operations could be mapped onto an intuitor (e.g., "This operator narrows the beaker, and this widens it, so the first will be fuller because the liquid in it goes up, whereas it goes down in the other"). At the age of 14, subjects managed to solve two kinds of problems: single-operator problems in which the operators resulted in within-half comparisons and multiple-operator problems in which the operators resulted in intuitor-dependent relations. Thus, as this age, problems high on only one of the dimensions defining difficulty can be solved. At the age of 16, subjects appeared able to solve multiple-operator and counterintuitive problems. The only difference between the 16-year-olds and the college students was that the performance of the latter was essentially unconstrained by the number of operators or by the type of the relations involved. It should be stressed that the four QR-N problems proved soluble at the ages of 12, 14, 16, and 21 years, respectively.

The concept of an intuitor is also useful in attempting to understand the vertical structure of the *causal-experimental SSS* hierarchy. It seems that here the basic intuitor is what might be called the *effective connection* intuitor—a scheme that directs the system to look for sequences in which a given event (or element B) can be ascribed to the previous occurrence of an event (or of element A). When such a sequence is found, then a causal connection directed from A to B is assumed, whereas, when it is not, no causal relation is seen in the data. However, the intuitor's tendency to find a positive relation is so strong that it imposes direct one-to-one causal relations even when these are not present in the data. This happens because an effect to be explained in real life almost always coexists with a host of seemingly causal but actually unrelated factors. Thus, this intuitor enables the person to identify necessary and sufficient cause-effect relations—when they are present. At the same time, however, when it is applied indiscriminately, the intuitor results in the reduction of necessary and not sufficient and of not necessary and sufficient relations to necessary and sufficient relations simply because a seemingly privileged event A occurred before B. Thus, the intuitor makes the person inattentive to the possible role of other events that may have co-occurred with A. The negative side of the intuitor that would result in the realization that two events are causally unrelated (i.e., in the conception of not necessary and not sufficient relations) is frequently overridden by its positive side. As a result, an ineffective or neutral factor N may be considered to be related to event B simply by virtue of its coexistence with the causal factor A.

The set of items addressed to these relations strongly suggests that the development of causal understanding progresses from indiscriminate application of the intuitor to a refined inquiring approach to causal relations. At 12 years of age, children were able to solve all problems whose solutions could be directly derived from the intuitor, that is, all those involving necessary and sufficient or sufficient and not necessary relations. Even sufficient and not necessary relations can be grasped when there is an effect but no single factor can be invoked as an explanation. In this case, one factor is regarded as being the main cause, and the other is taken to be the "assisting factor." At 14 years, subjects were able to solve the necessary but not sufficient relation problems and, at 16, the not necessary and not sufficient relation problems. Finally, at the age of 21 years, subjects were able to solve the incompatibility relations problems. Thus, from the age of 14 years, the intuitor begins to be refined into an inquiring scheme that directs the person to make cross-comparisons between a series of relations connecting the *explanatum* B with a series of possible *explanants* $A_i, \ldots, A_j$. At the age of 16, this differentiation results in a clear strategy that directs the person to examine each relation from the perspective of the others. Eventually, all types of main and interaction effects become, in principle, understandable.

Interestingly enough, the 12-year-old subjects managed to solve the first two of the CE-N and the first two of the CE-I tasks. However, the remaining tasks appeared related to age in a spiral-like fashion. The 14-year-olds solved the level-III task of the CE-I battery, the 16-year-olds solved the level-III tasks of the CE-N battery, and, finally, the level-IV tasks of both batteries were solved by the 21-year-olds, although the CE-I tasks were clearly easier than the corresponding CE-N tasks (see Fig. 3).

Causal Relations between and within Sequences

Identifying developmental sequences does not of itself demonstrate how abilities are interrelated either within or across sequences. How, then, are the abilities represented in our various batteries interrelated during development? The model shown in Figure 4a was used as a means of obtaining an answer to this question with regard to the QR SSS. Specifically, all QR-I items that proved soluble at a given age were grouped together regardless of their original level characterization so that a QR-I factor specific to this age could be identified. In this way, four age-specific factors were identified, each representing those QR-I items that could be solved at each of the four ages tested. The scores attained on each of the four QR-N tasks were used in an identical fashion, given that the tasks addressed to levels I, II, III, and IV proved to be soluble at the four age groups represented in the study, respectively. It can be seen that the basic assumption built into the model is quite simple. Each next level in each of the two QR sequences was regressed on the *previous* level of both its own and the other sequence. In this way, we could see directly how performance at each level is accounted for by performance known to have been attained earlier in the same and in the other family of skills.

Two conclusions are clearly suggested by the regression values obtained. First, the flow of causality ("causality" here is of course statistical rather than instrumental) within each of the two sequences is very strong. This is indicated by the fact that all causal paths within a sequence are significant and high; the lower values in the case of the QR-N sequence are due to the fact that they connect observed variables. Second, between the ages of 12 and 14, the abilities represented by the two sequences interact on a reciprocal basis. This is indicated by the fact that the paths going from the first level of the sequence to the second level of the other were both significant and practically equal. From the age of 14 years on, the intersequence effects seem to become unilateral and decreasing. That is, the paths go from the QR-I to the QR-N sequence until the age of 16 years and then become almost null. Thus, it seems that, in the early phases of the representational transformation that occurs in early adolescence, the mastering of quantitative intuitors opens the way for the processing of complex quantitative relations stated in mathematical language. Operation through numerical symbolism facilitates in turn the emancipation of quantitative processing from the need to operate with the support of intuitors. In other words, the two developmental hierarchies get off the ground by mutually

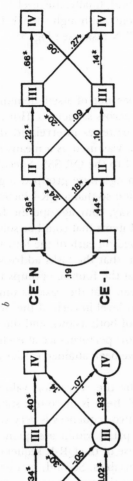
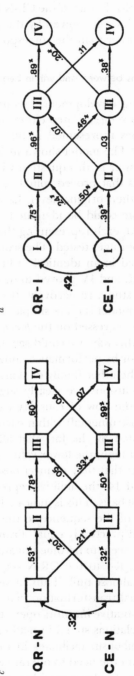

Fig. 4.—The models representing causal relations between levels within and across SSSs.
The values shown in the figure are standardized regression coefficients. An asterisk indicates that a value is significant. The Roman numerals I, II, III, and IV stand for tasks solved at the age of 11, 13, 15, and 20 years, respectively. (Causal relations within SSSs and symbol systems are much higher than relations across SSSs and symbol systems. Mutual exchanges of causal effects are also observed.)

supporting each other. After that, however, each appears to draw on itself in order to develop further, although the general representational flexibility afforded by the differentiation of intuitors into directed processing of relations still seems to be useful for the development of mathematical abilities represented by the QR-N battery.

The same approach was adopted to specify the interrelations between CE sequences. Two models were tested: the model shown in Figure 4*b* involved the CE-N battery and the first part of the CE-I battery. It can be seen that intrasequence relations were again stronger than intersequence relations. In line with the findings regarding the QR SSS, both mutual-interaction paths again proved to be significant between the ages of 12 and 14, However, in the case of this SSS, the transfer of causal effects interchanged regularly from one age level to the next from 14 years on. It can be seen that, between the ages of 14 and 16, only the I → N path was significant; however, between 16 and 21, the N → I path was significant. The model involving the second part of the CE-I battery (which directly addressed the different kinds of causal relations) was basically identical. Thus, the development of causal intuitors into systematic inquiring strategies required for deciphering causal relations seems to provide the basis for the development of experimentation proper. The latter, in turn, makes the mind receptive to more complex interactions between factors and thus provides the representational flexibility needed to move from intuitor-based causal understanding to what might be called "free search" causal understanding.

The same approach was used to examine inter-SSS relations. Specifically, the general model that we described above was independently applied to the two N-biased (Fig. 4*c*) and the two I-biased (Fig. 4*d*) batteries. The results are clear and consistent across the two models. In the interval between 12 and 14 years of age, the causal interaction between the two SSSs is perfectly mutual. This is suggested by the fact that the QR → CE path and the CE → QR path were significant in both models for this age interval. In the 14–16-year age interval, the QR SSS appeared to dominate. This is suggested by the fact that the QR → CE path was still significant and considerably stronger than the previous QR → CE path, whereas the CE → QR path dropped to almost zero in both models. It has to be emphasized here that the QR → CE paths between 12 and 14 years and between 14 and 16 years in the I-biased model (Fig. 4*d*) were higher than the corresponding CE → QR paths. The causal interactions between the two SSSs vanished in the 16–21-year age interval.

Mutual support at the initial phases of development therefore helps both SSSs get off the ground. In the intermediate phase, the QR SSS does not gain much from the CE SSS—probably because it becomes mathematized. However, the representational flexibility afforded to the cognitive system as a result of this process is helpful in the person's attempt to grasp complex causal connections and work with them. Eventually, both systems reach a stage at which they are more or less self-sufficient in developmental momentum.

CONCLUDING COMMENTS

The present study has shown, first, that performance on cognitive tasks is constrained by the forces represented by the organizational principles proposed by the theory. This is suggested by the fact that structural modeling revealed networks of relations that can be identified with the dimensions and systems specified by the theory (the reader is reminded that the G, the QR-CE, and the N-I factors were postulated to reflect the vertical, the horizontal, and the depth dimensions, respectively).

With regard to development, the results clearly show that quantitatively defined complexity accounts for only a part of the sequencing and timing in the acquisition of cognitive skills. Other factors, such as the nature of the intuitors available to an SSS at a particular developmental phase, are equally important in this respect. Thus, the distance between structural and developmental equivalence is a function of the number of factors taken into account: the more factors are taken into account, the more developmental equivalence approaches structural equivalence.

Finally, development of each of the skills that we investigated appears to be both self-propelling and externally supported. This indicates that development may be possible precisely because of the multidimensional and multifunctional nature of mind: a change in a given part of the system destabilizes other parts connected to it and pulls them to change in the direction that it is moving. We will return to this issue in Chapter VII. For now, suffice it to say that development seems to lead from intuitors to differentiated structural systems that, instead of simply running off, can be used flexibly in support of each other. This is not to devalue the importance of intuitors. In fact, these may be considered as the bridges connecting the mind in a coherent and meaningful way to different reality domains until development provides the individual with the ability to relate to a given reality domain in a personal way and to construct meaning by herself, very often despite appearances.

IV. STUDY 2:
EXPERIMENTAL MANIPULATION OF
INTERDIMENSIONAL RELATIONS

One might argue that the structural and developmental relations among dimensions and cognitive systems that we established in the previous chapter are specific to the abilities, the experimental design, or the type of analysis used in Study 1. Hence, establishment of the boundaries between systems was pursued further in the training study described in this chapter. Training is considered particularly conducive to delimiting structural boundaries because it is deemed to minimize performance difficulties that might hinder a person in realizing her structural capacity or optimum level (see Fischer & Farrar, 1988). Specifically, training can be used to test the functional autonomy of any two SSSs on the basis of two assumptions. First, if they are autonomous, then each SSS should display a distinct pattern of change in response to training, thus indicating developmental/functional peculiarities. Second, transfer of training from one SSS to the other should be limited. This is so because training is received through a particular procedural/conceptual/symbolic system rather than through an abstract operational structure such as those described by Piaget. If the systems were functionally interchangeable, any effects of training would transfer fully from one system to the other.

A further aim of Study 2 was to investigate the relations between general intelligence, as it has been operationalized by psychometric theory, and the cognitive systems described by our theory. Specifically, we aimed to test whether our SSSs represent dimensions of ability that go beyond general intelligence since it is only under this condition that one can claim—as we do—that the mind involves both general components shared by every cognitive skill and components specific to different families of skills. An additional goal was to specify the relative contribution of general and SSS-specific factors to the effectiveness of training.

METHOD

Subjects

The study involved 10-, 12-, 14-, and 16-year-olds. The numbers in each group were, respectively, 198, 294, 261, and 275. Upper-middle-class, working-class, and rural families, as well as both sexes, were about equally represented in each age group. All subjects were Greeks. Upper-middle-class and working-class subjects were drawn from schools located in the metropolitan area of Thessaloniki. Rural subjects were drawn from schools located in villages and small towns in central Macedonia (see Efklides et al., 1992).

Tasks

Two sets of tasks were given to the subjects: cognitive development tasks and general intelligence tasks. The first set consisted of the quantitative-relational-numeric and the causal-experimental-numeric tasks used in Study 1. Three of the general intelligence measures were selected from the Kit of Factor Referenced Tests (Ekstrom, French, & Harman, 1976) and one from a test devised by Gustafsson, Lindstrom, and Bjorck-Akersson (1981). These measures were as follows:

The *Letter Sets* (LS) test contains 15 items in which five sets of four letters are presented. The task is to find the rule that relates four of the sets to each other and to mark the one that does not fit the rule.

The *Figure Classification* (FC) test comprises 14 items consisting of two or three groups of three geometric figures that are alike in accordance with some rule. The task is to discover these rules and to assign each of eight additional figures to one of the groups.

The *Hidden Figures* (HF) test contains 16 items in which the task is to decide which of five geometric figures is embedded in a complex pattern. The HF test was constructed to measure field independence, or flexibility of closure, but it is known to be a good indicator of *g* as well (Gustafsson, 1984, 1988a, 1988b).

The *Number Series* (NS) test also addresses inductive ability. It contains 20 items showing a series of five or six numbers connected by a rule; the task is to abstract this rule in order to add two more numbers to each series (Gustafsson et al., 1981).

Design

The cognitive development batteries were given at both a pre- and a posttest and the general intelligence measures at only the pretest. With the pretest completed, subjects in each age group were divided into three equal groups and subjected to different training conditions. Specifically, one-third were trained on the quantitative-relational SSS, one-third were trained on the causal-experimental SSS, and the last third served as controls.

Training

Training was directed toward two goals. First, it aimed to improve metacognitive awareness of the nature and usefulness of the SSS concerned. To this end, subjects were given a demonstration task in which it was explained to them what sort of abilities one needs to use in order to solve this type of task as well as its relevance to understanding and solving similar problems in everyday life. The demonstration task was given in print so as to be available throughout the training phase, but it was also explained orally by the experimenter. The experimenter was a female graduate student.

Second, the training period was meant to give the subjects an opportunity to practice using the rules and algorithms needed to solve problems involving the given SSS. This was accomplished by providing a step-by-step demonstration of what exactly one had to do in order to solve the given type of task. A second problem, structurally equivalent to the one used in the demonstration, was given after the demonstration, and the subjects had to produce the solution in the same step-by-step manner; this was the training task. Subjects were also requested to compare their solutions with the one that had been demonstrated and to locate their mistakes by themselves, after which feedback was given to them about the solutions they had produced. Each subject was trained to one level above his pretest performance level. In sum, we systematically attempted to ensure that the subjects would profit as much as possible from the training we provided and, thus, not only exhibit their optimum level but even surpass it.

In essence, this study was designed to maximize generalization. That is, it involved tasks similar in structure, content, and symbolic bias, and the subjects were provided with both environmental support in understanding the tasks and practice in solving them. In this, the design of the study was biased against the predictions of experiential structuralism.

Procedure

All testing was conducted in groups and carried out in the pupils' regular classrooms. The pretest session lasted for approximately 2 school hours. The training session was held about 2 weeks later and was followed immediately by administration of the eight SSS-specific tasks as "posttests." The training session lasted approximately 30 min. The training leaflets were matched to each subject's assignment to the experimental groups and the level achieved at the pretest.

The presentation order of the three batteries was counterbalanced across subjects at both the pre- and the posttest. At the training session, the experimental group subjects were instructed to study the problems, the solution, and the explanations provided so as to profit as much as possible from the opportunity to gain practice on the particular type of task. At the posttest, the subjects in the control group were instructed to do their best and to try to attend to the details of the tasks now that they were familiar with their requirements; it was particularly stressed that all must try to improve their performance. No time limit was imposed on any of the three phases of the experiment.

RESULTS AND DISCUSSION

The Structure of Abilities

In order to investigate the questions specified in the introductory section of this chapter, the data were analyzed through a sequence of confirmatory factor analyses and structural equations models, fitted with the EQS program (Bentler, 1989). It was assumed in these models that all 12 tests administered at the pretest are related to one latent variable or factor that would be interpreted as an index of general intelligence. It was also assumed that the four quantitative-relational tasks and the four causal-experimental tasks would additionally be related to two other factors, which could then be interpreted as indexes of the quantitative-relational and the causal-experimental SSS, respectively. In other words, it was assumed that the performance on the four fluid intelligence tasks can be accounted for by the general factor only whereas performance on the other two sets of tasks can be decomposed into parts that can be accounted for by this general factor and by an SSS-specific factor.

This general model was first fitted separately to each age group's pretest performance, following the factor-nested method that has been proposed by Gustafsson (1988a, 1988b, in press) and that was described in the previous chapter. These series of analyses aimed to test the relative importance of the three factors across the four age groups represented in this study. The relatively large number of subjects involved in each age group provides the opportunity to test whether the importance of the dimensions represented by the factors is stable despite any developmental changes in individuals' relative standing on these dimensions. Verification of the stability of the dimensions would, of course, provide great support for our theory: it

TABLE 4

Results of Tests of Fit of Nested-Factor Models, in Each Age Group, of the Fluid Intelligence, the Quantitative-Relational (QR), and the Causal-Experimental (CE) Tasks Used in Study 2

Age Factors	Model Statistics				Change		
	χ^2	df	p	CFI	$\Delta\chi^2$	Δdf	Δp
10 years:							
G	127.466	54	.00	.597			
+QR	107.385	50	.00	.686	20.081	4	.001
+CE	83.175	46	.00	.769	24.210	4	.001
+Res	48.181	43	.27	.972	34.181	3	.001
12 years:							
G	186.642	54	.00	.808			
+QR	135.251	50	.00	.877	51.391	4	.001
+CE	94.651	46	.00	.930	40.600	4	.001
+Res	53.482	40	.08	.981	41.169	6	.001
14 years:							
G	159.756	54	.00	.789			
+QR	135.699	50	.00	.836	24.057	4	.001
+CE	96.935	46	.00	.903	38.764	4	.001
+Res	55.336	42	.08	.975	41.599	4	.001
16 years:							
G	147.231	54	.00	.747			
+QR	131.783	50	.00	.778	15.448	4	.001
+CE	88.213	46	.00	.885	43.570	4	.001
+Res	53.101	41	.10	.967	35.112	5	.001

Note.—The organization of this table is the same as the organization of Table 3. The fit of the model involving only the general factor was poor across all age groups (see first row of each age group). Adding each of the SSS-specific factors results in a highly significant improvement of model fit (see the corresponding difference statistics).

would show that the constructs described by the theory, be they general or specialized, are permanent components of the human cognitive apparatus. Besides its general theoretical significance, specification of the status of constructs with increasing age is also necessary from the perspective of a training study such as the present one. It would show whether there always exists a module to assimilate the training of a set of skills supposedly related to this module or whether, at least at some points in development, such training is mediated by general purpose mental devices or modules with which the given set of skills is not affiliated.

The significance of each of the three factors was tested in each of three successive runs performed for each of the four age groups. The models fitted in the first, second, and third runs involved, respectively, only the general, the general plus the quantitative-relational, and these two plus the causal-experimental factors. The statistics of these models are shown in Table 4. It can be seen that introduction of each factor results in significant improvement of the model fit in all four age groups.

Having established the significance of the general and the two SSS-specific factors separately in each of the four age groups, a multisample analysis was run to test the fit of the three-factor model to the performance of the four groups, simultaneously. The advantage of this process is that it allows testing whether the relation between the observed and the latent variables is the same across the different groups. This is effected by imposing the restriction that the parameter estimates (i.e., the loadings of the tasks on the factor that they are presumed to represent) be equal across groups. The fit of this constrained model to the data, $\chi^2(224) = 307.597$, CFI = .953, $p = .001$, was very good but significantly different from the data and therefore not acceptable from the statistical point of view. However, the model did fit the data once the across-groups equality constraints were released, $\chi^2(164) = 181.248$, CFI = .990, $p = .169$. This is the model shown in Table 5.[4]

Three conclusions are suggested by the findings summarized above. First, all three factors are needed to account for performance on the 12 tasks at all ages represented in this study. However, some changes with age in the relation between tasks and factors can be seen. For instance, the contribution of the general factor to the variance of all tasks is higher at the ages of 12 and 14 years than its contribution at 10 or 16 years. In general, the loadings at these youngest and oldest ages tended to be rather unsystematic. From a methodological point of view, this is evidently a major reason for having to reject the model assuming equality of parameters across ages. From a substantive point of view, this finding might imply that these ages mark the activation points of major reorganizations in cognitive functioning. In fact, the studies to be presented next indicate that major changes are indeed observed in the functioning of the two domain-free systems at these age levels. (The reader should recall here that the age of 10–12 years is associated with a major representational change and that the age of 14–16 years is associated with a structural change.)

Second, the general factor is involved in the level of performance attained on almost every task: this is indicated by the fact that the loadings of almost all the tasks on this factor were significant (see Table 5). However, this factor is clearly much more involved in the processing of the quantitative-relational than the causal-experimental tasks: loadings of the former were always considerably higher than the corresponding loadings of the latter.

Third, the four tasks addressed to each of the two SSSs are not equally strong in representing the SSS that they are presumed to measure. The two easier quantitative-relational tasks proved to be much more closely related

---

[4] The correlation matrices, means, and standard deviations for each of the four age groups involved in Study 2 are shown in Appendix Table A3.

TABLE 5

LOADINGS OF THE TASKS USED AT PRETEST ON THE FACTORS EXPECTED BY THE THEORY IN THE SEPARATE ANALYSIS OF EACH AGE GROUP

FACTOR	GENERAL FACTOR (GF)				QUANTITATIVE-RELATIONAL (QR)				CAUSAL-EXPERIMENTAL (CE)			
	10 Years	12 Years	14 Years	16 Years	10 Years	12 Years	14 Years	16 Years	10 Years	12 Years	14 Years	16 Years
FD	.40*	.48*	.62*	.58*								
NI	.65*	.75*	.72*	.50*								
LI	.52*	.72*	.47*	.44*								
FI	.28*	.43*	.36*	.41*								
QR1	.30*	.56*	.49*	.37*	.41*	.35*	.87*	.10				
QR2	.45*	.54*	.57*	.44*	.66*	.84*	.21*	.27*				
QR3	.28*	.44*	.47*	.43*	−.05	.04	.08	.47*				
QR4	.01	.32*	.55*	.39*	.24*	.11	−.08	.52*				
CE1	.27*	.12	.21*	.22*					.13	.05	.15	.14*
CE2	.09	.24*	.22*	.15					.00	.09	.25*	.23*
CE3	.16	.53*	.32*	.27*					.99*	.85*	.80*	.96*
CE4	.28*	.26*	.36*	.27*					.30*	.34*	.36*	.37*

NOTE.—The symbols FD, NI, LI, and FI refer to the embedded figures, the number, letter, and figure induction tests, respectively. The numbers 1, 2, 3, and 4 stand for the developmental level of the task. An asterisk indicates that the loading is significant (i.e., $Z > 1.96$ for each loading, in every case a loading is denoted as significant).

to the quantitative-relational factor than the two more difficult ones, the loadings of the latter being much lower on this factor than those of the former. This relation is reversed at the age of 16 years, when it is the two most difficult tasks that are more closely related to the quantitative-relational factor. The best representatives of the causal-experimental SSS across all four age levels tested were the two most difficult tasks. Taken literally, this finding implies, in agreement with the finding of the first study, that the formal equivalence of developmental levels does not necessarily imply that they are related in the same way to the underlying functional dimension they represent.

These three conclusions lead one to expect that the two systems should differ in their overall modifiability as a result of training. In addition, the two systems should show differential sensitivity to training at the same age level if the task level is held constant and, conversely, at the same task level, provided that the age is held constant. The differential relations between each of these SSSs and the general factor imply that the two systems are differentially able to mobilize general resources in the service of their own functioning. The interaction between task level and age in regard to the association between the four tasks addressed to a system and the respective factor suggests that the mobilization of SSS-specific forces also varies as a function of age and task complexity.

Training Effects

Structural Relations

The first question that needs to be answered in a training study such as the present one is whether training drastically alters the relative standing of the individuals on the vertical dimension (induced by performance) of the abilities concerned. Were this the case, one would be justified in assuming either that random factors operate at the pre- or posttest that cause misclassification of subjects or that the vertical dimension does not represent a necessary developmental sequence, or both. However, if satisfactory pre- to posttraining stability were found, one would be able to go on and look for the "sheer" effectiveness of training. To put these issues under scrutiny, the analysis applied on the pretest scores was extended to include the eight SSS-specific posttest scores. Thus, the two latent posttest SSS-specific factors could also be identified and related to the corresponding pretest factors. In this model, the residuals of the eight cognitive tasks at the posttest were allowed to correlate. This manipulation was meant to purify the SSS-specific variance from variance due to the contribution of the general factor. The manipulation was made necessary by the fact that the general factor could not be identified directly at the posttest since the four fluid intelligence tasks in which this factor was anchored at pretest were not used in the posttest.

The analysis permitted estimating the autocorrelations between the pre- and the posttest SSS-specific latent variables. Estimated separately for each of the three treatment groups, the autocorrelations of the quantitative-relational SSS for the control, the quantitative-relational, and the causal-experimental SSS training groups were .94, .84, and 1.00, respectively. The corresponding values for the causal-experimental SSS were .86, .94, and .80. Since these r values are very high, we can conclude that the degree of stability of individual differences was considerable, even though there were some changes in the rank ordering of the subjects' level of performance. It must be noted here that the pre-/posttest autocorrelation of both SSSs was always lower for subjects who had been trained; we return to this finding later because it may be revealing with regard to how learning experiences operate to produce change.

Nature and Size of Effects

Having established the stability of individual differences, we can go on to two fundamental questions that a training study like the present one must be able to answer. The first concerns the effectiveness of training. That is, was the training experience provided to the subjects successful enough to raise their performance relative to the controls on the specialized structural system trained? The second issue concerns the prerequisites of training effectiveness. In other words, how does posttest performance on each SSS vary as a function of pretest performance on these as well as on the general factor? To answer these questions, the model described above, which involved both the pretest and the posttest scores, was extended into a multisample structured means model. The models of this kind are identical with the models employed earlier insofar as the testing of structural relations between observed and latent variables is concerned. Additionally, they allow testing for possible differences between groups in the degree of attainment of the constructs represented by the observed or latent variables involved. This is made possible by involving the means of the observed variables in the analysis in addition to the covariances (see Bentler, 1989).

In this study, the model described above was extended in two respects. First, in order to test the effectiveness of training (see the first question above), in each of two analyses this model involved (i) the control group and the group trained on the quantitative-relational SSS and (ii) the control group and the group trained on the causal-experimental SSS. Second, each of the two SSS-specific posttest factors was regressed on all three factors identified at the pretest (see the second question above).

The basic technical specifications of this model need to be mentioned. First, the paths from the intercept to the observed variables[5] were specified as free parameters in each group; however, each intercept was constrained to be equal across the two groups in both analyses. In this way, the intercepts may be taken as a kind of baseline level for the variables. Therefore, any differences in the means of the variables across groups must result from other sources. Second, the factor loadings of all pretest variables were also constrained to be equal across groups. This constraint is based on the assumption that the structure of performance of the three groups involved in this study would have to be identical before the intervention of training. This equality constraint was not imposed on the posttest factors (although the same factors were specified) because it was assumed that training may alter the exact relation between each of the variables (i.e., the tasks) and the factors with which they are associated. This assumption is based on the fact that different subjects were trained on different levels (see the methods section above). The across-groups equality constraint was also not imposed on the regressions of the posttest on the pretest factors. Finally, the intercepts of the factors were fixed at zero in the control group but defined as free parameters in the experimental group. Thus, any deviation from zero in the intercepts of the experimental group can be taken to indicate that the attainment of this group in whatever is represented by a given factor differs from the corresponding attainment of the control group.

Two basic predictions can be derived from our theory in relation to the two questions stated above. With regard to group differences, it must be predicted that there would be no difference between the control and the training groups in the two pretest factors to indicate the equality of the groups before training. However, each of the training groups would differ from the control group only on the posttest factor on which it has been trained. This would indicate that, although it is domain specific, training is able to accelerate development. With regard to between-ability relations, the models presented earlier suggest that the condition of the posttest factors would depend primarily on the factor representing general intelligence and the condition of the same factor at pretest.

Part A of Table 6 shows the regressions of the posttest factors on the pretest factors, the factor intercepts, and the respective statistics that were produced by the model that contrasted the control with the quantitative training group and the control with the experimental training group.[6] It can be seen that these figures are generally in line with the two predictions

---

[5] In the conventions of structural modeling, the intercept defines the means of the variables.

[6] The correlation matrices, means, and standard deviations for each of the three treatment groups involved in Study 2 are shown in Appendix Table A4.

stated above. Regarding group differences, the intercepts of the pretest factors in the two runs of the model were low and nonsignificant, indicating that the two experimental groups did not differ from the controls at pretest. However, in the quantitative training group, the posttest intercept of the quantitative-relational factor (.08, $z = 1.870$, $p < .10$) was marginally significant and considerably higher than the intercept of the causal-experimental factor, which was very low (.01, $z = .369$, $p > .1$). In the experimental training group, it was the posttest intercept of the causal-experimental factor (.05, $z = 1.574$, $p > .1$) that, although nonsignificant, was higher than the intercept of the quantitative-relational factor (.03, $z = .728$, $p > .1$). Therefore, training did raise the performance of the subjects on the SSS trained. Admittedly, however, the effects of training were not strong enough to reach statistical significance.

A possible explanation for this finding may be the fact that a considerable number of subjects involved in the two experimental groups did not profit from the training provided to them. Thus, we decided to test the structured means model described above on the performance of those subjects who did profit from training. Technically, a subject was regarded as profiting from training if she was able to provide a solution to the training task that closely reproduced the demonstration task (see the methods section above). This restriction decreased the number of subjects in the quantitative-relational training group from 335 to 222 and in the causal-experimental training group from 330 to 166. The results of this analysis are shown in part B of Table 6. It can be seen that the model that involved the control and the quantitative training group yielded results fully consistent with the prediction. That is, the pretest factor intercepts were nonsignificant, and, of the posttest factor intercepts, only that of the trained quantitative-relational SSS was significant (.94, $z = 2.419$, $p < .05$). The results of the model that involved the control and the causal-experimental SSS can be considered only indirectly consistent with the prediction. Specifically, the pretest factor intercepts proved to be negative and significant. This indicates that the removal of the subjects who failed the training task from the causal-experimental training sample yielded a group that started lower than the control group in both SSSs. However, the intercept of the posttest trained causal-experimental factor was positive and of the same size (.095, $z = .756$, $p > .1$) as the intercept of the posttest quantitative-relational factor in the quantitative training group. The intercept of the posttest nontrained quantitative training group was very low ($-.005$, $z = -.042$, $p > .1$). Therefore, the training of the causal-experimental SSS was successful enough to invert a significant difference favoring the control group to a difference favoring the experimental group only in the trained SSS.

The factor regressions were practically identical in the two sets of analyses. These suggest the following conclusions. First, the dependence of both

TABLE 6

INTERCEPT OF PRE- AND POSTTEST FACTORS AND RAW (and Standardized) REGRESSION COEFFICIENTS OF THE POSTTEST FACTORS ON THE PRETEST FACTORS ACROSS TREATMENT GROUPS AND SSSs

A. MODELS INVOLVING ALL SUBJECTS IN EACH TREATMENT GROUP

PRETEST FACTORS: CONTROL GROUP vs. QUANTITATIVE-RELATIONAL TRAINING GROUP

POSTTEST FACTORS	GF Regression	GF Z	QR Regression	QR Z	CE Regression	CE Z	Intercept	Z
QR:								
Control	.480 (.794)	9.805	.636 (.491)	4.817	.525 (.136)	1.805	.000	
Training	.441 (.754)	8.494	.418 (.274)	2.590	.574 (.174)	2.062	.077	1.870
CE:								
Control	.427 (.791)	8.564	.070 (.060)	.805	1.430 (.414)	2.862	.000	
Training	.412 (.756)	8.392	.028 (.020)	.231	1.698 (.552)	3.098	.014	.369
Intercept:								
Control			.000		.000			
Training			.069	1.273	.005	.265		

PRETEST FACTORS: CONTROL GROUP vs. CAUSAL-EXPERIMENTAL TRAINING GROUP

POSTTEST FACTORS	GF Regression	GF Z	QR Regression	QR Z	CE Regression	CE Z	Intercept	Z
QR:								
Control	.545 (.858)	10.913	.467 (.347)	3.957	.259 (.126)	1.878	.000	
Training	.562 (.910)	11.283	.399 (.330)	4.227	.090 (.041)	.632	.028	.728
CE:								
Control	.442 (.792)	9.002	.022 (.019)	.252	.791 (.437)	3.873	.000	
Training	.370 (.788)	7.785	.144 (.157)	2.281	.579 (.345)	3.397	.053	1.574
Intercept:								
Control			.000		.000			
Training			.035	.598	.027	.801		

B. Models Involving the Subjects Succeeding on the Training Task

Pretest Factors: Control Group vs. Quantitative-Relational Training Group

Posttest Factors	GF Regression	GF Z	QR Regression	QR Z	CE Regression	CE Intercept	CE Z
QR2:							
Control	.501 (.787)	10.082	.659 (.448)	4.482	.500 (.140)	.000	1.942
Training	.347 (.736)	5.806	.410 (.315)	2.341	.621 (.274)	.094	2.402 / 2.419
CE2:							
Control	.431 (.790)	8.604	.071 (.056)	.737	1.285 (.420)	.000	3.043
Training	.356 (.716)	6.270	.133 (.097)	.927	1.396 (.584)	.031	3.091 / .797
Intercept:							
Control			.000		.000		
Training			−.013	−.236	.001		.066

Pretest Factors: Control Group vs. Causal-Experimental Training Group

Posttest Factors	GF Regression	GF Z	QR Regression	QR Z	CE Regression	CE Intercept	CE Z
QR:							
Control	.561 (.824)	11.374	.847 (.497)	5.284	.369 (.159)	.000	2.533
Training	.841 (.815)	12.100	.575 (.254)	3.300	.051 (.017)	−.005	.259 / −.042
CE:							
Control	.507 (.825)	10.115	.135 (.087)	1.283	.864 (.411)	.000	4.226
Training	.757 (.700)	8.591	−.071 (−.030)	−.374	.341 (.106)	.095	1.489 / .756
Intercept:							
Control			.000		.000		
Training			−.455	−6.760	−.249		−4.669

Note.—The intercept of the control group (shown in italics) was set to zero. The critical values for the significance of Z are as follows: 1.64, 1.94, and 2.58 for $p < .10$, $p < .05$, and $p < .01$, respectively. According to prediction, the intercepts of the pretest factors should not be significant; of the intercepts of the posttest factors, only those of the factors trained should be significant.

SSSs at posttest on the pretest general factor is generally very strong. This is indicated by the fact that the regression coefficients of both SSSs on the general factor were always higher than their self-regressions. (When comparing regression coefficients, the reader is advised to inspect standardized values—shown in the table in parentheses—rather than raw values.)

Second, the second-best predictor of an SSS at the posttest is its own condition at the pretest: the self-regressions (shown in italics in Table 6) were always higher than the regressions on the other SSS across all groups. However, training appears to disturb this relation. The difference between self-regressions and the regressions on the other SSS decreased in the experimental groups as contrasted to the control group. In fact, the regression on the *other* SSS reached significance in both experimental groups (see the italicized regressions in pt. A of Table 6). This finding is interesting in that it shows that, at least initially, learning experiences function as a local destabilization factor. In other words, although learning experiences may speed up the rate of development, it is difficult to tell how and to what extent this will happen. It is equally interesting that these effects do not generalize to untrained systems since this indicates that learning experiences affect only the skill system concerned. However, the strengthening of the relations between SSSs in the experimental groups, as indicated by the significant between-SSS regressions mentioned above, may suggest that intensive learning experiences such as those provided here may direct the mental component affected to seek support from other mental components. Therefore, when generalization or transfer occurs, it has to be interpreted as a result of indirect and not easily traced transmissions from the directly affected component to any other components to which it is connected. This interpretation suggests that change propagates from a given component via chains of changes that travel from a given energy point in any direction and to any distance, depending on how good a conductor the different media are. As will be seen below (and in accord with the findings of Study 1), these effects vary as a function of the subject's developmental level and the SSS concerned.

The Nature of Change

The results presented thus far give a picture of the effects of training and of the underlying network of relations between mental components that, although accurate, is rather global. That is, this picture does not show who is changing, in what direction she is moving, or how far she is going. Table 7 shows results that address these issues. This table presents the percentage of subjects in each treatment group who regressed to a lower level (R), stayed at the same one (S), or progressed (P) to a higher level from pre- to posttest performance on each SSS. Note that these values

TABLE 7

PERCENTAGE OF SUBJECTS WHO REGRESSED (R), STAYED AT THE SAME LEVEL (S), OR PROGRESSED TO A HIGHER LEVEL (P) AS A FUNCTION OF EXPERIMENTAL CONDITION AND PRETEST PERFORMANCE

| | PRETEST PERFORMANCE LEVEL | | | | | | | | | | | | | | |
| | 0 | | | 1 | | | 2 | | | 3 | | | 4 | | |
	R	S	P	R	S	P	R	S	P	R	S	P	R	S	P
Cont.:															
QR	...	69	*31*	30	33	*37*	35	37	*32*	12	52	*36*	21	79	...
CE	...	56	*44*	37	19	*44*	39	37	*24*	33	56	*11*	25	75	...
Quant.:															
QR	...	36	*64*	22	17	*61*	25	24	*51*	24	30	*45*	...	...	...
CE	...	61	*39*	31	18	*51*	37	28	*35*	33	42	*25*	28	72	...
Exper.:															
QR	...	46	*54*	29	08	*62*	22	48	*30*	33	42	*25*	30	70	...
CE	...	39	*61*	24	00	*76*	18	32	*50*	16	24	*59*	...	...	...

NOTE.—"Cont.," "Quant.," and "Exper." refer to the control, the quantitative, and the experimental SSS training groups, respectively. The symbols QR and CE refer to the quantitative and the experimental SSSs, respectively. Performance was scored 0 (failure on all tasks of the SSS to be trained; see Table 2), 1 (success on the first-level task only), 2 (success on the second-level task), 3 (success on the third-level task), and 4 (success on the fourth-level task). Subjects functioning at level 4 on both SSSs were allocated to the control group. Subjects functioning at level 4 on one of the two SSSs were trained on the other SSS. Thus, no subject functioning at level 4 of an SSS was trained on this SSS. The percentage of subjects progressing to a higher level is shown in italics.

include only those subjects who succeeded in solving the training task correctly, a restriction imposed to ensure that only subjects who "really" profited from the training were used in these comparisons.

Inspection of Table 7 makes it clear that the effect of training was very satisfactory. Averaging across subjects who progressed from any pretest level, a mean of 53% of those trained on the quantitative-relational SSS progressed to a higher level, compared to a mean of 34% of the controls. Similarly, a mean of 62% of subjects trained on the causal-experimental SSS progressed to a higher level in this SSS, compared to a mean of 31% of the controls. With regard to transfer effects, a mean of 38% of the quantitative-relational training subjects progressed in the nontrained causal-experimental SSS, and a mean of 43% of subjects trained on the latter progressed in the nontrained quantitative-relational SSS.

The profile of the subject who failed to profit from learning may be very revealing about the possible between-SSS differences or about intra-SSS differences between developmental levels. It is interesting to note that the failure of an individual to profit from the training experiences provided in this study is related to three factors: age, developmental level, and SSS. Specifically, the lower the age of a subject, the more probable it is that he will not be able to profit from training on the abilities investigated here: of the subjects trained on the quantitative-relational SSS, 41%, 31%, 33%, and 27% of the 10-, 12-, 14-, and 16-year-olds failed the training task, respectively; the corresponding percentages for the subjects trained on the causal-experimental SSS were 62%, 51%, 45%, and 40%. With regard to developmental level, training on level II was much more difficult than training on any of the other levels. This is clearly indicated by the fact that, of those found to operate on levels 0, I, II, and III of the quantitative-relational SSS at pretest, 15%, 24%, 55%, and 11%, respectively, failed the training task; the corresponding percentages for those trained on the causal-experimental SSS were 41%, 60%, 63%, and 26%. These results clearly indicate that an individual can profit from training if it aims to move him from level 0 to level I, from level I to level II, or from level III to level IV. However, it is very difficult to profit if training aims to move the individual from level II to level III. Therefore, it appears that the boundaries between levels II and III are deeper than the boundaries between the other levels.

Five conclusions are suggested by these findings. First, sheer practice with the tasks does have an effect on an individual's cognitive functioning. Second, however, the fact that almost twice as many trained subjects as controls progressed in the trained SSS indicates that specific training is needed if extensive change is to be obtained. Third, the transfer of training from one SSS to the other is very weak, if any occurs at all: progression in the nontrained SSS among the experimental subjects was only slightly higher than that obtained by the control subjects. However, the experience of learning seems to be able to direct the SSS affected to seek support from other SSSs. This is indicated by the fact that the cross-SSS regression coefficients became significant in the two treatment groups but not in the control group. Thus, learning may not generalize easily across mental domains. but it strengthens the mutual support between domains.

The fourth conclusion is equally interesting. A nonnegligible number of subjects regressed to a lower level from the pre- to the posttest.[7] It must be noted, however, that, when applied to these data, a model that claims that ideally no regression to a lower level would occur was confirmed by prediction analysis (Froman & Hubert, 1980) for all experimental groups and the two SSSs.[8] The phenomenon is nevertheless interesting from the perspective of microdevelopment because it occurs even among successfully trained subjects. It indicates that, whether intrinsically or extrinsically induced, the momentum pushing the system upward causes instability in at least some individuals and that this instability finds expression in a return to lower levels of functioning. This is what Strauss (1982) has called U-shaped behavioral growth. It is interesting to note that such instability is less pronounced among those who have been trained: among trained subjects, on average about one-quarter regressed, compared to about one-third of the controls. This suggests that spontaneous development may not be as steady as guided development.

Finally, it should be noted in this context that the difference between the two SSSs shows up again: more subjects were unable to profit from training or regressed to a lower level on the causal-experimental than on the quantitative-relational SSS. In general, training was more successful among those trained on the quantitative than on the causal-experimental SSS (79%, 76%, 45%, and 89% in the former group and 59%, 40%, 37%, and 74% in the latter of those operating at pretest levels 0, I, II, and III, respectively, succeeded on the training task). However, of those succceeding on the training task, more subjects progressed to a higher level at the posttest on the causal-experimental than on the quantitative-relational SSS. These differences in response to training indicate that the two SSSs are differently organized modules. The quantitative-relational SSS seems to be organized more tightly than the causal-experimental SSS; as a result, it is

[7] Attention is drawn to the double meaning of the term "regression": before it was used in its statistical sense; here it is used in its standard meaning of a return from a higher to a lower developmental level.

[8] The values of the application of prediction analysis to the data for the quantitative and the experimental SSS, respectively, in the various groups were as follows: control group: $\hat{V} = .320$, $U = .303$, $z = 5.782$, $p < .000$; $\hat{V} = .381$, $U = .289$, $z = 6.746$, $p < .000$; quantitative training group: $\hat{V} = .320$, $U = .303$, $z = 5.782$, $p < .000$; $\hat{V} = .381$, $U = .289$, $z = 6.746$, $p < .000$: experimental training group: $\hat{V} = .471$, $U = .338$, $z = 9.020$, $p < .000$; $\hat{V} = .333$, $U = .291$, $z = 5.940$, $p < .000$.

more accessible to the on-line monitoring system (see Demetriou & Efklides, 1989) but also less easily penetrated and transformed by experience. Once transformed, however, it preserves the acquired changes because they are incorporated in a tight structure.

A final word is in order regarding the pattern of successes on the training task as a function of developmental level. The fact that movement from level I to level II, or from level III to level IV, was easier than movement from level II to level III gives some credibility to Fischer's claim (personal communication, 1989) that tasks I and III tap two different main levels and that task II represents a generalization of task I and task IV a generalization of task III. Fischer, Hand, and Russell (1984) have shown that training helps the individual generalize her present optimum level to new and unfamiliar domains. However, it cannot by itself push the subject up to a new optimum level. Moreover, this aspect of training effects gives credibility to the notion that the developmental phase from ages 10–12 to age 14, during which time the tasks of the first two levels are solved, is structurally different from the phase following after age 14, during which the two higher-level tasks are primarily attainable.

CONCLUDING COMMENTS

In conclusion, Study 2 shows that the SSSs described by our theory represent systems of cognitive organization that go beyond traditionally defined general intelligence. Nevertheless, the two SSSs investigated here are tightly interconnected with general intelligence. In fact, it was found that general intelligence takes priority over the SSSs as a predictor of the effects of learning experiences. However, according to a series of analyses of the present data that are not presented here, as well as according to some other studies (Demetriou et al., 1992), these connections become looser with age, indicating that development strengthens the autonomy of SSSs. The reader is reminded that this conclusion was also suggested by the findings of Study 1 regarding the relations between SSSs (see the models shown in Fig. 4 above). Additionally, the different SSSs are differentially related to general intelligence. Together with the differences in their very organizations, this may explain the fact that the two SSSs were differentially amenable to training. In our theory, general intelligence is the sum of the processes and components involved in the two domain-general systems, that is, the hypercognitive and the processing systems. The studies presented next focus on these systems.

V. STUDY 3:
LOOKING THROUGH THE
METACOGNITIVE LOOKING GLASS

To function as the interface between SSSs and reality or among any of the SSSs, the hypercognitive-reflecting system should satisfy at least two conditions. First, it must have recourse to what might be called "the intellect's menu," which presents an overview of the available SSSs. Second, this menu must have a minimum degree of accuracy that is by and large independent of the developmental/functional status of the SSSs that it lists. Were the first condition to be violated, the subjective structure of cognitive abilities would not be a veridical reflection of its objective structure. Were the second condition to be violated, the hypercognitive-reflecting system would always lag behind cognition. Thus, while it might eventually result in a precise reflection of the structure of cognitive abilities, the system would not be able to direct the functioning of cognitive abilities and cause their evolution.

These assumptions were tested in a large project that involved subjects ranging in age from 12 to 40–50 years. The subjects were tested on four pairs of tasks addressed to four SSSs: the causal-experimental, the verbal-propositional, the quantitative-relational, and the spatial-imaginal. One of the paired tasks tapped abilities normally acquired at about 12–13 years of age and the other those normally acquired at about the age of 16–18 years. Among other things, subjects were asked, first, to solve all tasks and, second, to evaluate each task in terms of processing difficulty and success of the solution given. The subjects were also asked to evaluate the similarity of a number of task pairs (i.e., tasks similar in content but different in SSS affiliation, tasks similar in SSS affiliation but different in content, etc.) according to the thought operations that they employed while working on them.

The assumption of objective-subjective correspondence leads to the prediction that the same SSS-specific factor structures would be abstracted from both performance scores and metacognitive evaluation scores. To test this prediction, the performance, difficulty evaluation, and success evaluation scores were factor analyzed separately. Each of these analyses showed that the two tasks addressed to the same SSS loaded highly on the same factor and that each factor differed from the factors on which the other tasks loaded. It was also found that the vertical structure of abilities is preserved in subjects' metacognitive evaluations, to a large extent independently of their cognitive attainment. That is, the more advanced the subjects' performance, the less difficult they considered the tasks and the more successful they believed their solutions to be. Nevertheless, the subjects' relative standing on the tasks was preserved in the evaluations of those able to solve both the easy and the difficult tasks, only the easy tasks, or neither of the two task categories. It was also found that the covariation between performance and success estimation, as well as between estimation of success and of difficulty, was quite high. This indicates that, as is asserted by the theory, the hypercognitive system preserves the forces governing the organization of cognitive structures (Demetriou & Efklides, 1989). Finally, the results regarding similarity evaluation clearly indicated that, with increasing age and/or developmental level, similarity evaluation shifts at about the age of 12–13 years from being based on external cues, such as content, to focusing on internal, operating/representational task characteristics. However, the ability to analyze these evaluations is present only after age 16–17 years and was seen in only a portion of the subjects operating on the fourth abstract level of the SSS tested. In conclusion, the SSSs are symmetrically reflected in performance as well as in the hypercognitive system from early adolescence on, although the quality of this reflection improves with increasing age.

Taken together, these findings indicate that, at least from early adolescence on, all persons are able to evaluate several aspects of tasks and of their own performance—such as task difficulty and solution success—in a way that reflects their own developmental level as well as the SSS and the level of complexity of the tasks. The existence of fairly accurate evaluation-decision mechanisms that guide the on-line regulatory system proposed earlier is thereby implied. However, it is only in late adolescence that this mechanism becomes conscious and an object of reflection. This conclusion is supported by our study of postformal development, which showed that a conscious and analytic personal theory of cognitive structure and functioning is coextensive with the metasystematic stages of cognitive development that start to appear no earlier than about 18 years (Demetriou, 1990).

The study to be presented here aimed to provide a further test of this claim by generating more fine-grained evidence regarding the metacognitive differentiation of cognitive functions and processes. In our earlier study, subjects were asked simply to specify their experiences in relation to the tasks they performed or just to evaluate their performance on these tasks. Such a method can provide only a gross approximation of the hyper-cognitive map of mental functions. Many reasons—such as differential sensitivity to the processes activated by different tasks, unsystematic descriptions of mental experiences, and absence of consistent criteria for evaluating one's performance or inaccuracy in the application of these criteria—can grossly distort the individual's actual hypercognitive map. To cope with this problem, subjects in the present study were given specific descriptions of a variety of mental functions and skills. These were either SSS independent, such as short-term memory or attention, or SSS specific, such as isolation of variables or understanding of proportional relations or mental rotation. The subjects' task was to indicate to what extent they used each of these functions and skills when solving each of a set of six tasks addressed to three SSSs.

Thus, the current study goes well beyond our earlier one in at least three respects. First, it can show whether subjects are able to differentiate the various SSSs with reference to the specific skills that they involve. If so, then SSS-specific skills will be associated more strongly with tasks known to tap the given SSS than with tasks known to tap other SSSs. It is plausible to expect that associating skills with SSSs correctly would not be an all-or-nothing phenomenon. Therefore, a second advantage of the current study is that it can reveal the degree to which skills regularly associated with one SSS are also perceived to be related to the other SSSs, by the reflecting person herself. Such evidence may throw light on the issue of the communication among different SSSs. Although there is no firm basis for specific predictions with regard to this question, it is reasonable to assume that skills specific to the quantitative-relational SSS would be more easily ascribed to the causal-experimental SSS (and vice versa) than to the spatial-imaginal SSS. Such a finding would reflect the popular belief that science and mathematics are not really different from each other. Finally, this study can show how domain-independent general cognitive functions are associated by the person with different SSSs with reference to specific tasks. To our knowledge, no previous study has been concerned with this question.

METHOD

Subjects

In all, 78 subjects were tested. Groups of 13, 13, 16, 19, and 17 subjects were drawn from grades 7, 8, 9, 10, and 11, respectively. The sexes were about equally represented in each of these age groups. All subjects came from middle-class Greek families living in Thessaloniki.

Cognitive Tasks

Three pairs of tasks were used to address the causal-experimental, the quantitative-relational, and the spatial-imaginal SSSs.

The Causal-Experimental Tasks

The first task concerned isolation of variables. A depiction of eight rods instantiating all possible combinations of two levels of length (long and short), two levels of width (thick and thin), and two cross-sectional shapes (triangular and round) was shown to the subjects. Subjects were then asked whether a fair test of the hypothesis that long rods are more flexible than short rods would be provided by (1) a pair of one short/thick/round rod and one long/thin/round rod, (2) a pair of one long/thin/triangular rod and one short/thin/triangular rod, or (3) a pair of one long/thick/round rod and one long/thin/round rod. Subjects were asked to explain their answers.

In the second task, subjects were presented with an arrangement of object, screen, and light source and asked to describe what experiments they would conduct in order to find out how the size of the object's shadow is related to (1) the distance of the object from the screen, (2) the distance of the object from the source of light, and (3) the size of the object. A satisfactory test of each of these hypotheses required systematic variations of the factor referred to in the hypotheses while holding all other factors constant.

The Quantitative-Relational Tasks

In the first task, specifications to be followed in the construction of buildings in various parts of the country were given to the subjects. According to these specifications, (1) the framework of one-story houses built in non-earthquake-prone zones must be made of iron bars 6 m long and 2 cm wide, (2) that of multistory buildings built in non-earthquake-prone zones must be iron bars 12 m long and 2 cm wide, and (3) that of one-story houses built in earthquake-prone zones must be iron bars 9 m long and 3 cm wide. Subjects were to specify the dimensions of bars to be used for multistory buildings constructed in earthquake-prone zones. Therefore, this task required the application of proportional reasoning in a well-specified context.

The second task concerned the quantitative relations among the three factors involved in the second causal-experimental task and the size of the shadows. A table containing the following information was given to the subjects: (1) the shadow of a ring 6 cm wide, at a distance of 5 m from the light and 5 m from the screen, would be 12 cm wide; (2) the shadow of a ring 12 cm wide, placed 5 m from the light and 5 m from the screen, would be 24 cm wide; (3) the shadow of a ring 12 cm wide, at a distance 10 m from the light and 5 m from the screen, would be 18 cm wide; and (4) the shadow of a ring 12 cm wide, placed 15 m from the light and 5 m from the screen, would be 16 cm wide. Subjects were asked to study these figures in order to discover exactly how each of the three factors is related to the size of shadows. They were then given two tasks to solve so as to demonstrate their understanding: (a) they had to specify the size of the shadow of a ring 8 cm wide, placed 5 m from the light and 5 m from the screen; and (b) they had to specify the size of a ring having a shadow 12 cm wide, given that it was placed 15 m from the light and 5 m from the screen.

The Spatial-Imaginal Tasks

The first task tapped the ability to formulate anticipatory mental images resulting from mental rotation and integration of figures that were separate before rotation. Specifically, the task shown in Figure 5a asked subjects to draw the geometric figures in their respective positions in the dashed rectangle AB, as they would appear if transparent planes A and B were rotated to come one above the other, as represented by rectangle AB.

The second task was based on Figure 5b. Subjects were told that each of the lights in an array was so tuned as to illuminate only one of the letters of the Greek word ΤΕΛΟΣ (telos, "end"); these letters were supposedly created by holes in a wooden rod. Thus, each letter could be projected onto a screen according to the direction of the light shining on it; the lights were arranged so as to make the letters appear on the screen in the reverse order (ΣΟΛΕΤ). The five letters were also reflected from the screen in a mirror, the normal order of the letters being restored in the mirror image. The subjects' task was to write the word as it would be projected both on the screen and on the mirror.

Our attempt systematically to manipulate the complexity and the content of the tasks should be apparent. The first of the two tasks addressed to each SSS was always simpler than the second (i.e., isolation of variables, extraction of a simple proportional relation, simple superimposition of fig-

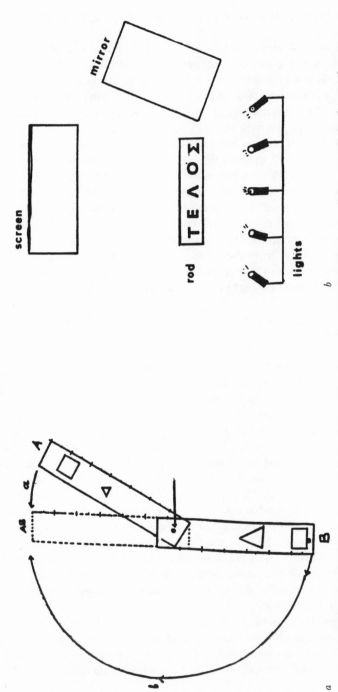

FIG. 5.—The spatial-imaginal tasks used in Study 3. *a*, The subject was asked to draw on parallelogram AB the figures shown on rods A and B. *b*, The subject was asked to draw on the screen and the mirror the projection of the word ΤΕΛΟΣ (*telos*, "end") appearing on the rod in front of the lights.

ures after rotation vs. design of a series of rather complex experiments, extraction of multiple proportional relations, and coordination of a series of figural arrangements related in complex ways). However, the first task was always concerned with rods and the second with shadows. Thus, the tasks addressed to the same SSS were different, whereas tasks addressed to the different SSSs were the same with regard to both developmental level and content. This manipulation was designed to show whether the hyper-cognitive system bases its decisions on the processing or on the phenomeno-logical characteristics of the tasks. If decisions concerning task-SSS or task-specific component affiliation are based on the feelings of difficulty that are related to the developmental level or to the phenomenological characteris-tics of tasks, then a given component or process would tend to be ascribed to tasks that are similar in level or content rather than to those similar with regard to SSS affiliation. However, if the affiliation process is geared to the processing aspects of tasks (as is assumed by the principle of formal-procedural specificity), the system would be able to circumvent the illusory effects of effort or content and to associate tasks with the cognitive processes directed to the attainment of the task goal.

Scoring the Tasks

Performance on each task was scored on a three-point scale. In the case of the two causal-experimental tasks, a score of 0 was given for responses indicating that the subject was unable to apply the scheme "all other things being equal but the factor tested" (task 1) or to design an experiment in which the manipulations were mapped onto the hypotheses (task 2). A score of 1 was given for responses indicating the unsystematic application of these abilities and a score of 2 for responses indicating errorless isolation of vari-ables and systematic design of experiments according to the hypotheses tested.

In the case of the quantitative-relational tasks, a score of 0 was given to incorrect responses that indicated that the subject was unable to approach the problems in relational terms. A score of 1 was given for correct but unexplained responses indicating the application of relational processing; correct and sufficiently explained responses, indicating the full mastery of the processes necessary to specify the relations involved, were scored 2.

In the case of the spatial-imaginal tasks, 0 was assigned to responses indicating that the subject was unable to formulate the images suggested by the transformations applied to the original figural arrangements. Images involving both correct and incorrect elements, indicating an incipient ability to produce an image out of another image as a result of the application of a specific transformation, were scored 1, and fully correct images, indicating

83

that the spatial-imaginal ability of the person was flexible enough to integrate the results of any transformation of an image into a new image, were scored 2.

The Hypercognitive Battery

The hypercognitive battery was designed to allow subjects to specify the degree to which they thought that each of a number of general or specialized cognitive processes or skills is associated with the processing of the six tasks. This battery consisted of two parts: the first was concerned with general cognitive functions or processes and the second with SSS-specific skills or components. In each instance, a statement was provided describing a function or a skill, together with an example instantiating how this function or skill may be used when solving common, everyday problems. The six tasks were listed in a column to the right of each of the statement-example blocks. Subjects were instructed to indicate for each task "how much [they] used" the skill described in the left-hand column on a five-point scale (1 = not at all; 2 = a little; 3 = quite; 4 = much; 5 = very much).

General Cognitive Processes

Five general functions were included: attention, short-term memory, long-term memory, comprehension, and reasoning. The first two were represented by two and the rest by three statements. Examples of the statements addressed to each of these functions follow:

Attention.—"This problem requires a degree of concentration such that any disturbance in the environment makes it very difficult to understand and solve the problem (e.g., when somebody talks to you while you are reading a very difficult text and giving it all your concentration in order to understand what is written)."

Short-term memory.—"To solve this problem, you have to hold in your mind many elements of the data you have been given (e.g., when you try to add up in your head two very large numbers such as 43,781,931 and 5,635,781)."

Long-term memory.—"To solve this problem, you first have to know a lot of things that are directly related to the problem (e.g., to find the houses you want in a town, you have to know the numbers, the districts of the town, where the various buses go, etc.)."

Comprehension.—"To solve this problem, you have to understand each new piece of information given to you fully so that you can use it when necessary (e.g., you must first understand all the chapters in your mathematics book before you can try to solve the exercises at the back of the book)."

Deduction.—"The facts presented in this problem are not very clear, so you have to go beyond those facts in drawing your own conclusions (e.g., in the morning when you see that the earth is wet, you realize that it has rained during the night)."

SSS-Specific Processes

Each of the three SSSs was represented by three statements addressed to a different component among those presumably constituting the given SSS. The three statements representing the causal-experimental SSS referred to the combinatorial, the isolation-of-variables, and the hypothesis-formation abilities. Those representing the quantitative-relational SSS referred to the processes enabling one to apply the basic arithmetic operations, order things along a quantitative dimension, and estimate proportional relations. Finally, the statements addressed to the imaginal-spatial SSS referred to the processes enabling one to apply mental rotation, integrate the different perspectives from which one can see an object, and integrate the different pieces of an image into the integrated image. Examples of these statements follow:

Causal-experimental SSS: Isolation of variables.—"To solve this problem, you have to proceed to test each of its elements while making sure that all the others remain the same (e.g., if you suspect that either the juice, the honey, or the milk was responsible for a certain recipe not succeeding, you have to make a number of tests changing only one of these constituents each time in order to find out what was really to blame)."

Quantitative-relational SSS: Dimensional coordination.—"To solve this problem, you must first understand that two different measurements can change in the same way (e.g., when the one increases, the other increases also) or that they can change in different ways (e.g., when one increases, the other decreases) (in general, e.g., when you know the relation between width and height, you can find the measurement for one if you know the measurement for the other)."

Spatial-imaginal SSS: Mental rotation.—"To solve this problem, you have to imagine that a certain shape turns in space either as a whole or only in part and to know the form that it will have when it stops rotating (e.g., you are shown the position of the hands of a clock when the time is 3 o'clock and then asked to describe their position when the time is 12 o'clock)."

Procedure

All subjects were tested in groups during school hours by a graduate student. Two booklets were handed to each subject, one containing the six cognitive tasks and the other the hypercognitive questionnaire. The order of presentation of the cognitive tasks was counterbalanced across subjects. The hypercognitive questionnaire was always answered after the cognitive tasks had been completed. This constraint aimed to provide the subjects with experience related to all tasks before going on to express their judgments about the processes they used when processing each task.

RESULTS AND DISCUSSION

Structural Relations

General Functions by SSSs' Relations

The hypercognitive association between the general functions and the SSSs can take one of two forms (if one excludes the trivial possibility of no perceived relation between them). First, the general cognitive functions may be the pivotal dimensions of hypercognitive monitoring. Therefore, when a problem has to be processed, the individual creates a mental space defined by general cognitive functions and then searches in this space to specify the functions most relevant to solving the problem at hand. The second assumption reverses the priorities. In this view, each of the SSSs functions as a dynamic module that, once activated, points to the functions most relevant to the attainment of the problem goals. In other words, the claim is that the mental space is defined by the forces peculiar to the SSSs and that the general cognitive functions are subservient to these forces. According to our theory, these forces are associated with the domain and the computational specificity of the problem and its symbolic bias. Therefore, our theory is coextensive with the second assumption.

Confirmatory factor analysis was again used as a means for testing these assumptions. There were 13 hypercognitive statements regarding the general functions, each of which had to be ranked in relation to each of the six cognitive tasks, yielding a total of 78 scores. To reduce the number of scores to a manageable level and increase reliability, all scores given to statements associating a given function with an SSS were averaged, generating three scores per function. These scores can be regarded as an index of perceived association between the functions and each of the three SSSs. The models aiming to test the two assumptions outlined above were fitted on 15 scores: five general functions × three SSSs.

A model consistent with the first assumption involves five first-order function-specific factors: each set of three scores representing a function would be related to the same factor. A further assumption in this model was that these five factors would all be related to a higher-order factor. This factor might be considered indicative of the general self-monitoring abilities of the person implied by the principle of the subjective distinctness of cognitive processes. The fit of this model to the data proved to be poor, $\chi^2(85)$ = 150.888, p = .001, CFI = .769.

A model consistent with the second assumption involves three first-order SSS-specific factors. Here, each set of five scores associating all five general cognitive functions with an SSS would be related to the same factor. The second-order general factor would also be present to indicate the operation of the principle of subjective distinctness. The fit of this model to the data, $\chi^2(87)$ = 132.242, p = .001, CFI = .841, was much better than the fit of the first model. In fact, this model proved to have a very good fit to the data when a few of the residuals were allowed to correlate, $\chi^2(83)$ = 98.032, p = .124, CFI = .947. This is the model shown in Figure 6.[9]

SSS-Specific Processes

The analysis presented above shows that the domain-free functions are perceived by the person as organized according to their association with the various SSSs. This makes it more than plausible that the SSS-specific skills would also be perceived as organized according to their SSS affiliation. To test this assumption, the model shown in Figure 7 was fitted to the data. This model involves the nine scores assigned by the subjects to the nine SSS-specific skills involved in the study (i.e., three skills for each of the three SSSs) and the scores they attained on the six tasks. This model was built on three assumptions. First, each set of three hypercognitive scores regarding the same SSS would be related to the same factor, which would differ from the two to which the other sets would be related. Second, each pair of scores representing performance on tasks addressed to the same SSS would also be related to the same factor. Thus, each of the three SSSs would be reflected in both the hypercognitive and the actual performance scores. Third, there would be a general second-order factor to which all six first-order factors would be related. This would be taken to represent the general monitoring function of the hypercognitive system. The fit of this model to the data was excellent, $\chi^2(82)$ = 78.002, p = .604, CFI = 1.000.

Development and Perceived Strength of Association between Processes

The results presented above are informative concerning the perceived organization of domain-free functions and SSS-specific processes. However, they are not very revealing concerning the relative differentiation in the

[9] The correlation matrix, means, and standard deviations of the variables involved in the models tested in Study 3 are shown in Appendix Table A5.

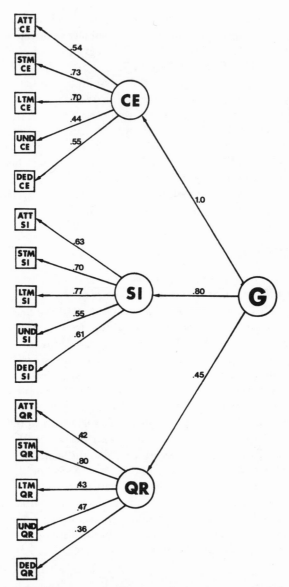

FIG. 6.—The model best fitting subjects' evaluations of the relations between general functions and SSSs.

The symbols ATT, STM, LTM, UND, DED, CE, SI, QR, and G stand for attention, short-term memory, long-term memory, understanding, deduction, the causal-experimental SSS, the spatial-imaginal SSS, the quantitative-relational SSS, and the general factor, respectively. (The model indicates that each of the general cognitive functions is perceived by the subject to have special relations with each of the three SSSs—the three SSS-specific factors. A general coordinating factor is also implicated—the second-order general factor.)

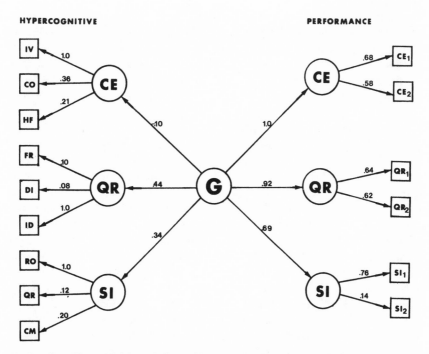

Fig. 7.—The model best fitting subjects' evaluations of the relations between the SSS-specific components and the SSSs and their performance on the six tasks.

The symbols IV, CO, HF, OP, DI, PR, RO, PI, and CM stand for the ratings given by the subjects to the statement referring to the use of, respectively, isolation of variables, combinatorial strategy, hypothesis formation, application of arithmetic operations, order values along a quantitative dimension, estimate proportional relations, mental rotation, integration of perspectives, and composition of an image. The symbols CE, QR, and SI stand for the causal-experimental, the quantitative-relational, and the spatial-imaginal SSSs, respectively. (The model indicates that metacognitive ratings of the perceived relations between components and SSSs, like performance on SSS-specific tasks, are organized in structures corresponding to the SSSs described by the theory. A higher-order coordinating function is also implicated—see the second-order G factor.)

strength of perceived relations between general functions or between SSS-specific processes and the particular SSSs represented in this study. They also do not address possible changes in these relations as a result of development. Analyses presented below focus on these issues.

General Functions by SSSs' Relations

A 5 (age) × 5 (function) × 3 (SSS) MANOVA with repeated measures on the last two factors was applied to the 15 mean scores representing the perceived association between the functions and each of the three SSSs. The results of this analysis indicated that the main effect of age was nonsignificant, $F(4, 72) = 1.38$, $p = .248$. However, the main effects of function,

$F(4, 292) = 12.27, p = .000$, Pillais index $= .411, p = .000$, and of SSS, $F(2, 146) = 19.88, p = .000$, Pillais index $= .295, p = .000$, were highly significant. The function × SSS interaction was also significant, $F(8, 584) = 4.08, p = .000$, Pillais index $= .334, p = .000$. Of the various interactions between age and the two between-subjects factors, only the age × SSS interaction was significant, $F(8, 146) = 3.21, p = .002$, Pillais index $= .214, p = .03$. These results are illustrated in Figure 8.[10]

With regard to the five functions, it can be seen that, overall, attention ($M = 2.843$) and comprehension ($M = 2.955$) were perceived as more usable than the other three general functions; interestingly enough, memory ($M = 2.523$) was perceived as the least usable of all functions. This finding probably indicates that the two functions scoring higher are more salient internally than the others. Thus, the effects of interference in attention can easily be detected because they cause interruption of the problem-solving attempt. However, the three processes scoring lower, long-term memory in particular, are more tacit and their effects on problem solving less direct than the others. For example, former knowledge may not be seen to be related to current processing of a problem because it may have led to automatic skills regarded by the person as "just being there."

With respect to the SSSs, it can be seen that the quantitative-relational SSS ($M = 2.952$) scored higher than the causal-experimental SSS ($M = 2.741$), which, in turn, scored higher than the spatial-imaginal SSS ($M = 2.511$). This finding is perfectly sensible: it indicates that subjects regard the quantitative-relational SSS as more intellectually demanding than the other two, the spatial-imaginal SSS in particular. The age × SSS interaction indicated that this differentiation between the three SSSs strengthens with increasing age. Whereas the three SSSs were rated on average about the same by the two younger groups, mean ratings of the quantitative-relational SSS tended subsequently to increase and to decrease in the case of the two other SSSs, especially the spatial-imaginal SSS. This finding indicates that awareness of the various SSSs changes with development. One possible explanation might be that the spatial-imaginal SSS involves skills that become automatic more easily, or earlier, than the skills involved in other SSSs. A different explanation might be invoked for the causal-experimental SSS, which usually shows a spurt in its development after 16 years of age. The persistent low degree of awareness of this SSS might indicate that our subjects had not as yet come to grasp it clearly; hence, the involvement of general processes in the execution of these skills evaded their awareness. The function × SSS interaction points to the same conclusion. What merits noting in this interaction is the very high score given to the use of short-term

---

[10] The mean metacognitive ratings (and standard deviations) on which Fig. 8 is based are presented in Appendix Table A6.

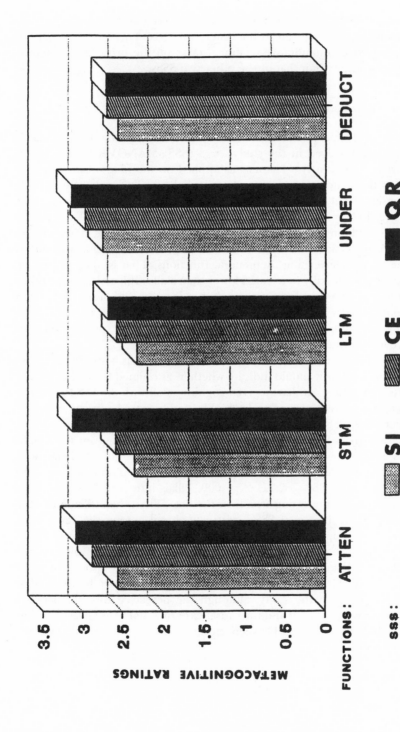

Fig. 8.—Mean perceived relations between general functions and SSSs

memory in solving quantitative-relational tasks as contrasted to the very low corresponding scores given to the other two SSSs. This indicates that the strain exerted by quantitative-relational tasks on the processing system is felt more strongly than that of the other two SSSs.

SSS-Specific Processes

A 5 (age) × 3 (mean of the scores assigned by subjects to the SSS-specific skills involved in the study) × 3 (SSS) MANOVA with repeated measures on the last two factors was applied on the nine mean scores involved in the structural modeling described above. The main effect of age was nonsignificant, $F(4, 72) = 1.29$, $p = .281$. However, the main effect of skills, $F(2, 144) = 8.02$, $p = .001$, Pillais index $= .150$, $p = .003$, as well as the age × skill interaction, $F(8, 144) = 2.48$, $p = .015$, Pillais index $= .150$, $p = .035$, were significant. These results point to the same conclusion as did the results concerning the general functions. That is, they reflect the fact that imaginal skills were rated lower than skills affiliated with the other two SSSs and that this difference tended to increase with age. Thus, from the point of view of the person, the spatial-imaginal SSS appears to be running with minimal direct involvement of general or specific processes relative to the other SSSs.

The most crucial effect to consider in this analysis is the skills × SSS interaction because it should indicate whether, as claimed by the theory, the subjects were able to affiliate a given cognitive skill with the SSS to which it belongs. This effect proved to be highly significant and in the expected direction, $F(4, 288) = 25.22$, $p = .000$, Pillais index $= .430$, $p = .000$. It can be seen from Figure 9 that the association between a given set of skills and its own SSS was always perceived as stronger than its association with the other SSSs.[11] Moreover, the age × skill × SSS interaction was also significant, $F(16, 288) = 2.71$, $p = .000$, Pillais index $= .344$, $p = .058$. This reflects two interesting trends in the data. First, the affiliation of the three skills with their own SSS is virtually absent among the 12-year-old subjects. It first appears among the 13-year-olds only as a differentiation between the spatial-imaginal and the two other SSSs. After this age, the quantitative-relational and the causal-experimental SSSs also begin to be differentiated. This differentiation becomes quite distinct for the oldest subjects involved in the study, although the perceived distance between the quantitative-relational and the causal-experimental SSSs always remains smaller than the distance between either of these two and the spatial-imaginal SSS.

[11] The mean metacognitive ratings (and standard deviations) on which Fig. 9 is based are presented in Appendix Table A7.

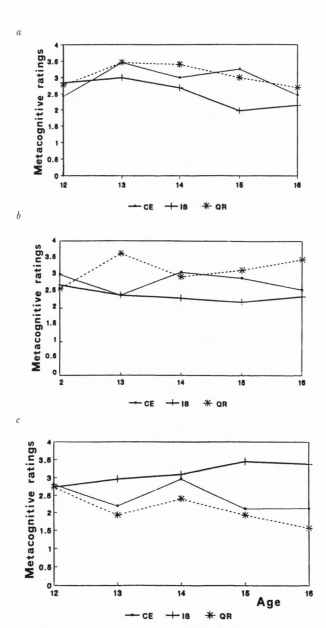

Fig. 9.—Mean perceived relations between SSS-specific components and the three SSSs as a function of age. *a*, The mean metacognitive ratings (averaged over the two tasks addressed to each SSS) indicating how much the subjects thought that they used a combinatorial strategy when solving the tasks addressed to each SSS. *b*, The mean metacognitive ratings given to the use of the strategy that aimed to specify the relations between two covarying dimensions. *c*, The mean metacognitive ratings given to the use of mental rotation when solving the tasks addressed to each SSS.

Each strategy is thought to be used more when solving tasks representing the SSS of which it is a component and less when solving tasks representing other SSSs—this tendency is very clear in the case of mental rotation.

CONCLUDING COMMENTS

Study 3 showed clearly that the SSSs are modules powerful enough to constrain how general cognitive functions or specific cognitive skills are perceived by the individual. Each of the general cognitive functions represented in this study tended to be perceived as differentially related to each of the SSSs. However, the various SSSs were not regarded as equally demanding in their use of the different cognitive functions; specifically, the spatial-imaginal SSS was viewed as generally less demanding than the other two. Moreover, processes such as attention or comprehension, which normally require more mental effort than others (e.g., long-term memory), were generally regarded as more involved in the processing of all problems. The SSS-specific skills were perceived as more closely related to their own than to other SSSs. However, some of the skills were more frequently found to be regarded as mutually interchangeable (i.e., the quantitative-relational and the causal-experimental) than others (i.e., the spatial-imaginal with the rest). These results are clearly also in agreement with the findings of the two studies reported in Chapters III and IV.

The large perceived distance between the spatial-imaginal SSS and the other SSSs may also signify the presence of more pronounced differences between this SSS and the causal-experimental or the quantitative-relational SSS. For instance, according to Baddeley (1991), working memory involves an executive component (which is very similar to our control of processing) and two storage systems: an articulatory loop specializing in the retention of acoustic information and a visual-spatial sketch pad specializing in the retention of visual-spatial information. Thus, the clear hypercognitive differentiation of the spatial-imaginal SSS from the other ones may reflect the subjects' sensitivity to their dependence on different storage components of the processing system.

It must be stressed, however, that sensitivity to the differential relations between general functions, or between specific skills and the various SSSs, is sharpened with development. This sensitivity was found to emerge at about age 13 years, and then only in relation to the SSS that is generally regarded as different from the others (i.e., the spatial-imaginal). At about the age of 16 years, hypercognitive monitoring appears to be sufficiently refined to involve very accurate maps reflecting intra- and inter-SSS connections with regard to general functions or specialized skills. Therefore, Study 3 also confirms the age points of major changes in the hypercognitive system that we specified in our previous research (Demetriou, 1990; Demetriou & Efklides, 1989).

VI. STUDIES 4 AND 5:
THE DEVELOPMENT OF THE PROCESSING SYSTEM AND ITS RELATION TO THE SPECIALIZED STRUCTURAL SYSTEMS

The following two studies focus on the development of the processing system and the relations between this system and the SSSs.

STUDY 4:
STORAGE SPACE, COGNITIVE LEVEL, AND SPECIALIZED STRUCTURAL SYSTEMS

This study concentrates on the development of the storage component of the processing system in order to answer two questions. First, are there really different kinds of storage space, such as dimensional and vectorial space, as is claimed by Case (1985)? The answer to this question touches on important issues regarding the very nature of development. As we noted in reviewing the work of other theorists (see Chap. II), development is considered by some to be a recycling process (Case and Fischer). For others (Pascual-Leone and perhaps Halford), development is an additive process in which cognitive functioning is rescaled from a lower- to a higher-level unit when the expansion of the storage component of mental power exceeds a certain number of units (usually two). Our own interpretation of cognitive development—which we view as a series of reiterated cycles of representational change leading from intuitors to differentiated and flexibly intercoordinated components—leans toward the recycling model (see Study 1).

The second question concerns the possible differential relations between storage space and the SSSs. Apart from experiential structuralism, all the models that we have discussed predict that the correlations between the two short-term storage space (STSS) tasks and the cognitive tasks should remain about the same because, according to these models, STSS is slotted into a certain number of units at a given age. Thus, it does not matter whether these units are occupied by numbers, words, or images: if no bias-ing mnemonic strategy is applied, STSS will show its—invariable—capacity.

In contrast, experiential structuralism assumes that the "standard infor-mation unit" (Demetriou & Efklides, 1988, p. 215) differs across SSSs. These differences may be located in the size, in the speed of processing, in the control needs they pose, or in the deactivation rate of the units characteriz-ing different SSSs. On the basis of this assumption, experiential structural-ism defines STSS in terms of the formula

$$STSS = f(Cp \cdot U_{SSS}), \tag{2}$$

where Cp is the general storage capacity available at the time of testing, and U_{SSS} is the SSS-specific information unit. The implication of this definition is very clear: a part of the variation in any measure of capacity is always due to the measurement instrument applied on capacity. Therefore, the degree of covariation between storage capacity and cognitive measures should be proportional to the number of common components (e.g., belong-ing to the same domain, encoded in the same symbol system, etc.) shared by the two kinds of measures.

To examine these two issues, Study 4 was designed to provide evidence regarding the growth of developmentally different manifestations of stor-age capacity, different SSSs, and cognitively different subjects. This design aimed to dissociate sheer age from cognitive level and hence permit estab-lishing whether STSS is age dependent, as all models presume, or depen-dent on the development of an SSS. To meet these specifications, some of the subjects involved in Study 1 were also tested with the counting (CST) and ratio (RST) span tests devised by Case and Kurland (1978), which ad-dress dimensional and vectorial operations, respectively.

Method

Subjects

In all, 72 subjects were involved in this study. Of these 72 subjects, 12, 16, 18, 12, and 13 were, respectively, 9, 11, 13, 15, and 20 years old. The 9- and the 20-year-olds were recruited for Study 4. Half the 9-year-olds were "good" and half "poor" students according to their teachers' evalua-tions. The 11-, 13-, and 15-year-olds were selected from subjects tested in Study 1 on the basis of their performance on the QR-N battery: half the subjects in each of these three age groups had shown the *lowest* and the other half the *highest* level of attainment on this battery (see Table 2 above).

Tasks

The CST assesses the person's ability to store in STSS, and to recall from it, a series of digits representing the results of counting. According to Case (1985), counting is a dimensional operation because the operations that it involves enable the subject to construct a single dimension that can be defined in terms of its elements, the relations between the elements, and its direction. In the present test, subjects were presented with three series of cards for each of the seven levels of the dimensional STSS investigated in this study. A number of red and green dots were depicted on each card. Subjects were instructed to count the red dots only, store the resultant digit in memory, and recall the complete series of digits on presentation of a white card. Thus, at levels 1, 2, . . . , 7, only one, two, . . . , seven cards, respectively, had to be counted before the presentation of a white card, for three consecutive trials.

The RST was identical, except that, in this instance, the subject was asked to evaluate, store, and recall the ratio between the red and the green dots ("How many green dots are there for each red dot on the card?"). This is a vectorial operation in that it requires the subject to coordinate two numerical dimensions rather than to work with just one.

Scoring

On both tasks, subjects were given a score corresponding to the highest level at which they succeeded on at least two trials in correctly recalling the results of counting. Subjects who were able to do so on only one of the three trials addressed to a level were assigned a score of .33.

Results and Discussion

The differentiation of subjects according to cognitive level (i.e., school performance or performance on the QR-N battery) aimed at revealing whether STSS is age dependent, as postulated by all the models, or cognitive-level dependent. In Case's words, STSS reflects "the maximum number of operational products the human neurological tissue can store" (1985, p. 427). If the "neurological tissue" is intact, it should be able to store whatever it is expected to store independently of its performance on cognitive tasks. According to all models, performance on cognitive tasks presupposes that the available capacity equals or exceeds the capacity demand of the task in question and that a minimum number of task-related strategies, skills, and schemes are available to the subject.

These considerations lead to the prediction that low-cognitive-level sub-jects should not fall short of the level of achievement expected for their age; expecting a slight advantage for the high-cognitive-level subjects is also reasonable because these subjects may possess memorization strategies not available to their low-cognitive-level age-mates. In any event, the STSS dif-ferences between the two groups should be smaller than the differences in their cognitive level.

Table 8 shows the mean attainment on the counting and the vectorial span test across age and cognitive level. To facilitate the evaluation of these findings, Table 8 also shows the expected attainment for each of the two tests at each of the years of age involved in this study. The specification of the expected values was based on Case's (1985) ascription of short-term storage capacity to different age levels. The mean level score attainment on the two cognitive batteries is also shown (the reader is reminded that the allocation of the subjects in the two cognitive-level groups was based on their performance on the QR-N battery). It can be seen in Table 8 that the foregoing prediction was fully supported by the evidence: in all but one case, the dimensional and the vectorial STSSs of the low-level subjects were slightly higher than those to be expected according to Case's theory. The conclusion suggested by these results is very clear. Age-related changes in the structures underlying the individual's capacity to store information are sufficient to bring about the minimum processing space required for age-related performance on cognitive tasks, even when performance itself on these tasks actually falls short of the level expected.

Is this age-dependent development consistent with the common-ceiling model or with the rescaling model? The common-ceiling model predicts that the CST score should level off at 11 and the RST score at 15 years of age. Beyond these ages, only minimal increases are to be expected, and in no case should these increases exceed 1 unit of STSS. The rescaling model predicts a linear increase in the CST score until at least the age of 15 years; it makes no specific prediction regarding the RST score.

Strictly speaking, our results support neither of these models. The re-scaling model must be totally rejected because even the most cognitively advanced subjects never approached the 7-unit limit; in fact, adults per-formed less well than 15-year-old adolescents on both tests. The results are closer to the common-ceiling model since, in accord with its prediction, the CST does essentially level off at 4 units by the age of 11 years. However, the most important deviation between expected and observed results was obtained with regard to the RST. The scores attained on this test, although always lower than those attained on the CST, proved to be higher than theoretically expected throughout the age range we studied. This fact con-tradicts the CST-RST relation that would have supported the recycling model of development—that is, that, before the counting span rises to 4

TABLE 8

Expected (Ex.) and Observed (Obs.) Mean Short-Term Storage Space (and Standard
Deviations) across Age, Cognitive Level, and Type of Operation

Age and Cognitive Level	Mean Level Score on the SSSs		STSS Tasks			
			Dimensional		Vectorial	
	QR	CE	Ex.	Obs.	Ex.	Obs.
9 years:						
Low	...	...	3.00	2.80	1	1.86
				(.65)		(.45)
High	...	...	3	3.90	1	2.57
				(.58)		(.49)
11 years:						
Low	.00	.86	4	3.42	2	2.76
	(.00)	(.83)		(.39)		(.89)
High	2.43	2.57	4	4.57	2	3.57
	(.73)	(.90)		(.83)		(.75)
13 years:						
Low	.14	1.43	4[a]	4.37	3	3.62
	(.35)	(1.12)		(.92)		(1.03)
High	3.38	3.12	4[a]	5.66	3	4.62
	(.48)	(1.17)		(.72)		(.68)
15 years:						
Low	1.00	2.67	4[a]	5.03	4	4.38
	(.82)	(.74)		(.83)		(1.41)
High	4.00	2.17	4[a]	5.44	4	5.11
	(.00)	(.68)		(1.51)		(.83)
22 years:						
Low	2.77	3.33	4[a]	4.88	4	4.37
	(.42)	(1.05)		(.38)		(1.05)
High	4.00	4.00	4[a]	6.00	4	4.91
	(.00)	(.00)		(.74)		(1.09)

Note.—Performance on each of the four tasks addressed to each SSS was scored 0, 1, and 2. Allocation of subjects to the "low"- or "high"-performance group in all but the 9-year-old subjects was based on the performance attained on the quantitative-relational tasks only. The allocation of the 9-year-olds was based on the evaluation of their teacher. The mean level score was calculated by averaging over the scores attained on the four tasks addressed to each SSS. The expected STSS scores were taken from Case (1985).

[a] These scores can be higher than expected by some unknown decimal value.

units, no vectorial unit can be stored; that 4 counting span units are equivalent to 1 vectorial unit; and that, after this, the storage of vectorial units
rises as specified for the successive age levels whereas the counting span
stays at the value of 4 units plus.

In sum, the results of Study 4 suggest that a weak version of the common-ceiling model—which one could call the *functional shift* model—might
be worth considering. This model presumes that, when the structures of a
given level reach a maximum degree of complexity, the system tends to
reorganize them at a higher level of representation or integration so as to
render them more manageable. This tendency might be neurologically or
functionally determined (the "or" here is not exclusive). Having created a

new mental unit, the system prefers to work with this rather than with previously used structures because of its functional advantages. However, the development of the earlier units may still continue, although at a much slower rate. Evidently, there are occasional advantages in returning to a lower-level unit. Moreover, functioning at each next higher level may exert positive effects on the management of the units processed at the lower levels.

Finally, the functional shift model does not presume an exact formal equivalence between the corresponding levels of successive developmental cycles. Recycling is thus to be conceived more as a gross correspondence between two or more hierarchies of ascending complexity than as a self-repetition of a single hierarchy across different contents or representation systems. This implies, on the one hand, that, for example, level-2 units in a given cycle Y are more complex than level-1 units in this cycle, just as it is the case with level-2 units relative to level-1 units in the preceding cycle X. On the other hand, however, it also implies that the same level units across the two cycles need not be structurally identical, as Case (1985) maintains. Thus, this model provides the vertical dimension of development with considerably more degrees of freedom to generate mental units that would satisfy the needs of successive developmental phases. The specific structural composition of the units of corresponding levels across cycles depends on the specific structural and representational characteristics of different phases.

The functional shift model can thus accommodate evidence that cannot be accommodated by the other two models. The common-ceiling model cannot accommodate the fact that age brings about STSS increments exceeding the ceilings specified by Case's theory; it also fails to predict the correspondence between dimensional and vectorial units. The rescaling model, on the other hand, cannot accommodate the fact that capacity development as expressed through the development of dimensional storage space is drastically inhibited as soon as functioning shifts to a new kind of unit (i.e., the vectorial storage space) and development starts to take place anew at the level of the new unit.

It should also be noted that the functional shift model is in line with recent views that conceive of short-term memory as a system built for efficient retrieval. According to MacGregor (1987), the limited capacity of such a system is due to the fact that there is an upper limit beyond which unorganized memory is less efficient than organized memory. Thus, when this limit is exceeded, the person shifts to memorization strategies such as chunking. MacGregor's analysis, which is consistent with empirical evidence (e.g., Broadbent, 1975), specified limits of four or six items for this shift to occur in, respectively, exhaustive and self-terminating search. This analysis also suggests that there are indifference points at which one- or two-level organizations are equally effective. For example, in the case of self-terminating search and with six items in storage, three chunks of two, two chunks of three, or six single items can be recalled with equal efficiency from short-term memory. What we propose here is that both the shift limits and the indifference points change with increasing age. This makes development of storage capacity appear, in Case's terms, to be recycling. Clearly, a study of changes in these limits and indifference points would be highly informative for cognitive developmental theory.

Short-Term Storage across Specialized Structural Systems and Symbolic Systems

Table 9 shows the correlations of the two STSS measures with the other cognitive measures used in Study 4. These correlations speak directly to the validity of the STSS-SSS relations specified in the formula given in equation (2). According to this formula, the correlations between the two STSS measures and the cognitive batteries should vary as a function of the operating/symbolic similarity between the STSS and the cognitive measures.

In this instance, the two STSS measures are based on numerical operations and representation. As far as the cognitive batteries are concerned, the quantitative-relational-numeric battery requires the systematic use of both of these, whereas the causal-experimental-imaginal battery requires the use of neither. The quantitative-relational-imaginal and the causal-experimental-numeric batteries share, respectively, numerical operations and numerical representation with the STSS measures. It is not known whether the operating or the representation system is more important in

TABLE 9

CORRELATIONS OF STSS MEASURES WITH AGE
AND SSS INDEXES ($N = 63$)

SSS AND SYMBOL SYSTEM	STSS TASKS	
	Dimensional	Vectorial
QR:		
N	.57	.46
I	.32	.22
CE:		
N	.44	.34
I	.29	.18
Age	.38	.18

NOTE.—The cognitive tasks used here are those used in Study 1 and described in Table 2.

determining the relation between two cognitive measures. It is generally supposed, however, that the imaginal mode of representation is particularly idiosyncratic insofar as encoding and processing are concerned (see Kosslyn, 1980). Thus, this mode may impose its own constraints on an operating system. Bearing these points in mind, one would predict that, from high to low, the correlations between the two STSS tasks and the cognitive tasks would be ordered as follows: quantitative-numeric → experimental-numeric → quantitative-imaginal → experimental-imaginal. The pattern of correlations shown in Table 9 fully coincides with this prediction.

It should be noted that these results are in line with the finding of Study 3 that the subjective distance between the spatial-imaginal SSS and the quantitative-relational or the causal-experimental SSS is clearly greater than the distance between the latter two SSSs. The low correlations obtained here between STSS and the imaginally biased versions of these two SSSs, as contrasted with the correlations between STSS tasks and their numerically biased versions, suggest that imaginal information may not be stored in the same space as phonological information. This differentiation is reflected in the hypercognitive awareness of the person.

How is level of attainment on STSS measures interpatterned with level of attainment on the two SSSs? The answer can show whether storage capacity is a necessary but not sufficient condition for the development of the SSSs (as it is assumed by the present theory) or whether these two partners of developing intellect are more closely related—as is assumed by other theories. Table 10 shows the interpatterning of performance on the CST and the two SSS measures; the corresponding distribution for the RST was virtually identical. It can be seen that only a few subjects were able to function on any of the developmental levels of the two SSSs without having attained a counting span of at least 4 units. However, subjects who attained this or a higher span may operate on any of the SSS-specific developmental levels. These results are in clear accord with the assumption that a minimum of storage capacity is required to permit certain cognitive constructions. However, satisfying this requirement is not sufficient in itself to ensure that these constructions will come into existence.

STUDY 5:
PROCESSING SPEED AND CONTROL

The aim of Study 5 was to investigate the relations between the three components of the processing system—namely, processing speed, control of processing, and working memory—and to examine the relations of these components with the SSSs. For the purposes of the present study, the quantitative-relational SSS was selected.

TABLE 10

BIVARIATE DISTRIBUTION OF PERFORMANCE ON THE COUNTING SPAN TEST (CST) AND THE
QUANTITATIVE-RELATIONAL AND THE CAUSAL-EXPERIMENTAL SSS MEASURES

SSS LEVEL AND MEASURE	CST LEVEL							
	0	1	2	3	4	5	6	7
0:								
QR	0	0	2	3	1^a	0^a	0^a	0^a
CE	0	0	0	3	2^a	1^a	0^a	0^a
I:								
QR	0^a	1^a	0^a	0^a	5	2	0	0
CE	0^a	0^a	0^a	1^a	4	1	2	0
II:								
QR	0^a	0^a	0^a	6^a	3	5	2	0
CE	0^a	0^a	1^a	1^a	5	4	5	0
III:								
QR	0^a	0^a	1^a	2^a	4	1	3	0
CE	0^a	0^a	0^a	1^a	6	2	1	1
IV:								
QR	0^a	0^a	1^a	2^a	8	5	2	0
CE	0^a	0^a	0^a	0^a	3	8	6	1

NOTE.—The necessary but not sufficient hypothesis was tested by prediction analysis.

[a] The model tested presumed that there would be no subjects in these cells. This model was confirmed in the case of the quantitative ($\hat{\nabla} = .43, U = .32, z = 3.17, p < .000$) and the experimental ($\hat{\nabla} = .39, U = .19, z = 2.11, p < .01$) SSS.

To measure processing speed and control of processing, we decided to make use of a phenomenon that at first sight does not appear related to cognitive development, namely, the Stroop phenomenon (Stroop, 1935). This phenomenon occurs when a sensory stimulus is composed of conflicting information and the subject has to respond to one of its attributes while suppressing competing responses evoked by the other attribute. In his classic experiment, Stroop presented the names of colors in various ink colors (e.g., the word "blue" was printed in red ink) and asked subjects to name the ink colors as rapidly as possible. The results of the experiment were impressive—subjects started stuttering and stumbling by the third or fourth name.

The phenomenon has been studied extensively since that time (see Hunt & Lansman, 1986). What is important to note from the perspective of the present study is that the reaction time to stimuli defined by compatible attributes that point to the same response (e.g., a color name written in the same ink color) is less than that required for response to stimuli that do not create a conflict (e.g., a color name written in black ink), and this, in turn, is less than the time required for responses to stimuli defined by incompatible and thus conflict-raising attributes, such as those used by Stroop (Hunt

& Lansman, 1986). The conflict effect is much more pronounced when the person is required to respond to the color rather than to the meaning of the word. This has been ascribed to the fact that responding to the meaning of words is the dominant and automated response: people are used to reading the words rather than naming the color of the ink in which they are written.

Automated responses to facilitating stimuli can generally be regarded as indicative of the individual's processing potential at a given age since automation, together with the facilitation built into a given condition, brings processing and response emission close to the person's limits. Therefore, from the point of view of our theory, the reaction time to the meaning of a word written in the same ink color can be regarded as a good approximation of the individual's processing speed. Conflict-raising stimuli require control in the execution of the required response. Hence, it is justifiable to assume that the response time to any condition in which the color name and the ink color are incompatible will indicate both the person's processing speed and his ability to control processing so as to inhibit response to the irrelevant attribute and direct it toward the relevant one. Consequently, the difference between reaction times to the meaning of a word under compatible and incompatible conditions can be regarded as a measure of the efficiency of the control component of the processing system. In fact, the more automated the response to be repressed, the more active the control would normally have to be.

Regarding storage, we again used the tasks devised by Case (1985) to address the dimensional and the vectorial storage space (see previous section). Tests directed to the last two of Case's developmental cycles were selected because the cognitive abilities assessed in Study 5 (i.e., quantitative-relational) correspond to these cycles. As noted earlier in this chapter, dimensional units are produced by dimensional operations such as the number of digits produced by counting and vectorial units by vectorial operations that integrate dimensions such as a relation between two numbers. Thus, the dimensional storage space appears more related to the execution of processes required by the two lower levels of our three quantitative-relational thought batteries, whereas the vectorial storage space seems more associated with the two highest levels of these batteries.

Study 5 was designed to test a number of predictions about the structure of the processing system and its relations to the development of problem-solving abilities. Regarding structure, we expected to identify the distinct contribution of each of the three components of the processing system to performance. Regarding the relations between the processing system and the development of cognitive abilities, it was expected that, the more efficient the individual's processing system, the more advanced this person would be in solving cognitive tasks.

Method

Subjects

The main sample involved 65 subjects selected from among subjects participating in a large project concerned with the structure and development of the quantitative-relational SSS (see Demetriou et al., 1991). Specifically, subjects attaining the lowest and those attaining the highest performance scores on the arithmetic operations battery to be described below were retained for testing on the Stroop and the working memory tasks. "Lowest performance" is equivalent to functioning at level I or below of the arithmetic operations battery and "highest performance" to functioning on level III or IV of this battery. Performance on the arithmetic operations battery was used as a basis for subject selection because our study of the quantitative-relational SSS had shown it to be the best discriminating battery for the age range with which the current study is primarily concerned.

On the basis of these criteria, 8 low and 8 high, 8 low and 9 high, 8 low and 8 high, and 6 low and 10 high scorers were selected from among third-, fourth-, fifth-, and sixth-grade subjects, respectively. Males and females were equally represented in each cognitive-level group. All subjects were Greek and came from upper-middle-class families.

The subjects were tested twice. The first testing session took place in April and the second in October 1990. At the second testing, all school-age subjects moved to the next grade (i.e., the fourth, fifth, sixth, or seventh, respectively). It should be noted here that the subjects who were in the third grade at the first testing were examined on all but the proportional reasoning and the algebraic ability batteries to be described below. According to our earlier research (Demetriou et al., 1991), third-grade children fail these two batteries. However, the two batteries were given to these children when they moved to the fourth grade. Thus, the analyses involving all the children were based on the data obtained from the second testing. Additionally, 10 first-year university students were also tested at the first testing session for comparative purposes.

Tasks

The Stroop task.—This task involved a total of 28 cards (21 × 15 cm), each card bearing the name of a color; 18 cards were used for the main task. These were organized in a 2 (attribute: word vs. color naming) × 3 (control: color name written in black ink; compatible: color name written in the same ink color; conflict: color name written in another ink color) design. The same three Greek color words were used for each of the six attribute × ink combinations: πράσινο (green), κίτρινο (yellow), and κόκκινο (red). These color names were used because they are each composed of seven letters. Of the remaining 10 cards, four were used for demonstration purposes; these contained color names different from those used in the main task. Finally, six cards were used for practice, three on word reading and three on color naming. The color names used for practice were the same as those used in the main task, and all cards represented the conflict condition; the aim was to give subjects practice on the most difficult and unfamiliar condition of the experiment.

The working-memory tasks.—The counting (CST) and the vectorial (VST) span tests used in Study 4 were again used in the current investigation. However, a variation between the version of the CST task used in the two instances should be noted. In Study 4, subjects were asked to count and subsequently remember the number of only the red dots, whereas, in the first testing of Study 5, they were asked to count both. This variation was introduced in order to make the CST equivalent to the VST in all respects but the vectorial operation of finding the ratio between the two sets of dots. Unexpectedly, this manipulation rendered the CST more difficult than the VST; hence, at the second testing, both versions of the CST were used.

The Quantitative-Relational Tasks

The arithmetic operations battery.—This battery involved tasks addressed to the ability to perform the four basic arithmetic operations in combination with each other. Subjects were given a series of standard arithmetic equations in which an arbitrary symbol was presented in the place of the arithmetic operation. Subjects' task was to specify the missing operation. These tasks were made to tap four levels of difficulty. At the first, the second, the third, and the fourth levels, subjects were required to identify one (e.g., $5 * 3 = 8$), two (e.g., $[3 * 5] * 5 = 10$), three (e.g., $[3 * 2 * 4] * 5 = 7$), and four (e.g., $[3 * 2] * 4 = [12 * 1] * 2$) unknown operations, respectively (the asterisks stand for the arithmetic operations to be specified by the subject).

The proportional reasoning battery.—The second battery was addressed to proportional reasoning; it too involved tasks spanning four developmental levels. Following the paradigm devised by Noelting (1980), subjects were asked to judge the relative intensity of the color of two mixtures involving part pure paint and part solvent. The first-level mixtures involved fully equivalent ratios (e.g., $[1, 1]:[2, 2]$, each pair of numbers referring to one mixture and the first and second numbers in each pair denoting how many paint and how many solvent parts, respectively, are in a mixture). The second level involved partially equivalent ratios (e.g., $[4, 2]:[2, 1]$). The third level involved ratios of ordered pairs with two corresponding terms being multiples of one another (e.g., $[2, 1]:[4, 3]$). The fourth level involved ratios without corresponding terms (e.g., $[5, 7]:[3, 5]$). Thus, lower-level items provided intuitive support to the processing of the proportional relations involved, whereas higher-level items required exact quantification.

The algebraic ability battery.—The third battery was addressed to the ability to solve algebraic equations. At the first level of difficulty, the solution to the problems could be directly deduced from the elements given or defined by operating on them (e.g., $a + 5 = 8$; $a = ?$). The problems at the second level required coordination of two well-defined structures so as to specify the value of a third unknown element (e.g., $m = 3n + 1$; $n = 4$, $m = ?$). The third-level items required operation on undefined structures (e.g., $r = s + t$; $r + s + t = 30$, $r = ?$). The items at the fourth level required coordination of undefined structures and understanding of the role of letters as generalized numbers or symbols of variables (e.g., "When it is true that $L + M + N = L + P + N$?"). Thus, the four levels represented a movement in using symbolization from well- to ill-defined and from reality- to representation-referenced structures.

Procedure and Scoring

The Stroop task.—Subjects were tested individually by the third author. Experimenter and subject were seated facing each other. The experimenter told the subject that they were going to play a game in which the subject's task was either to read the word that was written on each card or to name the color of the ink in which the word was written, depending on the instruction "word" or "color" given with the presentation of the card. Subjects were instructed to "respond as fast as possible but to be careful not to make mistakes." The task was explained by using the demonstration cards, following which the six practice cards were given to the subject. Once it was clear that the subject could easily carry out the instructions, testing proceeded to the main task. The presentation order of the 18 test cards was randomized across the six conditions to rule out the possibility that a response set might contaminate the results. Performance on the main task was tape-recorded.

The reaction time of each subject to each card was measured by an electronic device from the audiotapes. It was defined as the time elapsed between the first phoneme of the instruction spoken by the experimenter ("word" or "color") and the first phoneme of the subject's response. The subject's reaction time to each of the six attribute-by-ink conditions was determined by the average of his or her reaction time to the three different color names contained in each condition. Reaction time was not scored if the response to the instruction was wrong; however, this occurred extremely rarely, and in no case did a subject's reaction time to a condition involve responses to less than two words (see below).

The memory tasks.—Subjects were again tested individually. Following the procedure described in Study 4, they were instructed to recall the results of counting (CST) or ratio evaluation (VST) of the dots appearing on the cards. All materials used to test memory in this study were the same as those used in Study 4.

In both memory tasks, each subject was given a score corresponding to the highest level at which he or she succeeded in correctly recalling the results of counting or ratio evaluation in at least two of the three trials. If the subject was able to recall the results in only one of the three trials addressed to a level, he or she was given a score of .33.

The arithmetic operations battery.—Responses to each item were scored pass (1) or fail (0). A subject was considered to have passed an item if he or she was able to specify *all* unknown operations in this item.

The proportional reasoning battery.—Performance on each item was scored as follows: 0 = no response or nonsense responses; 1 = wrong response justified by an explanation indicating an intuitive grasp of ratio and proportional relations; 2 = right response but no explanation; 3 = right response justified by a proper, although incomplete, explanation; and 4 = right response justified by a proper and fully complete explanation.

The algebraic ability battery.—Performance on the items in this battery was also scored pass (1) or fail (0).

The Structure of Abilities

Study 5 is unique among the studies presented in this *Monograph* with regard to task construction. It involves tasks that represent processes ranging from the very basic level of the speed of processing to advanced SSS-specific abilities in a clearly nested way. At the most basic level, there are tasks that represent processing speed only (e.g., the compatible Stroop conditions). At the next level there are tasks requiring both processing speed and control of processing (e.g., the incompatible Stroop conditions). At the next level there are the working memory tasks, which presuppose both processing speed and control of processing in addition to a storage buffer or function. At the next level, the arithmetic operations tasks presuppose all these three components in addition to requiring the basic quantitative-relational skill for executing arithmetic operations. Finally, the algebraic and proportional reasoning tasks require more specialized quantitative-relational skills in addition to all four antecedent components.

A model consistent with this analysis involves at least five factors. Specifically, measures representing processing speed must be related to only one factor. Measures representing control of processing should be related to the first factor and also to a second factor. Measures representing working memory should be related to these two plus a third factor. Measures representing arithmetic operations should be related to a fourth factor in addition to the first three factors. Measures representing the algebraic and the pro-portional reasoning abilities should be related to an additional fifth factor. So defined, factors 1, 2, 3, 4, and 5 will represent speed of processing, control of processing, working memory, a basic quantitative-relational abil-ity, and an advanced quantitative-relational ability, respectively. Finally, a sixth factor might be needed to represent specialized skills such as those used when processing proportional reasoning tasks. This model is depicted in Figure 10.

Structural modeling requires relatively large samples to yield reliable results (Tanaka, 1987). Given the rather limited number of subjects used in Study 5, we tried to deal with this problem by reducing the number of variables included in the analysis. Thus, the model specified above was tested on 12 variables, using two measures for each of the constituents. The reader is also reminded that the models to be presented below—which involve all abilities—were tested on the data of the second testing because, at this testing, subjects were examined on all batteries.

In reducing the number of variables, reaction time to the word-compatible (i.e., a response under facilitating conditions) and the word-control (i.e., a response under standard conditions) conditions was taken to represent speed of processing. The difference between reaction time under the color-control and the word-compatible condition and the color-incompatible and the word-compatible condition was taken as the two mea-sures representing the control of processing component. Using the dif-ferences between measures indicating the functioning of the control mechanism and the measure ideally suited to represent speed of processing aimed to isolate effects of the control mechanism from the possible effects of the speed of processing component. Selection of the color-control and the color-incompatible conditions was based on both conceptual and empirical grounds. The color-control condition requires inhibition of the dominant tendency to read the word in favor of recognizing its ink color. The color-incompatible condition requires the inhibition of both this tendency and the tendency to name the ink color suggested by the meaning of the word. In fact, it will be seen below that these two conditions yielded the highest response times of all six conditions used in the study.

Performance on the two Case tasks given at both testing occasions (i.e., the version of the CST used in Study 5 and the VST) was taken to represent working memory. Performance on each of the three quantitative-relational SSS batteries was represented by two half scores, each representing the mean score on half the items involved in each battery; all developmental levels and content variations were represented in each half score.

Correlations between the pairs of tasks were high ($M = .733$, SD = .117); those between tasks belonging to different pairs, although satisfac-tory, were much lower ($M = .364$, SD = .150).

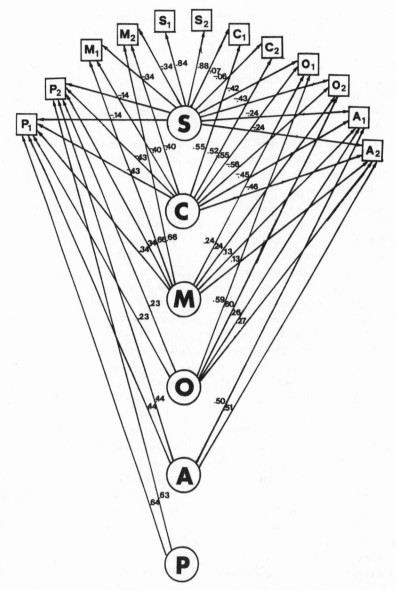

Fig. 10.—The nested-factor model best fitting subjects' performance on tasks assessing speed of processing, control of processing, memory, and the quantitative-relational tasks.

The symbols S, C, and M stand for the speed of processing, the control of processing, and the memory component of the processing system, respectively. The symbols O, A, and P stand for, respectively, the arithmetic operations, algebraic, and proportional reasoning abilities involved in the quantitative-relational SSS. The numerals 1 and 2 stand for the two scores representing each of the components specified above.

To test for the relative importance of each of the factors specified above, the model was tested following the nested-factor method proposed by Gustafsson (1988a, 1988b). In each of six successive runs, factor 1, factors 2–3, factors 1–3, factors 1–4, factors 1–5, and factors 1–6 were introduced. Each of these models was fitted under the constraint that the loadings of each pair of measures on each of the factors would be equal. The statistics for these models are shown in Table 11. It can be seen that introduction of each of the factors resulted in a highly significant improvement of the model fit up to factor 5; only factor 6 failed to result in improvement of fit. The model shown in Figure 10 above is the complete model involving all six factors.[12] The last row of Table 11 shows that the fit of this model to the data was excellent, $\chi^2(45) = 54.152, p = .160$. Note that, for all but the control of processing factor, the loadings were always much higher on the two measures representing the component associated with the given factor than on the measures representing the other components. This strongly suggests that the domain-free (i.e., speed of processing, control of processing, and storage) and the domain-specific components of developing intellect described by our theory have been identified in the data of Study 5.

It is interesting to consider the relative contribution of these components to the variance of tasks representing other components. Given that the loadings of the two members of each pair of measures were constrained to be equal on each of the factors to which they were allowed to relate, the contribution of each factor to the variance of each pair can be estimated by squaring the loading of any member of a pair on the factor. The speed of processing factor accounts for a substantially larger part of the variance of the basic arithmetic operations (i.e., 19%) and the working memory (12%) tasks than the variance of algebraic (6%) and proportional reasoning (2%) tasks. The very low contribution (practically null) of this component to the two measures representing control of processing indicates that our manipulation was successful in dissociating the two components.

The contribution of the control of processing factor to the variance of all other tasks was about equal and higher than that of the speed of processing component, accounting for 30%, 20%, 18%, and 16% of the variance of the arithmetic operations, the algebraic, the proportional reasoning, and the working memory tasks, respectively. Interestingly enough, the contribution of the memory component to the various quantitative tasks was rather weak, accounting for 12%, 6%, and 2% of the variance of the proportional, the arithmetic operations, and the algebraic tasks, respectively.

The basic quantitative operations factor accounted for a small portion of the variance of the algebraic (7%) and the proportional reasoning (5%)

---

[12] The correlation matrix, means, and standard deviations of the half scores involved in the models tested in Study 5 are shown in Appendix Table A8.

TABLE 11

Results of Tests of Fit of Nested-Factor Models to the Speed of Processing, Control of Processing, Working Memory, and Quantitative-Relational Tasks Used in Study 5

	Model Statistics				Change		
Factors	χ^2	df	CFI	p	$\Delta\chi^2$	Δdf	Δp
Sp.	302.272	60	.535	.00			
+Co.	131.658	55	.853	.00	170.614	5	.005
+Me.	86.844	51	.931	.02	44.814	4	.005
+Op.	63.400	48	.970	.07	23.444	3	.005
+Al.	55.152	46	.981	.15	7.741	2	.025
+Pr.	54.152	45	.982	.16	1.607	1	N.S.

NOTE.—The organization of this table is the same as the organization of Table 3. The inclusion of all but the last factor results in significant improvement of model fit. "Sp.," "Co.," "Me.," "Op.," "Al.," and "Pr." stand for, respectively, speed of processing, control of processing, working memory, arithmetic operations, algebraic reasoning ability, and proportional reasoning ability.

tasks. This is entirely comprehensible if one considers that there were two other quantitative SSS factors identified with performance on the two advanced quantitative-relational batteries. That is, performance on the algebraic and proportional reasoning tasks involves processing and representational skills that go well beyond the basic quantitative skills involved in the execution of arithmetic operations. In the present analysis, these advanced quantitative skills were captured by the algebraic and the proportional reasoning factors.

Demonstrating the presence of the components does not show whether they are organized in the way presumed by the theory. A model consistent with our theory would demonstrate that the three components of the processing system (PS) are organized into one general system and that the three subsystems of the quantitative-relational SSS are organized into another general system. Such a general model would involve two kinds of factors: six first-order factors to represent each of the processes and abilities indexed by each pair of measures and two second-order factors, namely, a general PS factor absorbing the three first-order processing factors and a general QR factor absorbing the three first-order quantitative-relational factors. Moreover, there should be a causal path running from the general PS to the general QR factor; this would indicate the SSS's dependence on general processing capacity. This model, which is shown in Figure 11, was found to fit to the data very well, $\chi^2(44) = 47.256$, $p = .341$, CFI = .994.

Structural Relations over Time

The longitudinal design of Study 5 permits investigating the dynamic relations among the various processes over time. To this end, three models

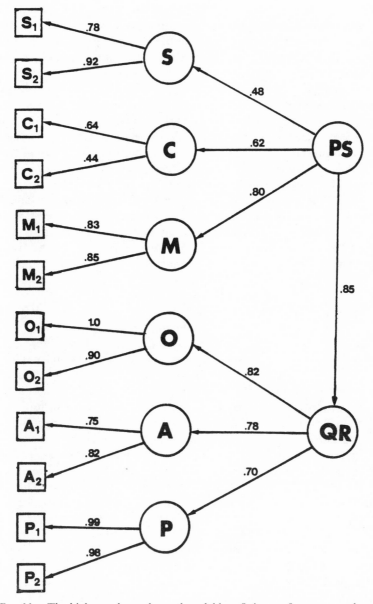

Fig. 11.—The higher-order and causal model best fitting performance on the speed of processing, the control of processing, the memory, and the quantitative-relational tasks.

The symbols S, C, M, O, A, and P stand for the same components specified in Fig. 10. The symbols PS and QR stand for the processing system and the quantitative-relational SSS, respectively.

were fitted to the performance attained on the Stroop, the memory, and the arithmetic operations tasks by the 65 subjects on each of the two testing occasions. (The reader is reminded that the youngest group of subjects was not tested by the proportional reasoning and the algebraic ability batteries at the first testing.)

The first of these was a standard autoregressive model that involved three basic assumptions: that the speed of processing, the control of processing, the working memory, and the arithmetic operations factors can be identified at each of the two testing waves; that the loadings of the two measures representing a factor will be equal both *within* and *across* testing waves; and that autoregressions (i.e., the regression of each factor identified at the second occasion on its corresponding factor identified at the first occasion) will be very high. The fit of this model was satisfactory and very close to statistical acceptability, $\chi^2(102) = 133.376$, $p = .02$, CFI = .950. All four autoregressions were significant and very high (speed of processing: .736; control of processing: .952; working memory: 1.000; arithmetic operations: .937). It is evident from these values that the stability of individual differences with regard to these factors over the 6 months intervening between the two occasions was almost perfect.

The second model asked whether there were mutual interactions among component processes beyond the inertial dynamics that characterize the course of change of a given process over time and that are represented by autoregressions. To identify these interactions, the second model was kept identical to the first in all respects but for the inclusion of a number of additional constructs regarding the relations between the first- and the second-occasion factors. Specifically, each second-occasion factor was regressed on the corresponding first-occasion factor as well as on all other preceding factors of the first occasion. Thus, the speed of processing factor was regressed only on itself, the control of processing factor was regressed on itself and the speed of processing factor, the memory factor was regressed on itself and the control and the speed of processing factors, and the arithmetic operations factor was regressed on all four first-occasion factors. The fit of this model to the data, $\chi^2(93) = 129.828$, $p < .02$, CFI = .951, was slightly, but not statistically, better than the fit of the first model. However, the fit of this model proved good, $\chi^2(91) = 112.875$, $p = .06$, CFI = .965, as well as significantly better than that of the first one, $\Delta\chi^2 = 16.953$ (for $\Delta df = 2$, $p < .001$), when some of the residuals of the first- and the second-occasion Stroop tasks were allowed to correlate. This is the model depicted in Figure 12.

In sum, the set of structural models presented in this section suggests that each of the components is a dynamic module that to a large extent draws on itself in order to change along the dimension of time. In other words, the condition of each of these modules at time t_2 is so strongly depen-

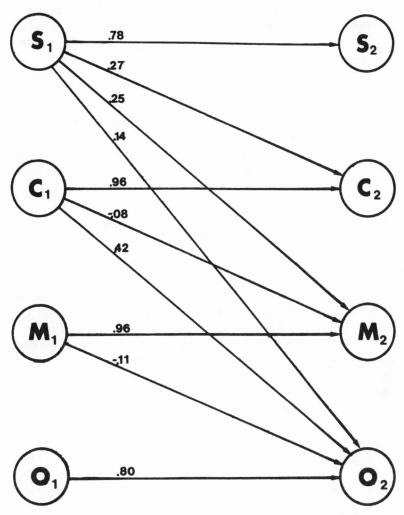

TIME 1   TIME 2

Fig. 12.—Causal relations between the speed of processing, the control of processing, the memory, and the arithmetic operations factors across the two testing occasions.

The symbols S, C, M, and O stand for the same components specified in Fig. 10. The values shown are standardized regression coefficients.

dent on its condition at time t_1 that very little room is left for effects generated by the other modules (see the autoregression models). However, at any given point in time, the modules are tightly intertwined in the sense that they are coactivated as required by the demands of the task at hand: the covariation among modules appears to be almost as strong as their autocovariation along the dimension of time (see the nested-factor and the hierarchical models). Thus, the change in each of the modules occurs in an environment of change in which every other module is also changing. This condition ensures that the system as a whole preserves a minimum of developmental momentum that can be used by the particular components to move up along their own developmental scales. This synergic causality is reflected in the coexistence of strong autoregressions with between-factor correlations in the third of the autoregressive models presented above. Moreover, this third model indicated that change tends to spread from the more basic to the more advanced modules of a system.

Differences between Processes and Patterns of Change

The results reported above concerned the structural relations among the processes represented by the various measures. The analyses to be presented in this section aim to show directly the status of the processes in question under the different testing conditions of the experiment. To this end, the children's performance on the Stroop task was first subjected to a 4 (age) × 2 (cognitive level) × 2 (testing wave) × 2 (attribute naming) × 3 (stimulus condition) MANOVA with repeated measures on the last three factors. Table 12 shows the means and standard deviations to which this analysis was applied. The main effects of age, $F(3, 57) = 4.16$, $p = .01$, and of cognitive level, $F(1, 57) = 18.80$, $p = .000$, were significant. The age × cognitive level interaction was nonsignificant, $F(3, 57) = .34$, $p = .796$, indicating that older subjects were always faster than younger ones over both cognitive levels. Similarly, the high-cognitive-level subjects were faster than the low-cognitive-level subjects over all ages. The effect of testing occasion was also significant, $F(1, 57) = 22.09$, $p = .000$, indicating better performance at t_2 on the part of all subjects. None of the interactions between this contrast and either age or cognitive level even approached significance. This finding is interesting in its implication that a 6-month interval was sufficient to result in significant improvements in speed and control of processing over all ages and over the two cognitive levels. Of course, one might ascribe this improvement to the effect of practice. We have recently tested this assumption and found that, although practice does have an effect, this is significantly lower than the difference between the two testings found here (see Platsidou, in preparation).

TABLE 12

Mean Response Times (and Standard Deviations) on the Stroop Tests across Age, Cognitive Level, and Testing Waves ($N = 65$)

Age	First Testing						Second Testing					
---	Word			Color			Word			Color		
	CO	CM	IN	CO	CM	IN	CO	CM	IN	CO	CM	IN
9 years:												
Low	1.233	1.197	1.031	1.184	1.207	1.829	1.134	1.084	1.320	1.293	1.131	1.478
	(.333)	(.283)	(.143)	(.192)	(.207)	(.508)	(.139)	(.209)	(.367)	(.266)	(.214)	(.292)
High	.984	1.005	1.004	1.195	1.015	1.420	1.000	.961	1.134	1.085	1.113	1.261
	(.156)	(.154)	(.192)	(.202)	(.245)	(.353)	(.214)	(.159)	(.329)	(.168)	(.220)	(.160)
10 years:												
Low	1.165	1.089	1.145	1.447	1.096	1.571	1.021	1.020	1.140	1.380	1.102	1.345
	(.230)	(.151)	(.226)	(.304)	(.165)	(.300)	(.121)	(.162)	(.100)	(.377)	(.165)	(.211)
High	.969	.890	.910	1.033	1.048	1.276	.953	.906	.974	.976	1.002	1.134
	(.162)	(.110)	(.190)	(.264)	(.243)	(.399)	(.208)	(.127)	(.216)	(.107)	(.271)	(.240)
11 years:												
Low	.961	.981	.990	1.316	.969	1.456	1.030	.922	.987	1.145	1.005	1.171
	(.215)	(.202)	(.180)	(.368)	(.190)	(.292)	(.185)	(.144)	(.238)	(.243)	(.249)	(.184)
High	.966	.950	.870	1.026	1.025	1.399	.905	.836	.969	.884	.846	1.027
	(.153)	(.140)	(.109)	(.157)	(.137)	(.348)	(.209)	(.189)	(.199)	(.138)	(.157)	(.275)
12 years:												
Low	1.160	.997	1.032	1.367	1.110	1.515	.943	.882	.972	1.190	.920	1.165
	(.310)	(.198)	(.269)	(.686)	(.298)	(.318)	(.253)	(.160)	(.319)	(.396)	(.141)	(.269)
High	.867	.860	.855	1.035	.907	1.280	.847	.834	.846	.864	.842	1.081
	(.179)	(.193)	(.164)	(.194)	(.213)	(.448)	(.152)	(.197)	(.230)	(.144)	(.166)	(.206)

Note.—The symbols CO, CM, and IN stand for the control, the compatible, and the incompatible conditions, respectively. Mean response times are given in seconds.

The effect of attribute naming, $F(1, 57) = 118.18, p = .000$, was highly significant, indicating that word naming was much faster than color naming. This finding is consistent with previously published results of both experimental (Dyer, 1973) and simulation (Hunt & Lansman, 1986) studies. It implies that color naming requires suppressing a highly familiar response (i.e., that of reading a word rather than naming the color of the ink in which it is written) and hence provides a stronger test of the person's mastery of the multiswitch mechanism referred to in Chapter II (see the section on the structure of the processing system).

The stimulus condition effect was also highly significant, $F(2, 114) = 50.33, p = .000$, Pillais index $= .666, p = .000$, indicating that reaction time under the compatible condition was lower than under the control condition and that this in turn was lower than under the conflict condition. The attribute $\times$ stimulus condition effect was also highly significant, $F(2, 108) = 29.00, p = .000$, Pillais index $= .512, p = .000$, indicating that the differences between the various stimulus conditions were smaller under the word naming than under the color naming condition.

Of the various between- $\times$ within-subjects interaction effects, the cognitive level $\times$ stimulus condition interaction was significant, $F(2, 114) = 4.32, p = .016$. This effect reflects the fact that the reaction time difference between low- and high-cognitive-level subjects under the compatible condition was smaller than under the control condition and that this was in turn smaller than in the incompatible condition. This was true under both the word and the color naming condition. In the same direction, the attribute naming $\times$ cognitive level interaction was marginally significant, $F(1, 57) = 3.67, p = .061$, indicating that the superiority of the high-cognitive-level subjects was more pronounced in the case of color than in the case of word naming. Overall, this pattern of results suggests that the advantage of the high-cognitive-level subjects is a function of the degree of control required by the stimulus: the more complex a stimulus is, and thus the more control it requires, the larger is the difference in favor of the high-cognitive-level subjects.

Finally, the occasion $\times$ attribute naming $\times$ stimulus condition interaction was highly significant, $F(2, 114) = 15.35, p = .000$, Pillais index $= .270, p = .000$. This effect captures two interesting trends in the data. On the one hand, the reduction in response times from the first to the second occasion was larger for color (average reduction $= .132$) than for word naming (.069) under all stimulus conditions. On the other hand, however, the reduction was much larger in the case of the incompatible (color $= .251$, word $= .150$) than the compatible (color $= .048$, word $= .044$) or the control (color $= .098$, word $= .014$) condition. It seems, therefore, that changes in the speed of processing are much slower than changes in the control of processing, indicating that speed of processing approaches ceiling much earlier than control of processing.

This conclusion is strengthened by the results of a 5 (the four high-cognitive-level school-age groups at the first testing occasion plus the college students) × 2 (attribute naming) × 3 (stimulus condition) planned contrasts ANOVA. Of the various results revealed by this analysis, only those involving age are presented here because these are concerned directly with developmental changes in speed and control of processing. The contrast of reaction times attained by the sixth-grade children with those attained by the college students showed a highly significant difference in favor of the latter, $F(1, 63) = 12.794, p < .001$. Moreover, this contrast interacted significantly with the word versus color naming contrast, $F(1, 63) = 11.026, p < .005$, indicating that, while the difference between word and color naming was large among the children, it almost vanished among the college students. We consider this to be a highly interesting finding. In line with what we have argued before, it indicates that the ability to take sufficient control of one's processing system to permit inhibiting a highly automated and therefore strong response in favor of weak but correct alternatives emerges quite late in development.

Incorrect responses were extremely rare: only 21 out of a total of 1,170 responses (i.e., 1.8%) were incorrect at the first testing occasion. However, most of these responses occurred among the low-cognitive-level subjects (16 of 21, or 76.2%) and under the incompatible conditions (14 of 21, or 66.7%). These findings indicate that, while the control mechanism is very successful in its functioning, the more demand is placed on this mechanism, the more probable it becomes that it will fail, especially in the case of subjects who are delayed in their cognitive development. Incorrect responses at the second occasion were fewer in number but similarly distributed.

The Memory Tasks

Average performance on the memory tasks used at the two testing occasions is shown in Table 13. These means were subjected to a 4 (age) × 2 (cognitive level) × 2 (testing occasion) × 2 (the CST and the VST that were used on both occasions) MANOVA. Of the various main and interaction effects, only two were significant: the effect of cognitive level, $F(1, 57) = 38.85, p = .000$, and the task effect, $F(1, 57) = 15.86, p = .000$. The first effect indicates that the performance of the high-cognitive-level subjects ($M = 3.24$) was higher than the performance of the low-cognitive-level subjects ($M = 2.01$) across all ages and both tasks by about 1 unit on the average, $F(1, 54) = 26.435, p < .001$. Unexpectedly, the second effect indicated that

TABLE 13

MEAN PERFORMANCE (and Standard Deviations) ON THE MEMORY TASKS
ACROSS AGE AND TESTING OCCASIONS

	FIRST TESTING			SECOND TESTING		
AGE	CST-A	CST-B	VST	CST-A	CST-B	VST
9 years	...	1.75	1.71	2.92	1.67	1.79
		(.56)	(.60)	(.75)	(.47)	(.50)
	...	2.50	2.87	3.87	2.58	2.62
		(.64)	(.71)	(.75)	(.73)	(.76)
10 years	...	1.75	2.33	3.29	1.87	2.29
		(.46)	(.56)	(.95)	(.64)	(.68)
	...	3.15	3.37	4.37	2.78	3.40
		(1.79)	(1.03)	(1.11)	(1.01)	(1.10)
11 years	...	2.00	2.37	3.29	1.79	2.41
		(.72)	(.82)	(.55)	(.73)	(.58)
	...	3.04	2.50	4.58	2.87	3.33
		(.84)	(.73)	(1.24)	(.80)	(.93)
12 years	...	2.00	2.61	3.35	1.66	2.05
		(.52)	(.49)	(.62)	(.52)	(.39)
	...	3.43	3.60	4.73	3.30	3.43
		(1.01)	(.86)	(1.00)	(1.15)	(.80)

NOTE.—CST-A and CST-B refer to the standard version of the counting span test and the version devised for Study 5, respectively.

performance on the VST ($M = 2.86$) was better than performance on the CST ($M = 2.38$).

The developmental implications of these results are particularly interesting. Specifically, the absence of any occasion effect indicates that a 6-month interval is not sufficient to result in changes in the storage component of the processing system, even though it was sufficient to result in considerable changes in its other two components, namely, speed and control of processing. We therefore conclude that a chain of developmental changes originates in basic processes and then gradually spreads over more complex processes. It is evident that this pattern of results is also consistent with the second structural model applied on the two testing occasions, which indicated that the chain of causal influences runs from the more basic and elementary to the more advanced and complex abilities (see Fig. 12 above).

The inferior performance on the CST is in all probability due to the fact that, in the version used in this study, the subject was also asked to count the set of dots that did not have to be remembered. Observation of the subjects' behavior during the experiment made it clear that counting this latter set of dots interfered with remembering the former set. Interference was not a problem in the case of the VST because this test required subjects to remember the ratio between the two sets, that is, only one digit.

This interpretation is strongly supported by the fact that performance on the standard CST used on the second occasion ($M = 4.38$) was much better, $F(1, 57) = 184.81$, $p = .000$, than performance on the "new" version of this test ($M = 2.32$) attained on the same occasion (the reader is reminded that the only difference between the two tests was the absence of the interference set in the standard version). This finding suggests that the distinction between different types of short-term storage span may still be necessary, but for reasons other than those assumed by Case (1985).

In fact, our findings may point to the reasons that would actually justify this distinction. The results outlined above can be taken to indicate that a shift in the kind of units that can be stored and processed in working memory may occur only when a change in the other components of the processing system takes place rendering the new units manageable. Note that vectorial units require more processing control than dimensional units since the former are derived from the combination of other units whereas the latter are stored as given. A person would, therefore, be able to work with vectorial units only after the control of processing had reached the threshold required for handling the information that is to be combined to give the vectorial units. Functioning below this threshold will result in processing failures in any instance in which the support of this process is mandatory. Operating under conditions of interference can certainly be considered to be such a case because the person must actively inhibit the intrusion into the storage space of units from the not-to-be remembered set. Thus, the shift from one developmental cycle to the next is not due to a change in any single component of the cognitive system; instead, it is a function of the dynamic relations among different components and systems. These issues will be dealt with in Chapter VII.

CONCLUDING COMMENTS

The results of the various analyses presented in this chapter converge to show that the three components of the processing system are interrelated. This implies that, the faster a person is as a processor, the more information units she will be able to process in a given standard time unit, and, consequently, the more efficient she will eventually become at distinguishing goal-relevant from goal-irrelevant units. In turn, the more efficient she is with regard to speed and control of processing, the better she will be at using her storage potential. This is so because the appropriate information units will occupy this potential for the minimum time required to grasp the concept defined by these units and to assemble the needed response. Eventually, this is reflected in superior performance on complex cognitive tasks tapping the various SSSs described by our theory.

However, each of the three components of the processing system may be differentially related to each of the various SSSs. The form of the relation seems to depend on how the information units particular to each SSS make use of each of the components of the processing system. That is, the more complex are the units characterizing an SSS as compared to the units characterizing another SSS, the more speed, control, or storage of processing they would require in order to be processed efficiently.

VII. GENERAL DISCUSSION: STRUCTURE, DYNAMICS, AND INDIVIDUAL VARIATION OF DEVELOPING MIND

THE STRUCTURE OF MIND AND THE NATURE OF REPRESENTATION

The results of the five studies that we have presented force the conclusion that no single structural system can suffice to describe, let alone explain, the growth and organization of cognitive abilities over macro- and micro-time as well as over different realms of knowledge. Instead, we need a family of structural systems capable of modeling the general and specific aspects of developing intellect at different levels and on different dimensions. Our conception of such a family of systems is depicted in Figure 13.

The General System

The inner cylinder shown in this figure corresponds to the most general system of intellect whose components are so pervasive that they enter into every form of intellectual endeavor. The results of Study 5 suggest that speed of processing, control of processing, and storage are its constituent components. But how is this general system itself to be defined? One answer might lie in Fodor's "First Law of the Nonexistence of Cognitive Science," which reads, "It goes like this: the more global (e.g., the more isotropic) a cognitive process is, the less anybody can understand it. *Very* global processes . . . aren't understood at all" (Fodor, 1983, p. 107). It therefore follows that, according to Fodor, this system cannot be defined by definition!

Fodor's law, however, need not end the matter here. In our opinion, the intellect's processing system is domain free because it is *protean* in nature: amorphous when inactive or in a latent state, once activated it takes the form of the operating and symbolic characteristics of the task responsible for the activation. In effect, this system is shaped on the pattern of the SSS with which the activating task is affiliated. Consequently, the intellect's

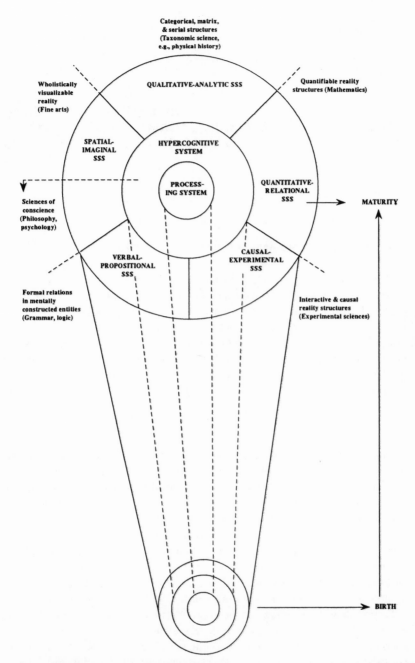

FIG. 13.—The general model of developing mind. The fields of knowledge primarily related to an SSS are shown in parentheses.

hardware can be understood only within a framework of *developmental and functional relativity*. The clearest demonstration of this postulate is provided by our two studies that focused on the relations between the processing system and the SSSs. Study 5 showed that the various components of the processing system are differentially nested in the different components of the same SSS, and Study 4 indicated that the same component of the processing system is differentially related to the various SSSs. Therefore, the task is, first, to specify how mental resources are allocated to problems at different developmental levels and, second, to delineate the functionally autonomous operating/representational domains and specify how each makes use of the available mental resources. The middle and the outer cylinders of the model depicted in Figure 13 represent our attempt at achieving these aims.

The Hypercognitive System

Specifically, it is assumed that there is a hypercognitive system of concepts and functions that underlies *meaning making* in the person-task encounters (the middle cylinder in the figure). As we use the term, "meaning making" is considered equivalent to activating the person's resources in order to construct a first representation of what a problem is about and then to ascribe the problem to an SSS for further processing. So defined, this system must necessarily involve two distinct sets of skills and strategies. The first is a set of on-line strategies for *handling* mental resources, general cognitive functions, and representations. The second is a "theory of mind" that functions to guide the task-SSS affiliation process. The results presented in Chapter V suggest that this domain-general system does involve these characteristics. The findings of Study 3 were very clear in this regard: subjects clearly distinguished between general cognitive functions, such as working memory and attention, on the basis of their differential involvement with the functioning of different SSSs, rather than the other way around. They also associated SSS-specific skills more with tasks known to represent the given SSS than with tasks known to represent other SSSs.

One might argue that invoking the hypercognitive system to explain how proper solutions are produced makes the theory vulnerable to the so-called homunculus (or "little man in the head") problem: the cognitive system's ability to do X is explained by positing some higher-order mechanism that does X and is therefore able to direct the system accordingly. The problem is that one is still left with having to explain how that higher-order mechanism acquired the ability to do X. It needs to be emphasized that, in our theory, the hypercognitive system does not "have" solutions to problems. It only directs the mind, when the latter is in a state of uncertainty, to select a course of action that seems the more relevant and promising, in the light of the current representation(s) of the problem goal. Changing intentions, overlapping reality structures, and overlapping symbol systems contribute to the creation of uncertainties that call on or activate this system, and the nature of its activity resembles a quickly rolling menu that displays pointers to how similar or analogous problems have been processed in the past. In other words, the hypercognitive system may be viewed as a conveyor that transfers experiences of the forces that affected cognitive performance from a given time t_1 to a time t_2. These forces must reflect the operation of the organizational principles at t_1; otherwise, the subjective structure of mind would not mirror its objective structure (see Study 3; see also Demetriou & Efklides, 1989, 1990).

This mechanism does not necessarily have to be entirely conscious at the time it is running. However, the by-products of its operation, such as feelings of difficulty in handling alternative representations, the satisfaction felt when representations can be mapped on a course of action, etc., as well as transient conceptions, ideas, etc. that are generated during this process, may later be reflected on and possibly codified. Once codified, they may then function as conscious pointers at a next run. It is in this sense that, in our theory, cognition and hypercognition are intertwined in a never-ending helix in such a way that the cognitive activity at time t_1 provides the input that will affect the form and functioning of the hypercognitive system at time t_2, which will in turn influence cognitive activity at time t_3, etc. We will return to an explication of this process below in the section on development.

Reality structures as such, however, are represented, operated on, and apprehended by the SSSs shown in the outer cylinder of the model. Being defined by the five specificity-bias principles (see Chap. II), these systems must be regarded as modular (Fodor, 1983). That is, once it has dominated as the appropriate system to be activated, the given SSS is characterized by informational encapsulation and processing momentum: it tends to draw on information related to itself rather than to other SSSs and to run through the networks of its own task-related computational chains quickly. In other words, the SSSs are complex modules involving concepts, mental acts, schemes, or operations interconnected into networks that make their coactivation possible for the sake of particular mental goals. These networks may be conceived as "abilities" in the literal sense of the word. That is, they make the person *able* to understand whole domains of reality, and they structure the action required for efficient interactions with the elements of these domains. In line with our earlier research (Demetriou, 1990; Demetriou et al., 1992), Studies 1 and 2 have shown that the SSSs are more encapsulated—and therefore free of influences from the two domain-free systems—in later rather than earlier stages in development and when applied on familiar rather than unfamiliar tasks.

It is evident that this analysis may be extended both below and above the level of the SSSs identified by our theory. Moving in one direction, one may analyze the subsystems or component abilities constituting an SSS, that is, the modes of mental activity that can be used to attain goals and that, under some circumstances, can stand on their own (e.g., combinatorial thought, hypothesis formation, experimentation, etc.). Our Studies 1, 2, and 5 indicated clearly that these subsystems do have an objective status, and Study 3 (as well as others; see Demetriou & Efklides, 1989) indicated that they also have an experiential-subjective status. In principle, there is no end to how far one can carry analysis in this direction since each of the component abilities may be analyzed into more "basic" units, and these into subunits, and so on. Moving in the other direction, one may analyze how the different SSSs, whole fields of knowledge, or even the knowing persons themselves may be coordinated with each other (e.g., in science or education; see Demetriou et al., 1992).

In sum, the mind is conceived by us as a network of relations connecting the intellectual units into systems that are functional vis-à-vis the demands of specific environments encountered by the individual rather than as an aggregate of static structures. In our theory, the construction of these networks is governed by the organizational principles that we summarized in Chapter II. It goes without saying that, besides those discussed here, there may be other principles in operation that are yet to be discovered.

Specification of Networks

Depending on the focus of one's analysis, these networks may be specified in a number of alternative ways. *Semantically,* it may be said that, the more any two (or more) mental units are alike vis-à-vis each of the organizational principles, the easier it will be for them to be interlinked with each other in networks of meaning and to be thus conceived by the knower. *Logically,* there should be a threshold of relatedness that, when exceeded, should make the mental units reducible to the same formal structure, such as those specified by categorical logic, propositional logic, and so on. *Mathematically,* it may be said that, the more alike the mental units are relative to the organizational principles, the more closely they will covary whenever they are appropriately measured. From a *technical* point of view, there should also be a threshold that, when exceeded, should make the mental units reducible to the same factorial or formal structure. Hence, the factor structures abstracted by the studies presented in this *Monograph* are nothing more than maps indicating the boundaries between dynamic networks of mental activity and meaning.

From the point of view of learning, these boundaries circumscribe the regions within which automatic transfer of learning is to be expected. Study 2 has shown that automatic transfer of learning within an SSS is possible, both within and across its components. However, transfer of learning did not seem capable of automatically crossing the SSS boundaries. These findings have been fully verified by Goossens's (1992) careful meta-analysis of a large number of training studies that looked for intra- and inter-SSS transfer; thus, it seems that inter-SSS coordination requires different types of mechanism than intra-SSS coordination.

We believe that the specification of the SSSs that we have proposed is not beset by the problems of what Bickhard (see Campbell & Bickhard, 1986) has called the "encodingism" approach to representation. In this approach, representation is viewed as some form of encoding, in such a way that reality elements and their relations are represented in the cognitive system via symbols or codes that stand in for them. There is no problem with this view of representation when the element to be represented is known. In such cases, the encoding could be taken to stand in for the known element; for instance, a number stated in the binary code can be defined with reference to the mathematical definition of the same number. However, a problem does arise as soon as one asks about the representational status of the mathematical definition of a number. This, of course, can be defined with reference to an everyday verbal definition of the given number; however, the attempt may degenerate into an infinite regress because, in principle, there may be no foundational encoding on which the edifice of meaning could be grounded.

To quote Campbell and Bickhard (1986, p. 37):

> Interactivism provides an alternative form of representation. Consider a goal-directed system interacting with the environment. The course of the interaction will depend both on the organization of the system and on the environmental conditions and responses that the system is interactively engaged with. The course of the interaction within the system will depend in part on the environment being interacted with: differing environments will yield differing final internal conditions within the system. . . . The possible final states of such a system, in other words, serve to differentiate possible environments according to the final state that an environment yields when interacted with. . . . The final states of an interactive system, thus, contain information—differentiating information or implicit definitional information—about the environment. This information may well be useful for the interactions of other subsystems of the overall system: the internal outcome of one subsystem may serve to differentiate the interactive strategy of another subsystem. Environments of type "outcome A" may require one subsystem or strategy to achieve a given goal, while environments of type "outcome B" may require some other subsystem.

It is hoped that the reader recognizes in Campbell and Bickhard's systems and subsystems our SSSs and SSS components. Evidently, the principles that we specified guide the interactions that determine what final states will be formulated in response to engagement with one or another aspect of the environment. Thus, our theory gives flesh to modern constructivism. This, of course, is not to assert that encodings do not exist or that an encoding process does not take place. On the contrary, it will be seen in the following section that development generates and presupposes symbol systems. However, these take and renew their meaning as they lean on the bridges—such as the SSS-specific intuitors—that link the organism with the environment.

In a Gibsonian sense, the SSSs described by our theory represent in the mind the differential perceptual and conceptual affordances of different reality domains: "The *affordances* of the environment are what it *offers* the animal, what it *provides* or *furnishes,* either for good or ill. The verb *afford* is found in the dictionary, but the noun *affordance* is not. I have made it. I mean by it something that refers to both the environment and the animal in a way that no existing term does" (Gibson, 1979, p. 127).

It is highly interesting that, basing their work on logical considerations, Turiel and Davidson (1985) have recently parsed the mind in a way that is very close to our parsing, which originated from empirical work. On the basis of an elaborate theoretical analysis of between-domains differences regarding (*a*) types of subject-object interaction, (*b*) types of knowledge generated by alternative types of subject-object interaction, and (*c*) elements, operations, and operational properties involved in alternative types of subject-object interaction, Turiel and Davidson argued that the map of cognitive territories includes three levels of structuring: realms, domains, and concepts. At the first of these levels, they distinguished between the social and the nonsocial realms. As far as the nonsocial realm is concerned, they distinguished the domains of logical knowledge, mathematical knowledge, spatial knowledge, temporal knowledge, physical knowledge, and causal knowledge; each of these is assumed to be autonomous. It seems evident that the first three domains correspond to the qualitative-analytic, the quantitative-relational, and the spatial-imaginal SSSs that we have described. The domains of temporal, physical, and causal knowledge are all involved in our causal-experimental SSS. Like our SSSs, each of Turiel and Davidson's domains comprises distinct but interdependent concepts.[13]

It is interesting to emphasize in this regard that recent research on infant development suggests that categorical (Soja, Carey, & Spelke, 1991), quantitative (Gelman & Gallistel, 1992), causal (Starkey, Spelke, & Gelman,

[13] It should also be mentioned in this context that Case (1992) has recently been moving from a V-model to an E-model. He now speaks of *central conceptual structures* that are computationally and domain specific; these structures are more or less coextensive with our SSSs.

1990), and spatial (Landau, Spelke, & Gleitman, 1984) abilities may be functioning as autonomous modules that guide the interaction with the respective domains of the environment from the very first months of life. In fact, students of infant development believe that these modules are innate. Also, a number of authors claim that even the person's theory of mind is innate and present from the first months of life (Anderson, 1992; Leslie, 1987). If taken for granted, these findings and claims would suggest that the research reported in this *Monograph* succeeded in locating and demarcating the basic categories of human mind. Therefore, our theory may be taken as a general frame able to unify different lines of research and theorizing on cognitive development.

Gardner's (1983) theory deserves special mention because, superficially, it appears similar to ours. Indeed, some of Gardner's intelligences do correspond to some of our SSSs—his spatial and verbal intelligences appear very similar to our spatial-imaginal and verbal-propositional SSSs, respectively. However, our other three SSSs are all undifferentiated parts of what Gardner has called "logicomathematical intelligence." Gardner also refers to domains of activity (i.e., musical and kinesthetic intelligence) that are beyond the current concerns of our theory. Some additional differences are even more important. Gardner's is a static theory: that is, it neither describes the development of the intelligences that he proposes nor involves explanatory concepts capturing the dynamics of development. The theory also seriously underestimates the regulatory role of hypercognition and the constraining role of the processing system. Thus, Gardner's theory is at best an E-model that describes some of the entries to be placed along the horizontal dimension.

THE CAUSATION OF DEVELOPMENT

Why does development occur in the first place? Our theory postulates that developmental causality is a *synergic force*. Specifically, it is assumed that developmental change is possible because the cognitive system consists of multiple but interconnected structures. Thus, a change in any of the three kinds of systems we have described, or in any structure within a system, is able to cause changes in any of the other systems. This is so because the systems are functionally tuned to each other and a change in any one of them is therefore a disturbance factor that puts the dynamic tuning of the whole system in jeopardy. The direction of change is dictated by the system that has changed first, which will then tend to pull the other systems in the same direction as that toward which it has already moved. We shall try to highlight how synergic developmental causality may operate by looking at each system in turn; it hardly needs saying that the theory of course recognizes that a causal chain of changes may be initiated by endogenous (e.g., maturation), individual (e.g., discovery or invention), or exogenous (e.g., imitation or teaching) factors.

Changes Led by the Processing System

A chain of developmental transformations can be set in motion by a change in the most basic components of the processing system, such as speed of processing. We have already seen (Study 5) that a change in speed of processing is followed by a change in the control of processing component. It is plausible to assume that the faster flow of information resulting from an increase in processing speed above a certain threshold makes it more necessary than before to screen incoming information. An improvement in handling the flow of information, in turn, enables the system to exploit its available storage space or capabilities better. Such improvement in storage potential may be experienced by the person as an "enlargement in the screen of conscience" and may make her realize that her information-handling strategies are no longer adequate. This would be a cause for reorganizations at the level of the hypercognitive system, which would then be reflected in the status of the SSSs. Alternatively, the changes in the processing system may first lead to the acquisition of a new SSS-specific skill and subsequently affect the functioning of the hypercognitive system.[14]

Changes Led by the Hypercognitive System

The starting point of a chain of transformations may reside in the hypercognitive system. We have seen (in Study 3) that, before the age of 12 years, children tend to identify the surface content characteristics of tasks with their operational characteristics. This tendency creates no problem on tasks such as intuitor-based tasks, for which ready-made or automated plans of action are directly activated by the task's surface characteristics. However, problems are likely to arise when no such ready-made plan of action is

[14] It may be noted here that the findings of Study 5, indicating that the speed of processing does increase with age, and the interpretation advanced above, about the effects exerted by this increase on the development of the hypercognitive system and the SSSs, are in disagreement with Anderson's (1992) claim that speed of processing does not change with age and that the development of specialized abilities is independent of the condition of the processing system. It seems that Anderson's attempt to formulate a theory that would be able to account for the cognitive functioning of special populations (like autistic children and idiots savants), which is characterized by inflexibility and one-sided cognitive performance, has prevented him from taking notice of the dynamic nature of the normal course of cognitive development.

available and the person must select some strategy applied in the past and adjust it to the needs of the present situation. The shift of the hypercognitive system from the surface to the computational characteristics of tasks at about age 13 partly explains why it is only after this age that the young adolescent becomes able to handle problems that require the design of *original* computational chains because no guiding model is available. Even when the new chain can be assembled from components of previously used chains, one needs quite an accurate set of criteria regarding the functions of these subparts and their functioning vis-à-vis each other and vis-à-vis different mental goals to be able to locate, detach, and reassociate them appropriately.

Changes Led by SSSs

The causality governing changes within each of the various SSSs seems also to be synergic and capable of propagating change in the domain-free systems or the other SSSs. This inference is suggested by the developmental interpatterning of the quantitative-relational and the causal-experimental abilities revealed by Study 1 as well as by our earlier studies of the development of the various SSSs (Demetriou et al., in press; Demetriou et al., 1991). Specifically, the reader is reminded that the 12-year-old subjects of Study 1 were able to solve very complex problems if the solution could be derived by elaborating on an intuitor, such as the "half boundary" in the case of the quantitative-relational SSS or the "first this and then this" scheme in the case of the causal-experimental SSS. Sooner or later, the suppositional mind succeeds in breaking the intuitors into their components. The eventual coordination of these components results in the ability to solve problems directly related to them, such as those involving symmetric covariation or the counterintuitive quantitative-relational and causal-experimental SSS relations. This ability can also be seen in other problems that require forward planning of the steps needed for solution, such as tasks requiring the specification of complex quantitative relations or the design of experiments. To be possible, forward planning requires that the representations of the successive steps be stabilized or fixed in a way that enables the person mentally to visualize them together and hold the image for some period of time.

This process clearly enhances the need for symbolization. According to our earlier studies on the development of the quantitative-relational (Demetriou et al., 1991), the causal-experimental (Demetriou et al., in press), and the spatial-imaginal (Demetriou et al., in preparation) SSS, it is precisely at this phase that the adolescent starts to be able to employ and coordinate complex symbol systems. The establishment of a facility in the manipulation of symbolic structures would obviously open the way for the processing of complex and counterintuitive structures. It would permit these structures to be decomposed and the results of decomposition to be re-represented and redefined as the problem goal requires, independently of what the intuitive structure of the problem might suggest. In fact, the facility to do so becomes established after the age of about 16 years.

This view of development has been nicely described by Karmiloff-Smith (1990, p. 79): "Development appears to involve reiterated cycles of representational change, from the simple running of automatized procedures, to redescriptions of internal representations specified as a sequentially fixed list, and then to internal representations specified as structurally yet flexibly ordered sets of features, that is, a manipulable concept. The sequential specification of a redescribed procedure constitutes a second phase, after behavioral mastery, in a complex cycle of internal redescription and explicitation, ultimately leading in some cases to conscious access and verbal report." To our knowledge, our Study 1 is the first to demonstrate this process in the strict language of structural modeling and in relation to complex cognitive systems such as quantitative and causal thought.

By its very nature, this is a process that transforms the person from one who thinks *with* to one who can think *about* concepts, operations, etc. This is so because it generates and shapes mental spaces that get progressively differentiated from each other as they are put into a kind of mental dialogue. In other words, this process enables the person to envision one mental space from the perspective of another; consequently, each of the spaces becomes a heuristic tool through which the thinker can "take a step back" and think about the others.

This is equivalent to saying that, according to our theory, the multistructural nature of mind is one of the main causes of its development. The interplay of structures during development causes the differentiation among the cognitive structures or skills as well as between the structures and the cognitive activity that generates them. This differentiation enables the person deliberately to make both her cognitive structures and her cognitive activity the object of further cognitive activity. This initiates a new cycle of changes in the structures themselves, and so on.

Our interpretation may appear very similar to the Piagetian notion of equilibrium. This is partly true: both theories are grounded on the assumption that the resolution of cognitive conflicts is the basic cause of cognitive change. However, our view differs from the Piagetian equilibration theory in at least two important respects.

The first difference lies in the role assigned to conflicts as causes of change. Our interpretation assumes that the cognitive system strives primarily for functional efficiency rather than for coherence per se. Thus, a conflict would be cause for change only to the extent that it makes the person less efficient than before it arose. Conflicts render the person less efficient when they lead to indecision; in such cases, there would be a need for change.

However, plain incoherence does not suffice in leading to change. In fact, conflicting representations can indeed exist side by side in the same individual without causing any change that would result in construction of a new representation that would either integrate or abolish one of them.

The second difference relates to the origin of conflicts. In Piaget's theory, the conflicts that trigger the equilibration process have nothing to do with the relations between functional-structural systems; since these systems do not exist in his theory, they are simply conflicts between concepts. In terms used by our theory, the Piagetian conflicts are limited to the intra-SSS level. By contrast, in our theory, the conflicts are located primarily at the intersystemic level. They may be not even conflicts in the literal sense of the word but rather primarily divergences in the functional efficiency of different systems. In this view, conflicts between concepts arise naturally as by-products of the fact that the diverging efficiencies of two systems result in different representations of the same reality structure. The cognitive system may be led to an impasse if noncongruent representations are simultaneously available because this requires that the person decide which of the two is to be used as the accepted interpretation of reality and the guiding plan of action. From our theoretical perspective, conflicts as defined by Piaget could not even exist on their own because, first, to be created, conflicts require autonomous systems that register the same reality in divergent ways and, second, to be recognized as conflicts for which no decision can be reached automatically, a higher-order system that registers the divergence is needed.

The same theoretical difference holds with regard to the "agreement" hypothesis proposed by Bryant (1986) as being superior to Piaget's equilibration theory. According to Bryant, Piaget's theory "accounts for the constraints but not for the eventual successes of intellectual development. Conflicts tell you that something is wrong, but they do not show you what to do about it. They may warn you about the existence of a problem, but they do not provide the solution to it" (p. 174). The agreement hypothesis is "the opposite of Piaget's conflict theory. It is that children progress when they realize that two ways of approaching the same problem produce the same result. When they see that, they realize that both strategies work. The children validate the one intellectual strategy against the other. That is the way that they find out whether to and when to adopt a particular strategy" (p. 176).

From the perspective of our theory, Bryant's agreement hypothesis is a useful complement to Piaget's conflict hypothesis. However, like the Piagetian hypothesis, it is not in itself a causal account of cognitive change because it does not explain how agreement or disagreement is recognized by the thinker in the first place. In our theory, this is the role of the on-line component of the hypercognitive system. We have already discussed how this component is guided by the principles of cognitive organization so as to make decisions about what SSS and what specific strategies need to be brought to bear on the task (see Chap. II). In the SSS procedures–task mapping process, procedures are necessarily compared to each other vis-à-vis the task requirements and the constraints of the activated SSS. It is more than plausible that these comparisons would eventually result in the integration, the differentiation, or the subordination of the procedures in question as alternative means to an end. Thus, like Piaget's notion of equilibration, Bryant's agreement hypothesis appears as a subcase of the general experiential control mechanism advocated by our theory.

To conclude, the equilibration process as defined by Piaget is nothing more than a subcase of the dynamic relations among the three broad systems constituting the intellect. Conflicts between concepts or components that belong to the same or different SSSs are recognized as such by the hypercognitive system. This is the agent that will orchestrate the resolution of the conflict by mapping the conflicting alternatives onto their past and present variations and related evaluations. It is actually a weight ascription process that results in the selection of whichever variation accumulates the higher weights, given the current evaluation of what would constitute a successful performance.

Our position is very similar to Campbell and Bickhard's (1986, pp. 46, 41–42) interactivism:

> A learning system must be able to detect the conditions of undefined or ill-defined problems in the underlying knowing system in order to try to recover the failed or failing interaction of the knowing system. If a system were to evolve that differentiated such conditions of process uncertainty in the knowing system and fed them back into the knowing system as an input, then the knowing system would be able to interact with its own internal condition of uncertainty. Such conditions of uncertainty would correspond to lack of knowledge of the environment or failure to anticipate the interaction.

> From the interactive perspective, then, learning cannot have anything to do with structures being stamped in or imported from the environment. Learning can only be understood as the construction of a new system organization that in practice succeeds in coping with the environment, and succeeds in differentiating it in usable ways. Learning must at its roots involve a metaprocess of constructive variation and ·selection, a process that varies and selects interactive process organizations. Interactivism then *necessitates* constructivism.

In our theory, this metaprocess is part of the hypercognitive system, and it is constrained by the condition of the processing system, the organization of the environment, and the organism-environment tuning. Thus, both interactivism and constructivism necessitate the positing of SSSs. In other words, our theory argues for *constrained constructivism*.

THE CHARACTER OF DEVELOPMENT

Is then development a continuous or a discontinuous process? Our answer is that it is both. When viewed from the perspective of the dynamics underlying structural changes, development appears to be continuous rather than discontinuous. This is so because of the very nature of the mind itself: being both an open and a self-regulated system, it is always in a state of microadaptations. Thus, to the extent that our measures are sufficiently refined to spot these microadaptations among different blocks of mental units, development would be shown to be a continuous process. The results of Study 1 were very clear in this regard. The developmental scales used in this study were refined enough to involve tasks tapping different levels as well as tasks addressed to the same level but differing in the complexity of skills required to implement a level's competence into performance. Pitting these scales against age, we showed that the rate of change in the two SSSs under consideration remained constant from 11 to 21 years of age. Thus, it is practically impossible to notice when the jump is made from the most complex manifestations of a given level L_1 to the next level L_2.

However, when viewed from the perspective of its end products, development is discontinuous. This is especially true when the shift is of the representational variety, such as the sensorimotor to symbolic or the denotational to suppositional shifts mentioned in the introduction. These shifts may be viewed as cutting points that demarcate the end of one developmental cycle and the beginning of another. The age phases coinciding with these shifts have traditionally been associated with an acceleration in the rate of change. This acceleration is considered to index the acquisition of a newfound potentiality whose transformation into actual skills occurs rather rapidly at the beginning and makes the system appear to spurt.

What kind of changes in the general systems of mind might underlie these major transformations in the representational nature of mind and therefore in its strategic orientation toward reality? Taken together, Studies 3, 4, and 5 indicated that the 10–12-year-old age phase is associated with changes in both the processing and the hypercognitive systems. If taken to the extreme, these findings could be taken to suggest that major representational—and hence probably structural—changes require the co-occurrence of changes in more than one system. For instance, the co-occurrence of changes in the processing and the hypercognitive systems causes a reexamination of the relations between concepts, which in turn results in major representational transformations. A reasonable assumption about the mechanism underlying these catalytic transformations is that, when the changes in one of the systems accumulate to a certain level, a change in the other system functions as a catalyst triggering the reorganization of the intellect as a whole at a new representational or structural level.

A complementary assumption is that none of the three major systems (processing system, hypercognitive system, SSSs) is privileged relative to the others as a source of change. This is so because changes confined solely to any one of these systems do not suffice to produce structural or representational change; at most, they result in the improvement of skills within the same representational or structural level. This conception runs contrary to the dominant view in neo-Piagetian theories (especially the theories of Case, 1985; Halford, 1988; and Pascual-Leone, 1988) that changes in the processing system are more important than any others as a source of cognitive restructuring. Changes in the processing system are given priority by these theories because they are thought to raise the general potential of the organism to assemble general strategies and to process SSS-specific information. It is indeed true that a change in the processing system raises the general potential of the individual; however, this is equally true for changes occurring in the other systems. We have already seen that changes in the hypercognitive system result in better management of the processing system. These changes may therefore afford potentialities that are practically equivalent to those initiated by a change in the processing system itself. Finally, it is the changes within the SSSs that result in the production of new conceptual networks and new symbolic tools.

How are the inter- and intrasystem changes effected? We have argued (Demetriou & Efklides, 1985; Demetriou et al., in press) that different kinds of change require different kinds of mechanisms in order to transform the potentialities they afford into cognitive actualities. Evidently, a change in general processing capacity is nothing more than an amorphous potential, and a change in the hypercognitive system is nothing more than a gross orientation. Thus, their SSS-specific formulation comes about via a process of differentiation that formulates the potential, or the general orientation, into actual strategies, rules, concepts, or operations that would be pertinent to the domain and computational specificity as well as the symbolic bias of each SSS. Deletion-substitution must be a mechanism complementary to that of differentiation. This permits the abandonment or rejection of skills or tactical abilities that ensue from the previous orientation and that are incompatible with the newly formulated skills or abilities.

Mechanisms such as Fischer's (1980) compounding or Flavell's (1985) inclusion seem more appropriate to describe changes that occur within SSSs. For instance, the compounding of combinatorial and isolation-of-variables abilities into a common scheme makes experimentation possible. The inclu-

137

sion of basic arithmetic operations and of algebraic ability into a common mental frame makes possible the processing of proportional relations. Finally, mechanisms such as intercoordination seem more appropriate to describe changes that refer to relations between two or more SSSs. For instance, the intercoordination of the model construction ability, which belongs to the causal-experimental SSS, with the algebraic ability, which belongs to the quantitative-relational SSS, results in the complex ability that enables one to quantify one's causal models of reality.

It is interesting to note that, in concluding his discussion of the postulates of several modern theories of cognitive development about mechanisms, Flavell (1984, pp. 207–208) has advocated a view that, although not well differentiated, is very similar in spirit to the position that we hold: "However, at some point we will have to face the likelihood that part of what mechanisms of cognitive development generate is other mechanisms of cognitive development. This implies that some of the agents (activities, knowledge, skills, or other mechanisms or processes) of our cognitive growth are not age independent functional invariants. . . . As in other areas of psychology, we may be obliged to devise specific theories for specific transitions, because different transitions may be accomplished in quite different ways."

INDIVIDUAL CHARACTERIZATION

The analysis advanced above suggests that specification of an individual's level of competence needs to be a three-level enterprise. At a first level, one may characterize individuals on the basis of their processing system only; for instance, one may measure the speed of processing or the working memory of an individual. Normally, it is to be expected that intra- or interindividual variation must be minimal with regard to this measure. However, this measure is nothing more than a cutting point between what the individual cannot do and what he might be able to do if provided with the chance to actualize the potentialities afforded this system to raise one or more components of the SSSs to a higher level of functioning. Hence, by itself, this measure does not lead very far in determining what the individual knows about himself or what he does with real tasks.

A further step would be to measure both general levels, that is, the person's capacity as well as the level of the hypercognitive system. One would then know not only what the individual might be able to do but also how she might go about doing it, that is, the individual's strategic orientation toward the world would also be known.

Nevertheless, the two measures do not tell us at what specific level the person is functioning across the different SSSs—to know about this level, one has to measure it. Having obtained measures of the two general systems and the five SSSs, one has then determined quite precisely the person's developmental zone for each of the SSSs, which is the distance between the person's two general levels and her SSS-specific levels.

How can one predict performance on a given Y task on the basis of one's knowledge of the subject's performance on an X task? According to the analysis that we presented, the relation between two tasks representing abilities X and Y is a function of the degree to which they are similar with regard to the organizational principles that we explicated in Chapter II and the level of the two domain-general systems. In practical terms, under the condition that the time spent on the two abilities is kept constant, this law implies that, the more two abilities are similar with regard to the organizational principles, and the higher the level of the general systems, the more similar their development will be, as they will—asymptotically—tend to match the general levels (see Demetriou & Efklides, 1981, p. 40; Demetriou & Efklides, 1988, p. 208). Axiomatically, this relation may be defined as

$$S_{X,Y} = fi(Pr, L_{DG}, t_{X,Y}),$$

where S is structuredness; Pr stands for the principles of the domain specificity, formal-procedural specificity, symbolic bias, and subjective distinctness of abilities; L_{DG} is the developmental level of the two domain-general systems; $t_{X,Y}$ is the time spent on each of the two abilities; and i is a not-yet-defined constant indicating the relative importance of each of these factors with regard to the organization process that integrates or subordinates abilities under common functional components and SSSs (see Demetriou & Efklides, 1988, p. 208).

In sum, our analysis suggests that, at the level of the processing system, development has to be viewed as the opening of possibilities. At the level of the hypercognitive system, it has to be viewed as the redefinition of a mind's relations with its past identity, reality, and other minds. At the level of the SSSs, development has to be viewed as a continuous emergence of new connections among mental units or as the modification, deletion, and redistribution of old connections.

To conclude, the theory presented in this *Monograph* is inspired by the assumption that the developing mind can be understood only if the strong points of the developmental, the cognitivist, and the psychometric traditions are allowed to converge and become integrated into a comprehensive system. A system that integrates these three traditions should be more successful in generating solutions to important practical problems than systems coming from a single tradition, and we expect this approach to be very helpful in our attempts to answer important but as yet unanswered questions. For instance, we still do not know exactly how each of the various SSSs makes use of the different components of the processing system. Answering this question will eventually enable us to decide if there is indeed a common pool of resources shared by the various SSSs or if the resources themselves are also specialized and/or modular. A reasonable assumption suggested by Studies 3 and 4 is that there may be different processing systems for the processing of acoustic and visual information. Thus, the question becomes, How does each of the SSSs make use of each of the two processing systems, and how do these relations change with development? This question is now being investigated in our laboratory. Another question that we are pursuing is how each of the SSSs is activated in the service of the effective functioning of another SSS. This project will throw some light on the intriguing fact that a differentiated and multistructural mind operates as a well-integrated whole, an issue that raises the question of the relations between the hypercognitive and the other systems. For instance, how are subconscious control of processing acts transformed into planned self-regulatory schemes? How do social influences intervene in this process? A series of projects currently being conducted in our laboratory is systematically directed at the pursuit of answers to these questions.

APPENDIX

TABLE A1

Correlation Matrix, Means, and Standard Deviations of the 16 Variables Used in Study 1 ($N = 163$)

	1	2	3	4	5	6	7	8	9	10	11	12	13	14	15	16
1 QR-N I	1.000															
2 QR-N II	.567	1.000														
3 QR-N III	.561	.513	1.000													
4 QR-N IV	.365	.379	.478	1.000												
5 CE-N I	.332	.415	.269	.208	1.000											
6 CE-N II	.308	.325	.315	.131	.411	1.000										
7 CE-N III	.386	.403	.463	.255	.262	.235	1.000									
8 CE-N IV	.430	.475	.478	.195	.259	.311	.668	1.000								
9 QR-I I	.385	.397	.291	.228	.225	.219	.251	.404	1.000							
10 QR-I II	.446	.330	.341	.199	.225	.213	.338	.344	.410	1.000						
11 QR-I III	.349	.316	.281	.223	.176	.250	.224	.356	.452	.427	1.000					
12 QR-I IV	.394	.489	.339	.240	.198	.152	.223	.424	.367	.376	.491	1.000				
13 CE-I I	.348	.318	.328	.115	.265	.253	.177	.325	.369	.348	.404	.335	1.000			
14 CE-I II	.139	.027	.168	.071	.125	.018	.046	.122	.170	.132	.159	.110	.259	1.000		
15 CE-I III	.212	.205	.252	.026	.130	.068	.262	.300	.191	.225	.154	.077	.202	.209	1.000	
16 CE-I IV	.277	.242	.300	.100	.201	.143	.232	.234	.182	.226	.268	.163	.394	.235	.169	1.000
M	1.319	1.239	1.024	.552	1.773	1.546	1.196	.865	2.037	1.196	1.411	1.595	1.264	1.086	.571	1.503
SD	.921	.928	.882	.833	.622	.730	.881	.843	1.030	1.094	1.029	1.004	.852	.652	.770	.723

NOTE.—The symbols N and I stand for the numerical and imaginal tasks. Roman numerals indicate the developmental levels of the tasks. The model shown in Fig. 1 is based on this matrix. The original of this and the other matrices presented below involved seven decimal digits.

TABLE A2

Mean Logit Attainment (and Standard Deviations) across Age and SSS
(Study 1)

	SSS	
Age	QR	CE
12 years	−.501	−.207
	(.807)	(.988)
14 years	.107	−.030
	(1.194)	(1.154)
16 years	.834	.485
	(1.079)	(1.106)
21 years	1.69	1.822
	(1.626)	(.965)

Note.—Figure 3 is based on this table.

TABLE A3

Correlation Matrices, Means, and Standard Deviations across Age of the Variables Used in Study 2

A. 10-Year-Olds ($N = 198$)

	1	2	3	4	5	6	7	8	9	10	11	12	13	14	15	16	17	18	19	20
1 PRE-QR1	1.000																			
2 PRE-QR2	.409	1.000																		
3 PRE-QR3	-.012	.108	1.000																	
4 PRE-QR4	.089	.169	-.059	1.000																
5 PRE-CE1	.050	.122	.036	-.156	1.000															
6 PRE-CE2	.095	.029	-.112	-.039	.260	1.000														
7 PRE-CE3	.052	.019	.050	-.008	.168	.004	1.000													
8 PRE-CE4	.100	.164	.127	.027	.034	-.005	.347	1.000												
9 POST-QR1	.342	.243	.063	.089	.064	.101	-.076	.056	1.000											
10 POST-QR2	.296	.354	.108	.087	.049	.116	.027	.134	.498	1.000										
11 POST-QR3	.032	.138	.374	-.135	.073	.065	.010	.226	-.040	.102	1.000									
12 POST-QR4	.072	.156	.036	.236	.111	.096	.074	.117	.155	.155	.067	1.000								
13 POST-CE1	.094	.193	.093	.005	.120	.145	.124	.117	.155	.282	.130	.030	1.000							
14 POST-CE2	.183	.156	.022	-.029	.196	.318	.091	.155	.082	.179	.170	.048	.347	1.000						
15 POST-CE3	.063	.130	.197	-.021	.232	.080	.282	.314	.129	.288	.240	.208	.265	.187	1.000					
16 POST-CE4	.088	.029	.126	-.051	.198	.156	.389	.477	.140	.202	.252	.313	.152	.068	.470	1.000				
17 FD	-.016	.184	.148	-.053	.216	-.005	.092	.119	.010	-.054	-.053	-.020	-.015	-.106	.079	.135	1.000			
18 NI	.289	.291	.157	.036	.117	.118	.142	.195	.324	.433	.154	.100	.309	.253	.255	.130	-.004	1.000		
19 LI	.164	.191	.149	.023	.177	-.008	.016	.116	.238	.345	.185	.022	.144	.058	.268	.190	.140	.380	1.000	
20 FI	.112	.163	-.137	.032	.102	.119	-.099	.003	.107	.106	-.005	-.056	-.087	-.024	.018	.012	.161	.107	.211	1.000
M	1.172	.874	.293	.096	1.096	.515	.222	.081	1.066	.768	.379	.152	1.040	.763	.242	.106	4.278	7.556	4.303	41.581
SD	.918	.854	.456	.295	.751	.785	.474	.291	.918	.876	.536	.373	.799	.878	.506	.340	2.999	3.593	2.416	14.299

TABLE A3 (*Continued*)

B. 12-Year-Olds ($N = 294$)

	1	2	3	4	5	6	7	8	9	10	11	12	13	14	15	16	17	18	19	20
1 PRE-QR1	1.000																			
2 PRE-QR2	.598	1.000																		
3 PRE-QR3	.237	.277	1.000																	
4 PRE-QR4	.157	.267	.212	1.000																
5 PRE-CE1	.081	-.004	.074	-.017	1.000															
6 PRE-CE2	.216	.177	.122	.052	.199	1.000														
7 PRE-CE3	.233	.243	.307	.241	.099	.204	1.000													
8 PRE-CE4	.045	.137	.066	.149	.080	.063	.437	1.000												
9 POST-QR1	.473	.422	.229	.074	.084	.173	.301	.163	1.000											
10 POST-QR2	.513	.507	.256	.135	.091	.163	.363	.208	.617	1.000										
11 POST-QR3	.291	.313	.434	.110	.117	.160	.386	.277	.310	.398	1.000									
12 POST-QR4	.311	.287	.216	.346	.017	.186	.301	.124	.267	.313	.336	1.000								
13 POST-CE1	.280	.163	.166	.104	.221	.143	.252	.113	.281	.286	.142	.179	1.000							
14 POST-CE2	.252	.328	.248	.177	.143	.265	.266	.165	.292	.407	.218	.200	.369	1.000						
15 POST-CE3	.291	.322	.279	.281	.105	.175	.439	.206	.357	.404	.294	.357	.262	.369	1.000					
16 POST-CE4	.212	.231	.153	.195	.055	.052	.268	.257	.200	.233	.179	.317	.230	.234	.526	1.000				
17 FD	.249	.252	.102	.094	-.108	.031	.284	.126	.137	.285	.114	.165	.063	.120	.188	.071	1.000			
18 NI	.485	.404	.305	.235	.141	.212	.356	.224	.499	.423	.308	.306	.294	.397	.359	.203	.350	1.000		
19 LI	.398	.402	.321	.225	.082	.120	.389	.160	.335	.441	.347	.350	.247	.342	.420	.291	.360	.538	1.000	
20 FI	.191	.276	.174	.185	-.007	.182	.270	.193	.149	.206	.170	.161	.148	.260	.164	.181	.382	.296	.328	1.000
M	1.184	.891	.415	.174	1.133	.612	.245	.054	1.282	.969	.500	.276	1.027	.878	.422	.190	6.524	9.354	6.374	41.891
SD	.863	.906	.644	.446	.774	.842	.555	.268	.893	.884	.733	.574	.854	.919	.695	.442	4.090	4.338	2.860	13.570

C. 14-Year-Olds ($N = 256$)

	1	2	3	4	5	6	7	8	9	10	11	12	13	14	15	16	17	18	19	20
1 PRE-QR1	1.000																			
2 PRE-QR2	.467	1.000																		
3 PRE-QR3	.302	.292	1.000																	
4 PRE-QR4	.215	.359	.504	1.000																
5 PRE-CE1	.133	.148	.156	.072	1.000															
6 PRE-CE2	.092	.173	.111	.154	.226	1.000														
7 PRE-CE3	.215	.247	.127	.233	.185	.279	1.000													
8 PRE-CE4	.173	.213	.239	.218	.135	.172	.403	1.000												
9 POST-QR1 ...	.404	.278	.171	.157	.225	.125	.238	.164	1.000											
10 POST-QR2 ...	.354	.349	.205	.223	.102	.153	.197	.145	.581	1.000										
11 POST-QR3 ...	.278	.366	.403	.343	.188	.147	.192	.229	.318	.333	1.000									
12 POST-QR4 ...	.258	.377	.453	.551	.145	.119	.168	.296	.261	.276	.471	1.000								
13 PRE-CE1	.161	.310	.144	.173	.202	.272	.314	.269	.268	.347	.319	.299	1.000							
14 PRE-CE2	.173	.312	.278	.249	.258	.265	.324	.256	.188	.307	.255	.305	.495	1.000						
15 PRE-CE3	.271	.365	.252	.285	.154	.209	.479	.305	.289	.315	.304	.344	.424	.447	1.000					
16 PRE-CE4	.244	.240	.353	.311	.196	.205	.376	.406	.289	.294	.350	.421	.384	.412	.551	1.000				
17 FD	.112	.167	.302	.285	.124	.127	.129	.190	.123	.193	.237	.260	.254	.294	.252	.253	1.000			
18 NI	.347	.405	.327	.414	.105	.111	.194	.229	.294	.336	.324	.375	.294	.268	.334	.316	.461	1.000		
19 LI	.199	.263	.238	.201	.158	.256	.205	.226	.286	.330	.293	.193	.249	.232	.273	.301	.341	.311	1.000	
20 FI	.168	.096	.098	.228	.073	.053	.125	.116	.080	-.055	.118	.066	-.049	-.008	.057	.078	.252	.332	.155	1.000
M	1.531	.992	.633	.297	1.180	.945	.566	.203	1.457	1.320	.777	.418	1.238	.969	.750	.449	8.551	11.336	8.328	43.672
SD	.776	.920	.734	.624	.816	.906	.727	.449	.810	.863	.822	.687	.832	.941	.859	.744	5.297	4.372	3.278	13.638

147

TABLE A3 (*Continued*)

D. 16-Year-Olds ($N = 261$)

	1	2	3	4	5	6	7	8	9	10	11	12	13	14	15	16	17	18	19	20
1 PRE-QR1	1.000																			
2 PRE-QR2	.347	1.000																		
3 PRE-QR3	.185	.327	1.000																	
4 PRE-QR4	.218	.308	.407	1.000																
5 PRE-CE1	.090	.171	.241	.050	1.000															
6 PRE-CE2	.037	.057	.130	.080	.284	1.000														
7 PRE-CE3	.167	.232	.193	.187	.206	.266	1.000													
8 PRE-CE4	.082	.212	.196	.129	.130	.125	.425	1.000												
9 POST-QR1	.160	.195	.153	.137	.059	.020	.165	.190	1.000											
10 POST-QR2	.227	.369	.230	.173	.129	.067	.140	.148	.315	1.000										
11 POST-QR3	.159	.290	.462	.370	.138	.146	.152	.189	.248	.344	1.000									
12 POST-QR4	.248	.293	.357	.420	.070	.145	.201	.205	.171	.272	.517	1.000								
13 POST-CE1	.169	.191	.149	.055	.249	.109	.195	.104	.083	.191	.174	.186	1.000							
14 POST-CE2	.214	.192	.199	.100	.301	.308	.201	.171	.145	.114	.149	.242	.423	1.000						
15 POST-CE3	.155	.305	.253	.187	.294	.263	.378	.309	.053	.225	.169	.257	.254	.341	1.000					
16 POST-CE4	.184	.322	.335	.376	.194	.093	.353	.404	.133	.195	.266	.382	.117	.252	.481	1.000				
17 FD	.191	.212	.219	.261	.132	.048	.101	.181	.112	.184	.177	.163	.184	.142	.188	.249	1.000			
18 NI	.232	.209	.249	.179	.024	.031	.083	.047	.023	.120	.147	.190	.151	.234	.220	.219	.291	1.000		
19 LI	.163	.241	.184	.144	.186	.139	.063	.072	.126	.189	.151	.102	.170	.153	.206	.254	.254	.063	1.000	
20 FI	.096	.073	.116	.134	.034	.202	.126	.154	.029	.081	.080	.159	.075	.103	.031	.185	.284	.249	.173	1.000
M	1.624	1.464	.946	.563	1.548	.950	.793	.349	1.808	1.621	1.226	.839	1.632	1.352	1.169	.724	9.467	11.636	9.188	43.084
SD	.710	.834	.840	.775	.640	.891	.834	.605	.549	.711	.854	.858	.641	.849	.856	.851	5.697	4.187	3.424	13.047

NOTE.—The models shown in Tables 4 and 5 in the text are based on this table.

148

TABLE A4

Correlation Matrices, Means, and Standard Deviations across Treatment Groups of the Variables Used in Study 2

A. Control Group ($N = 344$)

	1	2	3	4	5	6	7	8	9	10	11	12	13	14	15	16	17	18	19	20	21	22
1 SUCCESS	1.000																					
2 AGE	.000	1.000																				
3 PRE-QR1	.000	.281	1.000																			
4 PRE-QR2	.000	.234	.483	1.000																		
5 PRE-QR3	.000	.240	.289	.325	1.000																	
6 PRE-QR4	.000	.268	.259	.376	.424	1.000																
7 PRE-CE1	.000	.186	.019	.011	.153	.030	1.000															
8 PRE-CE2	.000	.229	.070	.044	.141	.098	.285	1.000														
9 PRE-CE3	.000	.314	.227	.282	.173	.229	.200	.225	1.000													
10 PRE-CE4	.000	.172	.099	.236	.198	.138	.162	.101	.397	1.000												
11 POST-QR1	.000	.347	.449	.368	.236	.230	.076	.074	.263	.188	1.000											
12 POST-QR2	.000	.348	.430	.489	.274	.287	.108	.118	.287	.180	.572	1.000										
13 POST-QR3	.000	.321	.310	.335	.520	.379	.139	.183	.296	.240	.298	.429	1.000									
14 POST-QR4	.000	.356	.303	.367	.425	.549	.155	.149	.246	.232	.275	.362	.505	1.000								
15 POST-CE1	.000	.283	.256	.258	.227	.117	.230	.161	.266	.167	.284	.359	.279	.239	1.000							
16 POST-CE2	.000	.252	.250	.268	.260	.158	.275	.278	.258	.198	.254	.287	.221	.190	.435	1.000						
17 POST-CE3	.000	.386	.248	.365	.270	.277	.218	.200	.464	.260	.340	.403	.321	.294	.392	.405	1.000					
18 POST-CE4	.000	.318	.169	.268	.322	.309	.188	.103	.295	.436	.301	.307	.340	.358	.248	.297	.496	1.000				
19 FD	.000	.416	.188	.221	.246	.302	.166	.180	.221	.169	.229	.249	.269	.249	.242	.198	.344	.300	1.000			
20 NI	.000	.301	.413	.335	.349	.330	.058	.153	.213	.101	.399	.370	.357	.278	.304	.317	.389	.226	.426	1.000		
21 LI	.000	.556	.323	.355	.323	.286	.196	.273	.231	.187	.383	.429	.349	.277	.307	.280	.430	.282	.448	.371	1.000	
22 FI	.000	.028	.132	.156	.107	.182	.007	.168	.093	.081	.080	.095	.119	.097	-.008	.052	.108	.158	.292	.298	.225	1.000
M	9.000	166.691	1.363	1.029	.570	.282	1.221	.756	.471	.157	1.334	1.087	.753	.454	1.224	.936	.645	.343	7.468	9.948	7.378	42.718
SD	.000	26.290	.860	.916	.737	.586	.770	.896	.703	.424	.878	.893	.840	.698	.822	.920	.799	.624	4.952	4.469	3.853	13.412

TABLE A4 (Continued)

B. The Group Trained on the Quantitative-Relational SSS ($N = 327$)

	1	2	3	4	5	6	7	8	9	10	11	12	13	14	15	16	17	18	19	20	21	22
1 SUCCESS	1.000																					
2 AGE	.113	1.000																				
3 PRE-QR1	-.070	.171	1.000																			
4 PRE-QR2	-.247	.221	.441	1.000																		
5 PRE-QR3	.198	.308	.196	.300	1.000																	
6 PRE-QR4	.048	.154	.089	.194	.204	1.000																
7 PRE-CE1	.054	.267	.234	.273	.207	.019	1.000															
8 PRE-CE2	-.025	.144	.241	.222	.153	-.017	.285	1.000														
9 PRE-CE3	.045	.328	.131	.208	.302	.107	.186	.264	1.000													
10 PRE-CE4	.001	.272	.208	.197	.240	.159	.157	.172	.561	1.000												
11 POST-QR1	.069	.275	.093	.272	.231	.046	.276	.228	.200	.158	1.000											
12 POST-QR2	.125	.351	.255	.333	.294	.102	.208	.174	.227	.213	.565	1.000										
13 POST-QR3	.183	.410	.303	.380	.428	.201	.297	.227	.300	.282	.314	.394	1.000									
14 POST-QR4	.149	.360	.193	.301	.356	.190	.207	.273	.327	.290	.255	.320	.538	1.000								
15 POST-CE1	.044	.292	.195	.264	.206	.096	.327	.273	.300	.248	.280	.380	.303	.287	1.000							
16 POST-CE2	-.010	.189	.142	.271	.194	.105	.255	.370	.310	.251	.186	.296	.249	.287	.475	1.000						
17 POST-CE3	.113	.429	.253	.271	.312	.065	.300	.253	.510	.429	.241	.332	.352	.394	.360	.325	1.000					
18 POST-CE4	.112	.359	.166	.274	.283	.215	.213	.256	.480	.513	.181	.265	.360	.474	.319	.319	.534	1.000				
19 FD	.017	.375	.195	.254	.306	.154	.134	.154	.293	.292	.138	.221	.241	.232	.198	.192	.202	.248	1.000			
20 NI	.016	.318	.201	.383	.272	.106	.214	.181	.274	.192	.279	.368	.230	.293	.355	.319	.270	.294	.364	1.000		
21 LI	.062	.425	.327	.339	.294	.161	.256	.223	.300	.235	.309	.406	.368	.287	.379	.291	.377	.414	.363	.431	1.000	
22 FI	-.166	-.008	.258	.096	.048	.027	.110	.100	.096	.103	.023	.014	.027	.033	.053	.088	-.009	.054	.190	.163	.172	1.000
M	2.012	163.957	1.434	1.0469	.529	.177	1.208	.706	.385	.206	1.517	1.257	.703	.398	1.193	.933	.572	.342	7.309	10.165	7.061	42.712
SD	1.275	26.341	.818	.931	.704	.413	.759	.850	.668	.517	.802	.883	.818	.701	.838	.911	.783	.659	4.861	4.278	3.328	13.270

C. THE GROUP TRAINED ON THE CAUSAL-EXPERIMENTAL SSS ($N = 325$)

	1	2	3	4	5	6	7	8	9	10	11	12	13	14	15	16	17	18	19	20	21	22
1 SUCCESS	1.000																					
2 AGE	.207	1.000																				
3 PRE-QR1	.207	.204	1.000																			
4 PRE-QR2	.284	.218	.556	1.000																		
5 PRE-QR3	.210	.407	.283	.371	1.000																	
6 PRE-QR4	.253	.414	.301	.410	.551	1.000																
7 PRE-CE1	-.073	.161	.143	.191	.220	.153	1.000															
8 PRE-CE2	.077	.224	.195	.207	.134	.225	.190	1.000														
9 PRE-CE3	.211	.336	.344	.311	.340	.392	.242	.312	1.000													
10 PRE-CE4	.233	.307	.263	.285	.366	.456	.137	.219	.444	1.000												
11 POST-QR1	.239	.302	.500	.438	.281	.263	.181	.208	.325	.277	1.000											
12 POST-QR2	.333	.349	.502	.528	.334	.312	.155	.288	.374	.279	.599	1.000										
13 POST-QR3	.276	.406	.296	.375	.562	.441	.192	.193	.308	.375	.365	.410	1.000									
14 POST-QR4	.248	.342	.355	.400	.440	.657	.105	.158	.289	.339	.344	.375	.456	1.000								
15 POST-CE1	.282	.222	.313	.310	.224	.273	.191	.202	.316	.209	.310	.335	.257	.283	1.000							
16 POST-CE2	.248	.212	.241	.367	.331	.285	.233	.280	.277	.253	.316	.399	.346	.378	.436	1.000						
17 POST-CE3	.285	.392	.407	.463	.460	.466	.226	.305	.487	.399	.381	.483	.431	.509	.379	.482	1.000					
18 POST-CE4	.287	.366	.357	.351	.476	.522	.237	.174	.483	.401	.311	.364	.408	.524	.318	.349	.662	1.000				
19 FD	.270	.305	.243	.284	.350	.370	.103	.073	.221	.236	.216	.363	.281	.326	.210	.244	.372	.348	1.000			
20 NI	.334	.340	.438	.401	.409	.412	.169	.214	.322	.370	.439	.485	.391	.417	.296	.371	.473	.399	.423	1.000		
21 LI	.335	.437	.332	.336	.420	.352	.184	.184	.362	.263	.366	.490	.412	.359	.189	.294	.460	.439	.449	.494	1.000	
22 FI	.125	.116	.226	.223	.137	.220	.025	.128	.211	.236	.193	.169	.180	.193	.073	.165	.125	.179	.329	.307	.228	1.000
M	1.428	165.148	1.360	1.108	.662	.415	1.314	.843	.529	.145	1.418	1.225	.751	.449	1.314	1.129	.775	.443	7.311	10.200	7.175	42.655
SD	1.390	26.137	.837	.891	.763	.739	.782	.894	.752	.352	.834	.893	.810	.721	.805	.931	.890	.746	5.360	4.633	3.351	13.990

NOTE.—The values shown in pt. A of Table 6 in the text came out of models that were fitted to these matrices. The first of these models contrasted the control with the quantitative training group; the second model contrasted the control with the experimental training group. The matrices, means, and standard deviations that represent the performance of the subjects who solved the training task and that resulted in the models shown in pt. B of Table 6 are not presented here because of space considerations; they can, however, be obtained from the authors on request.

151

TABLE A5

CORRELATION MATRIX, MEANS, AND STANDARD DEVIATIONS OF THE VARIABLES
USED IN STUDY 3 ($N = 78$)

	1	2	3	4	5	6	7	8	9	10	11	12	13	14
1 ATTCE ..	1.000													
2 ATTSI ...	.602	1.000												
3 ATTQR ..	.342	.097	1.000											
4 STMCE ...	.442	.449	.119	1.000										
5 STMSI ...	.269	.541	−.023	.419	1.000									
6 STMQR ..	.116	.108	.279	.347	.254	1.000								
7 LTMCE ..	.317	.335	.113	.460	.468	.192	1.000							
8 LTMSI ...	.339	.456	.080	.467	.487	.128	.581	1.000						
9 LTMQR ..	−.084	−.087	.205	.159	.017	.330	.119	.077	1.000					
10 UNDCE ..	.255	.147	.083	.422	.188	.277	.213	.134	.119	1.000				
11 UNDSI ...	.268	.394	.124	.323	.433	.081	.264	.387	.033	.307	1.000			
12 UNDQR ..	−.044	−.154	.245	.123	−.020	.410	.044	.022	.159	−.022	−.009	1.000		
13 DEDCE ...	.269	.294	.136	.313	.204	.363	.504	.319	.286	.264	.116	.023	1.000	
14 DEDSI ...	.161	.304	−.101	.344	.379	.122	.330	.572	.068	.149	.347	.072	.268	1.000
15 DEDQR ...	.169	.198	.253	.180	.196	.259	.115	.153	.224	.266	.228	.112	.346	.059
16 CEIV	.486	.474	.192	.403	.247	.135	.237	.308	.088	.174	.212	−.066	.370	.229
17 CECO	.456	.230	.255	.500	.157	.141	.245	.216	.013	.328	.202	.226	.157	.143
18 CEHF	.150	.088	.330	.190	.074	−.024	.044	−.010	.094	.109	−.000	−.087	.181	−.094
19 SIRO	.070	−.094	.135	.075	−.095	−.066	.038	.050	.016	−.030	−.098	−.007	−.058	−.092
20 SIOP	−.130	−.017	−.060	−.162	−.082	−.014	−.174	−.055	.012	−.060	−.229	.070	−.078	−.072
21 SICM	.190	.209	.096	.216	.349	−.002	.205	.355	.173	.073	.196	−.059	.208	.238
22 QRPR	.024	−.090	.263	.110	−.197	.168	.089	.039	.423	.038	−.000	.304	.218	−.021
23 QRDI	.049	.099	.149	.169	.191	.154	.096	−.010	.179	.090	.179	.278	.096	−.061
24 QRID	−.067	−.038	.215	−.053	−.008	.064	.038	−.019	.007	−.091	.022	.050	−.146	−.031
25 SIA1	.055	−.199	.250	−.054	−.190	−.048	−.153	−.148	−.031	.019	−.072	.152	−.124	−.081
26 SIA2	.072	−.101	.040	−.116	−.206	.071	−.186	−.211	−.130	−.045	−.159	.212	.008	.003
27 CEP1	−.160	−.291	.314	−.065	−.425	.104	−.252	−.276	.194	.011	−.171	.241	−.103	−.163
28 CEP2	−.114	−.249	.348	−.297	−.290	−.122	−.260	−.225	−.135	−.113	−.168	.012	−.264	−.137
29 QRA1	−.198	−.254	.277	−.208	−.311	.253	−.334	−.232	.135	.029	−.151	.199	−.039	−.031
30 QRA2	.045	−.043	.338	.043	−.177	.070	−.119	−.095	.018	−.017	−.162	.274	−.080	−.001
M	2.880	2.556	3.094	2.583	2.349	3.128	2.573	2.316	2.680	2.971	2.747	3.147	2.699	2.588
SD	.796	.759	.732	.775	.880	.853	.685	.651	.729	.596	.803	.832	.649	.758

NOTE.—The symbols CE, SI, and QR stand for the causal-experimental, the spatial-imaginal, and the quantitative-relational SSSs, respectively. The symbols ATT, STM, LTM, UND, and DED stand for attention, short-term memory, long-term memory, understanding, and deduction, respectively. The symbols IV, CO, and HF stand for isolation of variables, combinations, and hypothesis formation, respectively. The symbols IV, CO, HF, RO, OP, CM, PR, DI, and ID stand for the ratings given by the subjects to the statement referring to the use of isolation-of-variables, combinatorial strategy, hypothesis formation, mental rotation, application of arithmetic operations, composition of an image, estimate proportional relations, order values along a quantitative dimension, and integration of perspectives, respectively. The models shown in Figs. 6 and 7 are based on this matrix.

15	16	17	18	19	20	21	22	23	24	25	26	27	28	29	30
1.000															
.238	1.000														
.192	.364	1.000													
.060	.250	.091	1.000												
−.085	.017	.218	.118	1.000											
−.070	−.063	−.124	.094	.127	1.000										
0.47	.165	.126	.308	.228	.195	1.000									
.038	.019	.062	.207	.024	.014	−.039	1.000								
.186	.180	.138	.182	.138	−.040	−.164	.015	1.000							
−.088	−.069	.060	.017	.239	−.053	−.061	.104	.084	1.000						
−.072	−.031	.095	.154	.263	.097	.164	−.027	.048	.095	1.000					
−.132	−.014	−.160	−.147	.001	.094	−.068	.086	−.061	−.076	.105	1.000				
−.035	−.135	.079	−.028	.187	.014	−.116	.101	.039	.303	.308	.103	1.000			
−.066	.068	.058	.130	.170	.154	−.078	.024	−.085	.434	.342	.049	.366	1.000		
−.089	−.165	−.012	.026	.208	.357	.023	.089	−.193	.118	.382	.136	.413	.366	1.000	
−.074	.007	.054	−.065	.138	−.014	−.055	.103	−.027	.276	.323	.034	.433	.251	.384	1.000
2.714	2.865	2.961	2.897	3.141	2.923	2.737	2.891	2.885	3.141	1.192	1.180	1.376	.539	.519	.910
.711	1.086	.990	.931	1.047	1.060	1.015	1.156	.967	1.125	.774	.528	.654	.733	.493	.900

TABLE A6

Metacognitive Ratings of General Cognitive Functions as a Function of Age and SSS

Age	Attention			Short-Term Memory			Long-Term Memory			Understanding			Deduction		
	CE	SI	QR	CE	SI	QR	CE	SI	QR	CE	SI	QR	CE	SI	QR
12 years	2.936	2.949	2.590	2.596	2.827	3.173	2.987	2.603	2.551	3.019	2.808	2.712	2.923	2.859	2.654
	(.449)	(.643)	(.637)	(.600)	(.672)	(.717)	(.427)	(.567)	(.629)	(.800)	(.849)	(.783)	(.626)	(.596)	(.709)
13 years	3.231	3.038	3.282	2.712	2.692	3.135	2.628	2.526	2.628	3.135	2.981	3.000	2.808	2.859	2.859
	(.644)	(.752)	(.909)	(.871)	(1.296)	(1.313)	(.746)	(.775)	(.635)	(.712)	(.892)	(1.123)	(.666)	(.923)	(.860)
14 years	2.760	2.500	3.104	2.875	2.344	2.969	2.667	2.427	2.865	2.844	2.938	3.312	2.688	2.427	2.813
	(.985)	(.767)	(.779)	(.885)	(.694)	(.991)	(.765)	(.686)	(.761)	(.473)	(.873)	(.698)	(.620)	(.758)	(.694)
15 years	2.825	2.263	3.184	2.408	2.053	3.118	2.333	2.053	2.763	2.842	2.618	3.474	2.474	2.333	2.719
	(.838)	(.681)	(.636)	(.713)	(.827)	(.689)	(.451)	(.481)	(.624)	(.522)	(.747)	(.825)	(.589)	(.683)	(.606)
16 years	2.745	2.265	3.225	2.397	2.059	3.250	2.392	2.127	2.549	3.074	2.485	3.074	2.706	2.608	2.549
	(.864)	(.675)	(.607)	(.755)	(.659)	(.566)	(.821)	(.639)	(.950)	(.514)	(.670)	(.611)	(.735)	(.759)	(.761)

Note.—Figure 8 is based on this table.

TABLE A7

Metacognitive Ratings of SSS-Specific Components across Age and SSSs

A. Ratings of the Causal-Experimental Components Given to the Three SSSs

Age	Causal-Experimental			Spatial-Imaginal			Quantitative-Relational		
	IV	CO	HF	IV	CO	HF	IV	CO	HF
12 years	3.154	2.423	2.885	3.000	2.846	3.038	2.808	2.769	2.654
	(1.049)	(.703)	(.982)	(.842)	(.899)	(.853)	(1.217)	(1.092)	(1.088)
13 years	3.308	3.462	2.885	3.000	3.000	2.615	3.769	3.462	2.692
	(1.362)	(.989)	(.845)	(1.323)	(1.291)	(.893)	(1.252)	(.853)	(1.146)
14 years	2.433	3.000	2.900	2.033	2.700	2.767	2.533	3.400	3.000
	(.980)	(1.035)	(.737)	(1.125)	(.775)	(.961)	(1.356)	(1.198)	(.866)
15 years	2.921	3.263	3.000	2.079	1.974	3.026	2.842	3.000	2.789
	(.917)	(.963)	(1.080)	(.961)	(.772)	(1.073)	(1.001)	(.816)	(1.032)
16 years	2.735	2.676	2.882	1.765	2.147	2.941	2.559	2.706	2.500
	(1.017)	(.967)	(.993)	(.773)	(.931)	(.899)	(1.249)	(.830)	(.968)

155

TABLE A7 (Continued)

B. Ratings of the Quantitative-Relational Components Given to the Three SSSs

Age	Causal-Experimental			Spatial-Imaginal			Quantitative-Relational		
	FR	DI	ID	FR	DI	ID	FR	DI	ID
12 years	2.462	2.615	3.000	2.615	2.846	2.692	2.654	2.808	2.577
	(1.108)	(1.121)	(.979)	(.982)	(.774)	(.925)	(1.107)	(1.128)	(.976)
13 years	2.731	3.192	2.385	2.269	2.731	2.385	2.923	2.962	3.615
	(1.285)	(.693)	(1.064)	(1.301)	(.857)	(1.044)	(1.484)	(.853)	(.795)
14 years	2.733	3.100	3.067	2.200	2.667	2.300	2.967	2.800	2.933
	(.961)	(.949)	(1.163)	(.882)	(1.160)	(1.265)	(1.232)	(1.066)	(1.237)
15 years	1.895	2.947	2.895	1.605	2.368	2.184	3.184	2.921	3.132
	(.756)	(.896)	(1.088)	(.636)	(.879)	(.820)	(.916)	(.902)	(1.141)
16 years	1.971	2.941	2.559	1.794	2.706	2.353	2.706	2.941	3.441
	(.910)	(1.029)	(.808)	(1.187)	(1.091)	(1.042)	(1.160)	(1.029)	(1.223)

C. Ratings of the Spatial-Imaginal Components Given to the Three SSSs

Age	Causal-Experimental			Spatial-Imaginal			Quantitative-Relational		
	RO	OR	CM	RO	OR	CM	RO	OR	CM
12 years	2.808	2.500	2.846	2.731	3.154	3.038	2.731	2.962	2.769
	(.723)	(.935)	(1.068)	(1.013)	(1.144)	(.946)	(.971)	(.828)	(.780)
13 years	2.192	2.538	2.346	2.962	2.423	2.500	1.923	2.654	2.462
	(1.128)	(.989)	(1.162)	(.923)	(1.188)	(.866)	(1.205)	(.966)	(1.089)
14 years	2.967	2.833	2.367	3.100	2.867	2.733	2.400	2.467	2.700
	(1.260)	(.772)	(1.172)	(1.228)	(1.141)	(1.252)	(1.198)	(1.026)	(1.320)
15 years	2.105	2.421	2.211	3.447	3.053	2.684	1.921	2.263	2.237
	(1.008)	(.886)	(1.018)	(1.117)	(.985)	(1.057)	(.731)	(.903)	(.918)
16 years	2.118	2.735	1.824	3.382	3.059	2.765	1.559	1.794	2.441
	(.977)	(.752)	(.789)	(.801)	(.917)	(.986)	(.966)	(.772)	(1.223)

Note.—Figure 9 is based on this table.

TABLE A8

CORRELATION MATRIX, MEANS, AND STANDARD DEVIATIONS OF THE HALF SCORES OF THE VARIABLES USED IN STUDY 5 ($N = 65$)

		1	2	3	4	5	6	7	8	9	10	11	12	13	14	15	16
1	IWCO	1.000															
2	IWCM	.643	1.000														
3	IWIN	.581	.496	1.000													
4	ICCO	.417	.325	.444	1.000												
5	ICCM	.502	.428	.325	.195	1.000											
6	ICIN	.419	.585	.353	.342	.338	1.000										
7	ICSTA	−.296	−.368	−.383	−.322	−.122	−.242	1.000									
8	IVST	−.378	−.484	−.274	−.241	−.268	−.334	.678	1.000								
9	IIWCO	.390	.399	.381	.423	.320	.467	−.238	−.209	1.000							
10	IIWCM	.502	.643	.494	.434	.388	.610	−.313	−.330	.728	1.000						
11	IIWIN	.345	.566	.440	.251	.225	.429	−.313	−.193	.619	.618	1.000					
12	IICCO	.369	.409	.450	.552	.291	.431	−.367	−.293	.467	.523	.518	1.000				
13	IICCM	.270	.515	.306	.275	.404	.511	−.149	−.272	.587	.712	.538	.499	1.000			
14	IICIN	.492	.561	.425	.435	.401	.561	−.238	−.354	.613	.568	.495	.487	.602	1.000		
15	IICSTA ...	−.340	−.302	−.315	−.288	−.316	−.444	.575	.452	−.400	−.412	−.280	−.429	−.374	−.442	1.000	
16	IICSTB ...	−.284	−.333	−.404	−.295	−.268	−.355	.736	.667	−.270	−.290	−.228	−.366	−.254	−.357	.659	1.000
17	IIVST	−.258	−.306	−.254	−.203	−.217	−.356	.665	.626	−.270	−.331	−.272	−.436	−.348	−.300	.511	.708
18	IDIF1	.025	−.288	.143	.812	−.067	−.015	−.099	.056	.182	.042	−.096	.307	−.039	.094	−.105	−.093
19	IDIF2	.113	.095	.124	.217	.148	.863	−.067	−.108	.325	.348	.174	.274	.306	.339	−.356	−.228
20	IIDIF1	.062	.006	.163	.326	.056	.056	−.198	−.100	.012	−.122	.151	.782	.060	.152	−.198	−.215
21	IIDIF2	.168	.133	.096	.157	.155	.161	−.023	−.147	.125	−.159	.074	.145	.123	.722	−.184	−.185
22	IOPER1 ...	−.368	−.375	−.286	−.376	−.278	−.440	.464	.470	−.341	−.350	−.285	−.515	−.311	−.448	.586	.556
23	IOPER2 ...	−.346	−.366	−.347	−.283	−.223	−.276	.526	.486	−.295	−.289	−.240	−.441	−.251	−.348	.548	.558
24	IIOPER1 ...	−.397	−.393	−.311	−.346	−.392	−.423	.478	.374	−.397	−.371	−.411	−.516	−.314	−.476	.581	.504
25	IIOPER2 ...	−.344	−.375	−.318	−.311	−.315	−.430	.527	.412	−.383	−.337	−.377	−.453	−.282	−.409	.605	.558
26	IALG1	.169	.305	.117	−.004	.168	.234	−.184	−.245	.258	.285	.376	.177	.315	.358	−.238	−.129
27	IALG2	.173	.307	.118	−.007	.181	.238	−.189	−.253	.263	.295	.379	.180	.324	.361	−.243	−.131
28	IPROP1	.090	.240	.035	−.070	.138	.189	−.090	−.163	.203	.203	.333	.070	.212	.253	−.094	−.003
29	IPROP2 ...	.089	.245	.038	−.067	.131	.193	−.086	−.180	.203	.215	.333	.063	.225	.259	−.096	.011
30	IIALG1 ...	−.241	−.341	−.175	−.185	−.294	−.290	.354	.410	−.262	−.256	−.267	−.370	−.324	−.370	.393	.390
31	IIALG2	−.199	−.279	−.262	−.082	−.191	−.154	.425	.387	−.136	−.178	−.240	−.372	−.291	−.223	.429	.381
32	IIPROP1 ...	−.300	−.124	−.262	−.204	−.209	−.140	.387	.319	−.121	−.138	−.111	−.324	−.279	−.240	.486	.470
33	IIPROP2 ...	−.307	−.147	−.270	−.137	−.203	−.092	.397	.330	−.059	−.133	−.122	−.305	−.266	−.216	.454	.440
M	....	1.027	.990	.973	1.188	1.041	1.458	2.506	2.710	.976	.929	1.038	1.090	.992	1.204	3.870	2.373
SD	....	.241	.203	.198	.333	.221	.400	1.107	.933	.195	.182	.282	.289	.223	.259	1.083	.983

NOTE.—The symbols W and C stand for word and color, respectively. The symbols CO, CM, and IN stand for compatible, control, and incompatible, respectively. Thus, e.g., the complex WCO denotes the word-compatible condition in the Stroop task. The symbols CSTA, CSTB, and VST stand for the standard version of the counting span test, the revised version of the counting span test, and the vectorial span test, respectively. The symbols OPER, ALG, and PROP stand for the tasks representing arithmetic operations, algebra, and proportionality. The numerals 1 and 2 associated with the cognitive tasks indicate half scores. The symbol DIF stands for difference, and it represents the scores based on the difference between the color-control and the word-compatible (DIF1) and color-incompatible and word-compatible condition (DIF2). The Roman numerals I and II stand for the two testing occasions. The models shown in Figs. 10, 11, and 12 are based on this matrix.

17	18	19	20	21	22	23	24	25	26	27	28	29	30	31	32	33
1.000																
−.016	1.000															
−.246	.161	1.000														
−.265	.326	.065	1.000													
−.081	.077	.115	.285	1.000												
.507	−.149	−.307	−.344	−.244	1.000											
.515	−.060	−.110	−.302	−.175	.841	1.000										
.515	−.108	−.275	−.329	−.259	.867	.823	1.000									
.520	−.083	−.295	−.280	−.207	.821	.806	.897	1.000								
−.299	−.193	.098	−.003	.189	−.131	−.061	−.175	−.213	1.000							
−.302	−.197	.100	−.006	.185	−.132	−.062	−.173	−.212	.999	1.000						
−.250	−.219	.082	−.067	.132	−.021	.075	−.073	−.098	.953	.952	1.000					
−.234	−.219	.085	−.084	.130	−.013	.083	−.061	−.083	.952	.951	.994	1.000				
.295	.024	−.143	−.244	−.229	.585	.556	.571	.562	−.064	−.069	.052	.064	1.000			
.314	.090	−.015	−.303	−.118	.460	.516	.499	.538	−.275	−.271	−.138	−.133	.604	1.000		
.424	−.130	−.095	−.276	−.172	.542	.536	.475	.574	−.294	−.299	−.112	−.091	.497	.609	1.000	
.423	−.047	−.021	−.258	−.147	.483	.492	.421	.550	−.351	−.357	−.160	−.141	.481	.619	.967	1.000
2.720	−.017	.468	.109	.275	.608	.503	.685	.582	2.444	2.387	3.217	3.215	.390	.233	1.373	1.369
.951	.201	.325	.222	.216	.330	.401	.296	.358	3.780	3.813	3.525	3.532	.211	.222	1.301	1.392

REFERENCES

Ackerman, E. (in press). From decontextualized to situated knowledge: Revisiting Piaget's water-level experiment. In I. Harel & S. Papert (Eds.), *Constructionism*. Norwood, NJ: Ablex.

Anderson, M. (1992). *Intelligence and cognitive development: A cognitive theory*. Oxford: Blackwell.

Baddeley, A. (1991). *Working memory*. Oxford: Oxford University Press.

Bandura, A. (1989). Regulation of cognitive processes through perceived self-efficacy. *Developmental Psychology*, **25**, 729–735.

Bentler, P. M. (1989). *EQS: Structural equations program manual*. Los Angeles, CA: BMDP Statistical Software.

Bickhard, M. H. (1988). Piaget on variation and selection models: Structuralism, logical necessity, and interactivism. *Human Development*, **31**, 274–312.

Biggs, J. B. (1992). Returning to school: Review and discussion. In A. Demetriou, M. Shayer, & A. Efklides (Eds.), *Neo-Piagetian theories of cognitive development: Implications and applications for education*. London: Routledge.

Bjorklund, D. F., & Harnishfeger, K. K. (1987). Developmental differences in the mental effort requirements for the use of an organizational strategy in free recall. *Journal of Experimental Child Psychology*, **44**, 109–125.

Brainerd, C. J. (1978). The stage question in cognitive developmental theory. *Behavioral and Brain Sciences*, **2**, 173–182.

Broadbent, D. E. (1975). The magic number seven after fifteen years. In A. Kennedy & A. Wilkes (Eds.), *Studies in long term memory*. London: Wiley.

Bryant, P. (1986). Theories about the causes of cognitive development. In P. van Geert (Ed.), *Theory building in developmental psychology*. Amsterdam: North-Holland.

Burtis, P. J. (1982). The development of short-term memory: Capacity increases or chunking? *Journal of Experimental Child Psychology*, **34**, 387–413.

Campbell, R. L., & Bickhard, M. H. (1986). *Knowing levels and developmental stages*. Basel: Karger.

Carey, S. (1985). *Conceptual change in childhood*. Cambridge, MA: MIT Press.

Case, R. (1985). *Intellectual development: Birth to adulthood*. New York: Academic.

Case, R. (1992). *The mind's staircase*. Hillsdale, NJ: Erlbaum.

Case, R., & Kurland, M. (1978). Construction and validation of a new test of children's M-space. Unpublished manuscript, University of Toronto, Ontario Institute for Studies in Education.

Case, R., Kurland, M., & Goldberg, J. (1982). Operational efficiency and the growth of short-term memory. *Journal of Experimental Child Psychology*, **33**, 386–404.

Chi, M. T. H. (1978). Knowledge structures and memory development. In R. S. Siegler (Ed.), *Children's thinking: What develops?* Hillsdale, NJ: Erlbaum.

Commons, M. L., Richards, F. A., & Kuhn, D. (1982). Systematic and metasystematic reasoning: A case for levels of reasoning beyond Piaget's stage of formal operations. *Child Development, 53,* 1058–1069.

Demetriou, A. (1983). *Psycho-logical development of the structures of concrete thought: Experimental studies on the thought of children aged from 4 to 10 years* (Scientific Annals of the School of Philosophy, Suppl. No. 39). Thessaloniki: Aristotelian University Press.

Demetriou, A. (1989). Structural systems in the developing intellect, science, and education. *EARLI News* (European Association for Research in Learning and Instruction), **8,** 14–18.

Demetriou, A. (1990). Structural and developmental relations between formal and post-formal capacities: Towards a comprehensive theory of adolescent and adult cognitive development. In M. L. Commons, F. A. Richards, C. Armon, & J. Sinnot (Eds.), *Beyond formal operations: Vol. 2. The development of adolescent thought and perception.* New York: Praeger.

Demetriou, A., & Charitides, L. (1986). The adolescent's construction of procedural justice as a function of age, formal thought, and sex. *International Journal of Psychology, 21,* 333–353.

Demetriou, A., & Efklides, A. (1979). Formal operational thinking in young adults as a function of education and sex. *International Journal of Psychology, 14,* 241–253.

Demetriou, A., & Efklides, A. (1981). The structure of formal operations: The ideal of the whole and the reality of the parts. In J. A. Meacham & N. R. Santilli (Eds.), *Social development in youth: Structure and content.* Basel: Karger.

Demetriou, A., & Efklides, A. (1985). Structure and sequence of formal and postformal thought: General patterns and individual differences. *Child Development, 56,* 1062–1091.

Demetriou, A., & Efklides, A. (1987). Towards a determination of the dimensions and domains of individual differences in cognitive development. In E. de Corte, H. Lodewijks, R. Parmentier, & P. Span (Eds.), *Learning and instruction: European research in an international context* (Vol. 1). Oxford: Leuven University Press and Pergamon Press.

Demetriou, A., & Efklides, A. (1988). Experiential structuralism and neo-Piagetian theories: Toward an integrated model. In A. Demetriou (Ed.), *The neo-Piagetian theories of cognitive development: Toward an integration.* Amsterdam: North-Holland.

Demetriou, A., & Efklides, A. (1989). The person's conception of the structures of developing intellect. *Genetic, Social, and General Psychology Monographs, 115,* 371–423.

Demetriou, A., & Efklides, A. (1990). The objective and subjective structure of problem solving abilities: Metacognitive awareness from early adolescence to middle age. In H. Mandl, N. Bennett, E. de Corte, & H. F. Friedrich (Eds.), *Learning and instruction: European research in an international context: Vol. 2, pt. 1. Social and cognitive aspects of learning and instruction.* Oxford: Pergamon.

Demetriou, A., & Efklides, A. (in press). Dynamic patterns of intra- and interindividual change in the acquisition of complex thinking abilities from 10 to 17 years of age: A longitudinal study. *Scientific Annals of the School of Philosophy* (University of Thessaloniki).

Demetriou, A., & Efklides, A. (in preparation). Structure and development of qualitative-analytic ability.

Demetriou, A., Efklides, A., Papadaki, M., Papantoniou, G., & Economou, A. (in press). The structure and development of causal-experimental thought: From early adolescence to youth. *Developmental Psychology.*

Demetriou, A., Gustafsson, J.-E., Efklides, A., & Platsidou, M. (1992). Structural systems in developing cognition, science, and education. In A. Demetriou, M. Shayer, & A. Efklides (Eds.), *Neo-Piagetian theories of cognitive development: Implications and applications for education*. London: Routledge.

Demetriou, A., Loizos, L., & Efklides, A. (in preparation). Imagery and meta-imagery. Structure and development from childhood to adolescence.

Demetriou, A., Platsidou, M., Efklides, A., Metallidou, Y., & Shayer, M. (1991). The development of quantitative-relational abilities from childhood to adolescence: Structure, scaling and individual differences. *Learning and Instruction* (European Association for Research in Learning and Instruction), **1**, 19–43.

de Ribaupierre, A., & Pascual-Leone, J. (1979). Formal operations and M power: A neo-Piagetian investigation. In D. Kuhn (Ed.), *Intellectual development beyond childhood*. San Francisco: Jossey-Bass.

Donaldson, M. (1978). *Children's minds*. London: Fontana.

Dyer, F. H. (1973). The Stroop phenomenon and its use in the study of perceptual, cognitive, and response processes. *Memory and Cognition*, **1**, 106–120.

Efklides, A., & Demetriou, A. (in press). Image of cognitive self, task-knowledge, and cognitive performance. In S. McDonald & M. L. Commons (Eds.), *Adult development: Postformal stages* (Vol. **3**). New York: Praeger.

Efklides, A., & Demetriou, A. (in preparation). The structure and development of propositional reasoning ability: Cognitive and metacognitive aspects.

Efklides, A., Demetriou, A., & Gustafsson, J.-E. (1992). Training, cognitive change, and individual differences. In A. Demetriou, M. Shayer, & A. Efklides (Eds.), *Neo-Piagetian theories of cognitive development: Implications and applications for education*. London: Routledge.

Ekstrom, R. B., French, J. W., & Harman, H. H. (1976). *Kit of factor referenced cognitive tests*. Princeton, NJ: Educational Testing Service.

Elkind, D., & Flavell, J. (Eds.). (1969). *Studies in cognitive development: Essays in honor of Jean Piaget*. New York: Oxford University Press.

Eysenck, H. J. (1986). The theory of intelligence and the psychophysiology of cognition. In R. J. Sternberg (Ed.), *Advances in the psychology of human intelligence*. Hillsdale, NJ: Erlbaum.

Feldman, D. H. (1980). *Beyond universals in cognitive development*. Norwood, NJ: Ablex.

Fischer, K. W. (1980). A theory of cognitive development: The control and construction of hierarchies of skills. *Psychological Review*, **87**, 477–531.

Fischer, K. W., & Farrar, M. J. (1988). Generalizations about generalization: How a theory of skill development explains both generality and specificity. In A. Demetriou (Ed.), *The neo-Piagetian theories of cognitive development: Toward an integration*. Amsterdam: North-Holland.

Fischer, K. W., Hand, H. H., & Russell, S. L. (1984). The development of abstractions in adolescence and adulthood. In M. Commons, F. A. Richards, & C. Armon (Eds.), *Beyond formal operations*. New York: Praeger.

Fischer, K. W., & Silvern, L. (1985). Stages and individual differences in cognitive development. *Annual Review of Psychology*, **36**, 613–648.

Flavell, J. H. (1979). Metacognition and cognitive monitoring: A new area of cognitive developmental inquiry. *American Psychologist*, **34**, 906–911.

Flavell, J. H. (1984). Discussion. In R. J. Sternberg (Ed.), *Mechanisms of cognitive development*. New York: Freeman.

Flavell, J. H. (1985). *Cognitive development*. Englewood Cliffs, NJ: Prentice-Hall.

Flavell, J. H. (1988). The development of children's knowledge about the mind: From cognitive connections to mental representations. In J. W. Astington, P. L. Harris, & D. R. Olson (Eds.), *Developing theories of mind*. Cambridge: Cambridge University Press.

Flavell, J. H., & Wohlwill, J. F. (1969). Formal and functional aspects of cognitive development. In D. Elkind & J. H. Flavell (Eds.), *Studies in cognitive development: Essays in honor of Jean Piaget.* New York: Oxford University Press.

Fodor, J. A. (1983). *The modularity of mind.* Cambridge, MA: MIT Press.

Freyd, J. J. (1987). Dynamic mental representations. *Psychological Review,* **94,** 427–438.

Froman, T., & Hubert, L. J. (1980). Application of prediction analysis to developmental priority. *Psychological Bulletin,* **87,** 136–146.

Gardner, H. (1983). *Frames of mind: The theory of multiple intelligence.* New York: Basic.

Gardner, H. (1985). *The mind's new science: A history of the cognitive revolution.* New York: Basic.

Gelman, R., & Gallistel, C. R. (1978). *The child's understanding of number.* Cambridge, MA: Harvard University Press.

Gelman, R., & Gallistel, C. R. (1992). Preverbal and verbal counting and computation. *Cognition,* **44,** 43–74.

Gelman, R., & Markman, E. M. (1987). Young children's inductions from natural kinds: The role of categories and appearances. *Child Development,* **58,** 1532–1541.

Gentner, D., & Stevens, A. L. (1983). *Mental models.* Hillsdale, NJ: Erlbaum.

Gibson, J. J. (1979). *The ecological approach to visual perception.* Boston: Houghton Mifflin.

Goossens, L. (1992). Training scientific thinking in children and adolescents: A critical commentary and quantitative integration. In A. Demetriou, M. Shayer, & A. Efklides (Eds.), *Neo-Piagetian theories of cognitive development: Implications and applications for education.* London: Routledge.

Gustafsson, J.-E. (1984). A unifying model for the structure of intellectual abilities. *Intelligence,* **8,** 179–203.

Gustafsson, J. E. (1988a). Broad and narrow abilities in research on learning and instruction. In R. J. Sternberg (Ed.), *Advances in the psychology of intelligence* (Vol. 4). Hillsdale, NJ: Erlbaum.

Gustafsson, J.-E. (1988b, April). *Broad and narrow abilities in research on learning and instruction.* Paper presented at the Minnesota Symposium on Learning and Individual Differences: Abilities, Motivation, Methodology, Minneapolis.

Gustafsson, J.-E. (in press). Hierarchical models of intelligence and educational achievement. In A. Demetriou & A. Efklides (Eds.), *Intelligence, mind and reasoning: Structure and development.* Amsterdam: Elsevier.

Gustafsson, J.–E., Lindstrom, B., & Bjorck-Akersson, E. (1981). *A general model for the organization of cognitive abilities* (Report). Goteborg: Department of Education, University of Goteborg.

Halford, G. S. (1982). *The development of thought.* Hillsdale, NJ: Erlbaum.

Halford, G. S. (1988). A structure-mapping approach to cognitive development. In A. Demetriou (Ed.), *The neo-Piagetian theories of cognitive development: Toward an integration.* Amsterdam: North-Holland.

Halford, G. (in press). *Children's understanding: The development of mental models.* Hillsdale, NJ: Erlbaum.

Halford, G. S., Maybery, M. T., & Bain, J. D. (1988). Set-size effects in primary memory: An age-related capacity limitation? *Memory and Cognition,* **16,** 480–487.

Hunt, E., & Lansman, M. (1986). Unified model of attention and problem solving. *Psychological Review,* **93,** 446–461.

Inhelder, B., & Piaget, J. (1958). *The growth of logical thinking from childhood to adolescence.* London: Routledge & Kegan Paul.

Inhelder, B., & Piaget, J. (1964). *The early growth of logic in the child: Classification and seriation.* London: Routledge & Kegan Paul.

Jensen, A. R. (1982). Reaction time and psychometric *g*. In H. J. Eysenck (Ed.), *A model for intelligence*. Berlin: Springer.

Johnson, J., Fabian, V., & Pascual-Leone, J. (1989). Quantitative hardware stages that constrain language development. *Human Development, 32,* 245–271.

Just, M. A., & Carpenter, P. A. (1992). A capacity theory of comprehension: Individual differences in working memory. *Psychological Review, 99*(1), 122–149.

Kail, R. (1986). Sources of age differences in speed of processing. *Child Development, 57,* 969–987.

Kail, R. (1988). Developmental functions for speeds of cognitive processes. *Journal of Experimental Child Psychology, 45,* 339–364.

Karmiloff-Smith, A. (1990). Constraints on representational change: Evidence from children's drawings. *Cognition, 34,* 57–83.

Karmiloff-Smith, A., & Inhelder, B. (1974). If you want to go ahead, get a theory. *Cognition, 3,* 195–212.

Kosslyn, S. M. (1978). Measuring the visual angle of the mind's eye. *Cognitive Psychology, 10,* 356–389.

Kosslyn, S. M. (1980). *Image and mind*. Cambridge, MA: Harvard University Press.

Kuhn, D. (1983). On the dual executive and its significance in developmental psychology. In D. Kuhn & J. A. Meacham (Eds.), *On the development of developmental psychology*. New York: Karger.

Kuhn, D., Amsel, E., & O'Loughlin, M. (1988). *The development of scientific thinking skills*. New York: Academic.

Kuzmak, S. D., & Gelman, R. (1986). Young children's understanding of random phenomena. *Child Development, 57,* 559–566.

Kyllonen, P. C., & Christal, R. E. (1990). Reasoning ability is (little more than) working memory capacity? *Intelligence, 14,* 389–433.

Lakatos, I. (1978). *The methodology of scientific research programmes: Philosophical papers* (Vol. 1). Cambridge: Cambridge University Press.

Landau, B., Spelke, E. S., & Gleitman, H. (1984). Spatial knowledge in a young blind child. *Cognition, 16,* 225–260.

Leslie, A. M. (1987). Pretense and representation: The origins of theory of mind. *Psychological Review, 94,* 412–426.

MacGregor, J. N. (1987). Short-term memory capacity: Limitation or optimization? *Psychological Review, 94,* 107–108.

Markman, E., & Callanan, N. A. (1984). An analysis of hierarchical classification. In R. J. Sternberg (Ed.), *Advances in the psychology of human intelligence*. Hillsdale, NJ: Erlbaum.

Miller, P. H., & Aloise, P. A. (1989). Young children's understanding of the psychological causes of behavior: A review. *Child Development, 60,* 257–285.

Moore, C., Bryant, D., & Furrow, D. (1989). Mental terms and the development of certainty. *Child Development, 60,* 167–171.

Noelting, G. (1980). The development of proportional reasoning and the ratio concept: 1. Differentiation of stages. *Educational Studies in Mathematics, 11,* 217–253.

Pascual-Leone, J. (1970). A mathematical model for the transition rule in Piaget's developmental stages. *Acta Psychologica, 32,* 301–345.

Pascual-Leone, J. (1988). Organismic processes for neo-Piagetian theories: A dialectical causal account of cognitive development. In A. Demetriou (Ed.), *The neo-Piagetian theories of cognitive development: Toward an integration*. Amsterdam: North-Holland.

Pascual-Leone, J., & Goodman, D. (1979). Intelligence and experience: A neo-Piagetian approach. *Instructional Science, 8,* 301–367.

Piaget, J. (1952). *The child's conception of number*. London: Routledge & Kegan Paul.

Piaget, J. (1971). *Biology and knowledge*. Edinburgh: Edinburgh University Press.

Piaget, J. (1973). *Structuralism*. London: Routledge & Kegan Paul.

Piaget, J. (1974). *The grasp of consciousness: Action and concept in the young child*. Cambridge, MA: Harvard University Press.

Piaget, J. (1978). *Success and understanding*. Cambridge, MA: Harvard University Press.

Piaget, J. (1979). Correspondences and transformations. In F. B. Murray (Ed.), *The impact of Piagetian theory*. Baltimore: University Park Press.

Piaget, J., & Inhelder, B. (1967). *The psychology of the child*. London: Routledge & Kegan Paul.

Piaget, J., & Inhelder, B. (1971). *Mental imagery in the child*. New York: Basic.

Piaget, J., Inhelder, B., & Sheminska, A. (1960). *The child's conception of geometry*. London: Routledge & Kegan Paul.

Pinard, A., & Laurendau, M. (1969). Stage in Piaget's cognitive-developmental theory: Exegesis of a concept. In D. Elkind & J. H. Flavell (Eds.), *Studies in cognitive development: Essays in honor of Jean Piaget*. New York: Oxford University Press.

Platsidou, M. (in preparation). Practice effects of Stroop-like tasks.

Rasch, G. (1980). *Probabilistic models for some intelligence and attainment tests*. Chicago: University of Chicago Press.

Shayer, M., Demetriou, A., & Pervez, M. (1988). The structure and scaling of concrete operational thought: Three studies in four countries. *Genetic, Social, and General Psychology Monographs*, **114**, 307–376.

Siegler, R. S. (1988). Some general conclusions about children's strategy choice procedures. In A. Demetriou (Ed.), *The neo-Piagetian theories of cognitive development: Toward an integration*. Amsterdam: North-Holland.

Simon, H. A. (1981). *The sciences of the artificial*. Cambridge, MA: MIT Press.

Soja, N. N., Carey, S., & Spelke, E. S. (1991). Ontological categories guide young children's induction of word meaning: Object terms and substance terms. *Cognition*, **38**, 179–211.

Spelke, E. (1982). Perceptual knowledge of objects in infancy. In J. Mehler, E. C. T. Walker, & M. Garrett (Eds.), *Perspectives on mental representation*. Hillsdale, NJ: Erlbaum.

Spinillo, A. G., & Bryant, P. (1991). Children's proportional judgment: The importance of "half." *Child Development*, **62**, 427–440.

Starkey, P., Spelke, E. S., & Gelman, R. (1990). Numerical abstraction in human infants. *Cognition*, **36**, 97–127.

Sternberg, R. J. (1977). *Intelligence, information processing, and analogical reasoning: The componential analysis of human abilities*. Hillsdale, NJ: Erlbaum.

Sternberg, R. J. (1985). *Beyond IQ: A triarchic theory of human intelligence*. Cambridge: Cambridge University Press.

Sternberg, R. J. (1988). Mental self-government: A theory of intellectual styles and their development. *Human Development*, **31**, 197–224.

Sternberg, R. J., Conway, B. E., Ketron, J. L., & Bernstein, M. (1981). People's conceptions of intelligence. *Journal of Personality and Social Psychology*, **41**, 37–55.

Strauss, S. (Ed.). (1982). *U-shaped behavioral growth*. New York: Academic.

Stroop, J. R. (1935). Studies of interference in serial verbal reactions. *Journal of Experimental Psychology*, **18**, 643–662.

Tanaka, J. S. (1987). "How big is big enough?" Sample size and goodness of fit in structural equation models with latent variables. *Child Development*, **58**, 134–146.

Turiel, E., & Davidson, P. (1985). Heterogeneity, inconsistency, and asynchrony in the development of cognitive structures. In I. Levin (Ed.), *Stage and structure: Reopening the debate*. Norwood, NJ: Ablex.

Vygotsky, L. S. (1978). *Thought and language*. Cambridge, MA: MIT Press.

Wellman, H. M. (1985). The child's theory of mind: The development of conceptions of cognition. In S. R. Yussen (Ed.), *The growth of reflection in children.* New York: Academic.

Wellman, H. M. (1990). *The child's theory of mind.* Cambridge, MA: MIT Press.

Wohlwill, J. (1973). *The study of behavioral development.* New York: Academic.

Wright, B. D., & Masters, G. N. (1982). *Rating scale analysis.* Chicago: Mesa.

ACKNOWLEDGMENTS

This *Monograph* was first drafted when Andreas Demetriou was a visiting research fellow in the Department of Psychology, University of Melbourne, Australia, in 1988. We are grateful to this department for providing the facilities and the academic atmosphere needed for the completion of a long monograph that is concerned with complicated and rather esoteric issues. Special mention should be made of the support provided by Doreen Rosenthal. Without this, the actual writing of this *Monograph* might not have taken place.

The ideas presented in the *Monograph* have been shaped over a period of 15 years. Many persons have been, conspicuously or inconspicuously, instrumental in this process. Lambros Houssiadas and John Taplin have directed our research toward the roads it still follows. The impact of Jan-Eric Gustafsson on the adoption and use of the statistical methods applied on our data has been enormous. The long and often lively discussions between Demetriou and Robbie Case, which started many years ago and still continue, have affected the whole network of ideas presented in this *Monograph* in many subtle ways. The assistance of three anonymous reviewers in the refinement and wiring of ideas and in the restructuring of the *Monograph* has been invaluable. Thanks are also due to Robert L. Campbell for his critical suggestions on an earlier version of the *Monograph* and to Kurt W. Fischer for his contribution to the ascription of the tasks used in Studies 1 and 2 to developmental levels. Special thanks are due to Sara Economidou for her contribution to polishing our English.

Studies 1 and 2 were supported by a grant provided by the Swedish Council of Social Research (F404/89) to J.-E. Gustafsson, A. Demetriou, and A. Efklides. Studies 3 and 4 were supported by a grant (87EΔ178) provided by the Greek Secretariat of Research and Technology to A. Demetriou. Thanks are due to Nikos Makris for running the experiments reported in Study 3. Finally, special thanks must be extended to the Institute of Education for granting permission to conduct these studies in public schools. Without this, it would have been impossible to implement these studies.

EPISTEMOLOGICAL PROBLEMS FOR NEO-PIAGETIANS

Robert L. Campbell

The neo-Piagetian movement in developmental psychology began nearly a quarter century ago, with Pascual-Leone's (1970) announcement of a new approach to Piagetian stage transitions. Neo-Piagetianism is old enough now to warrant a good look at what it has accomplished, where it needs to grow, and where its limitations may lie. To their credit, its own adherents have taken the lead in summing up and reassessing what they have accomplished. For nearly a decade, Demetriou and his coworkers have been concerned with a fundamental problem for neo-Piagetian approaches: how to define developmental domains and characterize the course of development within them (Demetriou & Efklides, 1981). The studies and theoretical discussions presented in this *Monograph* by Andreas Demetriou, Anastasia Efklides, and Maria Platsidou take a major step forward in grappling with the domain problem and most commendably raise two others that have been largely overlooked in the neo-Piagetian literature: the nature of knowledge, or of representation, and the manner in which we are to account for the development of reflection or metacognition.

Neo-Piagetianism carries forward certain basic themes in Piaget's genetic epistemology. The primary legacy from Piaget is *structuralism*, the view that knowledge consists of cognitive structures and that development is change in such structures. There is a secondary commitment to *constructivism*, the view that there is no way to get knowledge (at least, not knowledge of transformations or operatory knowledge) by importing structures from the environment. Instead, new structures must be constructed, tried in the environment, and changed if their use fails to reach the goal of the interaction.

For Piaget, structures were algebraic: groups of spatial displacements,

one-way functions, the nine groupings incorporating the reversible operations of concrete thought, the combinatorial and INRC group of formal
operations. Neo-Piagetians prefer different formalisms. Pascual-Leone
(1970, 1980, 1984) uses various sorts of schemes, Halford (1982, 1992)
concepts and cognitive systems, Fischer (1980) skills, Case (1985) schemes
again, and Commons and Richards (1984) actions. Demetriou et al. revert
to the generic term "structures." Despite differences in notation and presentation, all these structures appear to behave like subroutines that can be
coordinated and organized into a hierarchy (Campbell & Bickhard, 1986).[1]

Piaget's conception of developmental constraints and mechanisms focused on equilibration, the natural tendency of structures to get applied to
the environment, to get modified when they do not work, and to tend, as
construction continues, toward desirable properties such as reversibility and
closure (Bickhard, 1988; Piaget, 1975/1985). A secondary concern of his
was with reflective abstraction, the process responsible for becoming conscious of one's own knowledge and of the properties of one's own actions
(Piaget, 1974, 1977). In place of equilibration, which Piaget came to define
quite broadly, neo-Piagetians emphasize the differentiation and coordination of skills or schemes (Case, 1985; Fischer, 1980). It is not clear whether
they have replaced reflective abstraction with anything at all; in fact, that is
one of the major questions raised by the present *Monograph*.

By contrast, most neo-Piagetian theories (those of Pascual-Leone, Case,
and Halford as well as the current view) emphasize the growth of working
memory capacity as a motor of development. In focusing on the number
of elements that can be coordinated at a particular point in development,
they have paid less attention to the manner in which the coordination is
supposed to take place or its sufficiency to bring about various kinds of
developmental change.

Of course, the first thing that English-speaking psychologists think
about when Piaget's name is mentioned is stages. Neo-Piagetian approaches
retain his commitment to developmental stages and in this respect can be
differentiated from information-processing conceptions of development,
some of which also rely heavily on growth in working memory capacity (Kail
& Bisanz, 1982). Stages are still defined in terms of characteristic structures,
although these are no longer groups and groupings and lattices. An original
contribution of neo-Piagetian theories has been a recurring or repeating
cycle of substages. Although Halford (1982) expressly rejected this idea,
both Case (1985) and Fischer (1980) propose four substages, based on in-

[1] There is one exception: in Halford's later (1993) model, the adoption of a connectionist architecture precludes a subroutine-hierarchy interpretation of what he calls "conceptual complexity."

creasingly elaborated types of coordination of schemes or skills, that repeat within each new major stage. Demetriou et al. endorse a similar conception.

Until recently, many neo-Piagetians have treated stages as exhibiting what Flavell (1982) and the authors of this *Monograph* call "horizontal structure." In other words, not only does development in each domain proceed through the same stages, but there is also synchrony—children reach the same stages in each domain about the same time. Piaget probably never believed in synchrony (Chapman, 1988), but he was widely read that way in the 1960s and 1970s, and a great mass of empirical evidence was generated to challenge the "horizontal structure" claim (e.g., Gelman & Baillargeon, 1983). Fischer (1980) declared from the beginning that décalage is the rule, not the exception. For many neo-Piagetians, however, horizontal structure was locked in because of the major role accorded to clockwork increments in working memory capacity (often thought to occur every 2 years). The earlier versions of Case's (1985) theory stated a thorough and explicit commitment to horizontal structure. Breaking free from horizontal structure in order to characterize developmental trajectories in different domains is now a leading-edge concern, both for Case (1992) and for Demetriou et al.

There are distinct limits, however, to neo-Piagetian borrowings from Piaget. The Piaget who late in his career (Piaget, 1972) conceded the nonuniversality of formal operations and became concerned with domain specificity exerted no influence on neo-Piagetian treatments. Neither did the dialectical Piaget (1980), or the Piaget who was concerned with the detailed workings of reflective abstraction and constructive generalization (Piaget, 1977; Piaget & Henriques, 1978), or the Piaget (1981/1987a, 1983/1987b) who wished to chart the procedural origins of possibility and necessity. For neo-Piagetians, the Piaget of interest is the structuralist, pre-1970 Piaget.[2]

Neo-Piagetianism draws on other sources of inspiration. There have been major, albeit highly selective, borrowings from information-processing (IP) theories. The primary concern has been working memory. Working memory has been a central concept in IP thinking from Newell and Simon (1972) to the present because it is implicated in every process of problem solving. The relevant symbols have to be present in working memory for the conditions of the production rules to be matched and for their actions to be carried out. Neo-Piagetians have focused not so much on the detailed

[2] An instance of this limitation in the current *Monograph* is the claim that disequilibrium cannot arise from lack of coordination between larger cognitive systems: "Piagetian conflicts are limited to the intra-SSS level" (p. 134). In Piaget's (1975/1985) later model, which incorporates cybernetic concerns, one type of equilibration is integration and coordination of subsystems. The possibility of "conflicting representations" coexisting without producing cognitive change is also treated as an argument against Piaget despite extensive discussion of this very outcome in Piaget's later work.

operations of working memory or its management as on its capacity and on methods for measuring that capacity. Many, but not all, neo-Piagetian models have recourse to regular increments in M-power (Pascual-Leone, 1970), short-term storage space (STSS; Case, 1985), or primary memory (Halford, 1993) to explain transitions to higher stages. Other characteristic ideas and research methods in the IP canon, such as computer simulation models of problem solving, including occasional simulations of development (Anderson, 1983; Klahr & Wallace, 1976; Newell, 1990; Siegler & Jenkins, 1989), have generally not been incorporated into neo-Piagetian practice (the "metasubjective task analysis" of de Ribaupierre and Pascual-Leone, 1979, is an exception, and the work of Halford, 1982, 1993, has been distinguished from the beginning by its thorough engagement with first IP and now connectionist architectures for cognition). It is of more than passing interest that, in a movement known as Genevan functionalism, a number of Piagetians have made their own attempts to incorporate IP ideas into their work (Cellérier, 1979; Inhelder et al., 1976; Inhelder & Cellérier, 1992). Perhaps because it has developed in very different directions from neo-Piagetianism, Genevan functionalism has been consigned to the same limbo as other post-1970 developments in Piagetian thought (Brown, 1988).

The approach taken in this *Monograph* incorporates one more special ingredient, drawn from Demetriou's educational research—the psychometric approach to the characterization of intelligence and to the measurement of individual differences therein: "Our theory is inspired by the assumption that the developing mind can be understood only if the strong points of the developmental, the psychometric, and the cognitivist traditions are allowed to converge and inform each other" (p. 3).

Although a good portion of the *Monograph* is taken up with the presentation of empirical work—five massive studies, all told—its primary purpose is to advance a specific neo-Piagetian theory of cognitive development and to resolve questions not previously addressed within the neo-Piagetian corpus: the problem of developmental domains, the problem of reflective abstraction or metacognition, and, most basic of all, the problem of representation. My comments and criticisms will focus on these three problems; the specific studies will be mentioned only when they have some bearing on them.

Domains

Contemporary developmental psychologists would soon be at a loss for words if the term "domain" were to disappear from their vocabulary. It has become a truism that development proceeds differently in different specialized areas of knowledge. The mildest version of domain specificity

(Fischer, 1980) would have it that development proceeds by the same process and through the same steps or stages but at a different pace in different domains. A medium-strength version (Feldman, 1980; Turiel & Davidson, 1986) would claim that there are different series of steps in different domains. An even stronger conception (Keil, 1990) would claim that the developmental process is different in different domains.

But there are serious perplexities lurking behind all the domain talk. Developmentalists cannot do without domains because "horizontal structure" claims do not hold up in the face of empirical evidence (Gelman & Baillargeon, 1983). Yet we do not have clear ways of identifying different domains. Do domains in turn harbor subdomains and sub-subdomains? Where does one domain start and the next leave off? Are domain boundaries fixed, or do they change with development (Richie, 1984)?

As some of the neo-Piagetians break out of their previous commitment to "horizontal structure," they are confronting these questions afresh. Demetriou et al. propose five domains: the qualitative-analytic, the quantitative-relational, the causal-experimental, the verbal-propositional, and the spatial-imaginal. Each domain has its own system within the mind, its own specialized structural system or SSS. (The "central conceptual structures" proposed by Case, 1992, bear more than a casual resemblance to SSSs.) There is also a hypercognitive-reflecting system, which is intended to account for reflective abstraction; although said to be domain general in its operations, it incorporates domain-specific knowledge (it encompasses a "personal theory of mind" and knowledge of philosophy and psychology).[3]

Concentrating for now on the five SSSs, we need to ask how they have been identified. How do we know that the ability to solve a particular problem (say, factoring a quadratic equation in algebra) belongs to the quantitative-relational SSS instead of another SSS? We could take an *external* approach, arguing that any problem within the field of mathematics belongs to the quantitative-relational domain and must be grist for the corresponding SSS. The external approach to domain definition has a long and distinguished history; it was practiced by Piaget himself, when he took his theory of the foundations of mathematics to indicate that classes, relations, and numbers all belong to the same domain (Piaget & Szeminska, 1941). More recently, Turiel and Davidson (1986) have carried out a general purpose external analysis of domains.

---

[3] It would seem that many of the products of hypercognition ought to belong to the SSS from whence they came. For instance, if one comes to understand that the inferential validity of deductive arguments depends on their form and not on the truth of their premises or conclusions (for a metacognitive treatment of this development, see Moshman, 1990), does this understanding remain as part of the verbal-propositional SSS?

The perspective that ought to prevail in developmental psychology is an *internal* one, the perspective of the developing organism. Just because an external observer regards certain facts, problems, and phenomena as belonging to the same *field,* it by no means follows that the learner treats these facts, problems, and phenomena as belonging to the same *domain* (Bickhard, 1991a; Richie, 1984). The classic Piagetian model of numbers and classes can be taken, for instance, as a claim that reasoning about classes and reasoning about numbers belong to the same field or to the same domain. As a claim about fields, the models poses few difficulties: an observer versed in set theory and the foundations of mathematics would recognize a deep affinity between class-inclusion reasoning and reasoning about addition/subtraction. As a claim about domains, however, the model says something different—that young children will treat both kinds of problems in similar ways. Children should use similar heuristics for identifying and solving class-inclusion and addition/subtraction problems; moreover, if both are in the same domain, we would expect developmental dependencies between some addition/subtraction abilities and some classification reasoning skills: "The working definition of a domain is in terms of the pattern of learning. If, for example, restrictions on possible hypotheses are unique to a specific body of the knowledge, that knowledge is considered a domain" (Keil, 1990, p. 139).

Once domains are differentiated from fields, it becomes clear that no a priori approach will suffice to specify them. Domain questions are empirical. Developmentalists have to identify what sorts of common problem-solving heuristics are being used, and we have to test claims about developmental relations. In the case of class inclusion, Piaget's class-relation-number model implies a developmental relation: success on certain addition/subtraction tasks will be a prerequisite for success on class-inclusion tasks. A test of the prerequisite claims (Campbell, 1991) suggests that this relation does not obtain. Assuming that Piaget and others have correctly identified the implications of belonging to the same domain, we may conclude that class inclusion and addition/subtraction reasoning do not belong to the same domains.

However, such findings do not establish what else goes in the same domain as class inclusion or what else goes in the same domain as addition/subtraction reasoning. The findings are consistent with a model that puts class inclusion in a classification domain and addition/subtraction in a mathematical domain, but they are equally consistent with a host of other domain distinctions. Demetriou et al. believe that class inclusion is handled by their qualitative-analytic SSS, which "enable[s] an individual to . . . operate on categorical, matrix, and serial structures" (p. 14). If correct, this would imply that class-inclusion problems are handled by the same heuristics for variation and criteria for selection that apply to any part of "the networks of declarative and categorical knowledge that we construct about the world we live in" (p. 16). But how do we know that class inclusion belongs to the same domain as all these other systems of knowledge and skill, including seriation and analogical reasoning (Table 1)?

Similarly, addition and subtraction (like the other basic arithmetic operations) are considered by Demetriou et al. to belong to the quantitative-relational SSS. So, however, are a broad span of other mathematical abilities, including the ability to reason about proportions and about probabilities. Do basic addition/subtraction abilities belong in the same domain as reasoning about physical quantities like amount and weight, especially for younger children, whose understanding of measurement is limited?

Demetriou et al. assert that their domain (and SSS) identifications have been made empirically: "It must be stressed that these particular five systems . . . were empirically identified in a number of cross-sectional as well as longitudinal, and experimental as well as psychometric, studies that were analyzed by a number of different methods" (p. 14). Judging from the data of Studies 1 and 2, some skepticism is in order. In Study 1, participants are presented with a graduated series of four quantitative-relational problems in the numerical mode (all pertaining to correlations between watering frequency and other independent variables, on the one hand, and plant growth, on the other) and four in the imaginal mode (all having to do with the effects of doubling and halving various dimensions of a beaker on its fullness). Participants also get a graded series of causal-experimental problems—in the numerical mode, experiments have to be designed to test the relation between various independent variables and plant growth, and, in the imaginal mode, experiments must be designed to test the effects of various dimensional manipulations on fullness. Now, these tasks are parallel in "content" and in substage within Fischer's (1980) abstract tier of cognitive development, which roughly corresponds to Piaget's formal operations.[4] When a confirmatory factor-analytic model that includes separate factors for the two SSSs turns out to fit the data well, that is evidence that the quantitative and the causal tasks do belong to different domains (leaving aside some doubts about the actual meaning of the "causal-experimental" factor).

Study 2 peeks at the same two SSSs (quantitative and causal) through the lens of training. Will training on causal-experimental problems (the same ones used in Study 1, in their numerical versions) lead to progress on quantitative-relational problems as well? Will training on quantitative-

---

[4] Interestingly, Fischer rates these tasks at lower substages than Demetriou does. Yet it does not matter which exact substages the four graded tasks belong to, so long as the sequences are parallel. Considering the implausibility of recycling substages (Campbell & Bickhard, 1922b), the lessened emphasis on them is a rather refreshing feature of the *Monograph*.

relational problems (identical to those in Study 1, numerical versions) lead to progress on problems in the other domain? The plan here is like that of Inhelder, Sinclair, and Bovet (1974), who examined the effect of class-inclusion training on number conservation performance, and vice versa, but this study is much bigger and more tightly controlled. Yet, where Inhelder et al. expected transfer, basing their predictions on Piaget's foundational model of number, Demetriou et al. do not: "First, if they are autonomous, then each SSS should display a distinct pattern of change in response to training, thus indicating developmental/functional peculiarities. Second, transfer of training from one SSS to the other should be limited" (p. 59).

All well and good. But notice again that the study includes only one graded set of problems (corresponding to a single developmental sequence) in each putative domain. Taken at face value, the factor analysis shows that the quantitative and causal problems belong to different domains, but not what those domains are. Moreover, only one method of training is used for each domain—one not as effective as hoped, especially for participants at the second of the four substages. Would another method of training have been more effective within the domain? If so, could that other method have led to cross-domain transfer? It is hard to draw strong conclusions from failure in a training study, especially when no other training methods have been explored. Further complicating matters is a fair number of regressions in developmental level over the course of the study. The authors waver between dismissing the regression as noise in the data (a conclusion consistent with the results of their prediction analysis) or treating it as a meaningful consequence of the process of transition between substages (if they are serious about this, they need to provide an analysis of the developmental progress, e.g., in the form of new goals, that underlies the behavioral regression—Karmiloff-Smith, 1986, 1992).

Demetriou et al. regard data sets like those of Studies 1 and 2 as sufficient evidence for the existence of the quantitative and causal SSSs and their corresponding domains. They do not seek other kinds of converging evidence, as Gardner (1983) does when he points to the differential effects of brain injuries or the existence of prodigies and idiots savants. Yet, if our aim is to establish the breadth and scope of different developmental domains and to locate their boundaries, we have to contend with issues of sampling and coverage. It is not enough to take one sequence of tasks from one putative domain and one from another; such limited sampling may tell us that there are different domains, but not what the domains are. In consequence, the domain claims made by Demetriou et al. have not progressed beyond a priori distinctions based on familiar and plausible ways of dividing up fields of knowledge.

Looking at domains empirically leads to questions about some other things. Demetriou et al. parcel out the more "cognitive" kinds of knowledge into five big domains; despite their disagreements over detail, Turiel and Davidson (1986) and Gardner (1983) also like big domains. Yet, as Keil (1990) points out, it is not clear whether domains should be broadly characterized or should be as narrowly defined as different kinds of expertise. Studies of computer programming (Campbell, Brown, & DiBello, 1992) suggest, for instance, that skill in procedural programming (in the FORTRAN or C languages) is quite distinct from, and does not transfer very well to, object-oriented programming (in the C+ + or Smalltalk languages). Such a mosaic of tiny domains cannot be reconciled with the broadly based approach unless domains have some kind of hierarchical or network organization. A related issue is whether domains change with development. Do their boundaries move around? Do new domains come into being? Do old ones split up or disappear? Like Gardner and Turiel, Demetriou et al. regard their domains as immutable, although perhaps prone to become more separate over time.[5] In Figure 13, the five SSSs extend unaltered from birth through maturity. On a view of domains as small areas of expertise, it is much easier to imagine that becoming an expert may actually create or differentiate a new domain for the learner.

None of this is meant to imply that other research has resolved these questions about domains—they have scarcely begun to be thought about. Indeed, Demetriou et al. are to be commended for their pioneering forays into some rather difficult territory.

Reflective Abstraction and Hypercognition

Although not well researched, domains are widely spoken of in developmental psychology. Reflective abstraction is not. Although his extended discussions of it have fallen into post-1970 limbo, some of the blame no doubt rests with Piaget; for him, reflective abstraction was a composite of "reflecting" and "reflected" abstraction. Reflected abstraction involves consciousness; reflecting abstraction does not. Although many examples of reflecting abstraction seem to involve coming to know properties of one's procedures for interacting with the environment, in Piaget's (1974, 1977) general statements, reflecting abstraction is hard to distinguish from equilibration, and reflected abstraction seems to be reflecting abstraction plus consciousness. When neo-Piagetians have thought about reflective abstrac-

[5] Demetriou et al. suggest that SSSs may become more autonomous from other SSSs over the course of development. Although this trend is sometimes called "modularization" (Karmiloff-Smith, 1992), a great many claims about the nature of knowledge have been packed into Fodor's (1983) modules, and their theoretical habitat is distinctly hostile to any conception of constructive development (Bickhard, 1991b; Campbell & Bickhard, 1987).

tion at all, it has simply been a mysterious process that causes transition to the next structurally defined stage. Case (1985, p. 22) equates reflective abstraction with the interiorization of actions and never mentions consciousness at all.

The lack of interest in reflective abstraction among neo-Piagetians is puzzling. Metacognition (knowledge about one's own cognitive processes and the properties thereof) has been a fixture in cognitive and developmental psychology since around 1970 (Flavell, 1971; Kreutzer, Leonard, & Flavell, 1975). In recent years, research and public disputation over "the child's theory of mind" have swollen to flood stage (Astington, Harris, & Olson, 1988; Gopnik, 1993; Perner, 1991; Wellman, 1990). Yet there is no treatment of conscious reflection, of knowledge about knowledge, anywhere in the works of Pascual-Leone, Case, Fischer, or Commons. In his earlier work, Halford (1982, pp. 336–337) considered metamemory simply a matter of mapping—it can be attained whenever one can build sufficiently complex structures. In his more recent work, he has gone on to develop computational models of the development of metacognitive strategies, the details of which deserve a good deal more attention than could be given them here (Halford et al., 1992). Still, metacognition seems to be primarily differentiated from cognition plain and simple by its degree of structural complexity—there is nothing special to knowledge *about* knowledge.

Against this background of neglect and reductionism, the attention that the *Monograph* gives to the hypercognitive-reflecting subsystem is most welcome. The hypercognitive system, like the processing system, is domain general, and so is the knowledge that gets constructed by it. The hypercognitive system is saddled with a great many responsibilities. It is responsible for the development and maintenance of a "personal theory of mind." At the same time, it is responsible for online self-understanding and self-management. What these online processes do is identify problems: they recognize similarity between the new problem and old, previously solved problems and between solutions to old problems and possible solutions to the new problem. The hypercognitive system applies acquaintance estimators, task-SSS affiliation estimators, and additional affiliation estimators—the problem is identified in terms of its degree of familiarity and the appropriate SSS to be brought to bear on it. Using processing load estimators and success estimators, the hypercognitive system also takes note of how difficult the problem might be and of the amount of effort required. Because such functions have to be carried out every time a problem is solved, one would expect the hypercognitive system to be omnipresent. Supposedly, it serves as "the individual-environment or the SSS-SSS interface" (p. 20).

How problems are identified and how a similarity gradient or topology of problem solutions is established and updated are very deep questions in psychology. Such questions have received very little attention (Bickhard &

Campbell, 1993). In the IP framework, possible solution paths revelant to the new problem take the form of an explicitly represented "problem space" that incorporates a featural analysis of possible solution states and of pathways toward solutions (Newell, 1990; Newell & Simon, 1972). It is not specified how the developing system might come to construct problem spaces; in IP simulations, such spaces are simply provided in advance by the programmer (Bickhard & Terveen, 1993; Winograd & Flores, 1986).

The older versions of Piaget's theory ignored problem identification. Some Piagetian writings (e.g., Inhelder & Piaget, 1955) create the impression that, once a cognitive structure is in place, it must be applied, without delay, to any and all relevant problems.[6] Demetriou et al. have this very difficulty in mind when they criticize V-models (those that focus on stage and sequence or the vertical dimension of development) because "the dominating strategies and the ensuing solutions to problems are always derivatives of the sole and omnipotent cognitive structure" (p. 12). Some latter-day structuralists (e.g., Overton & Newman, 1982) have tried to get around the "omnipotent structure" problem by insulating their structures with thick layers of "performance factors" and "information-processing issues." Performance insulation has a purely defensive function, absorbing the shock of questions like, If that learner already has formal operations, why can't she solve these problems? By taking problem identification seriously, Demetriou et al. are undertaking to fill a major gap in Piagetian theory.

Although Demetriou et al. are thus to be congratulated for their concerns, their equation of hypercognition with interactive learning suggests that there may be better places in their model for the processes that identify problems and relevant possible solutions. Attributing these functions to the hypercognitive-reflecting system embroils them in all manner of difficulties. Must problem identification be conscious? Does it always require reflective knowledge of one's own memory, comprehension, prior problem solutions, or whatever? If we base our account of problem identification strictly on our introspections as adults, we might be led to treat the process as metacognitive and conscious—and, clearly, we do sometimes identify problems consciously. It is distinctly odd, however, for a developmentalist to be claiming that problem identification must be conscious because metacognitive abilities are themselves subject to development. In many current theories (e.g., Bickhard, 1978, 1992; Perner, 1991), nothing of a metacognitive nature takes

---

[6] On the matter of problem identification, Genevan functionalism has made tremendous progress over classic structuralism. Inhelder and de Caprona (1992, p. 44) have gone so far as to raise the problem of "familiar schemes." Does the learner simply apply to the problem a scheme taken off the rack, or does a contextually appropriate, individualized scheme have to be tailored through a process of microgenesis? This work, however, is most recent and has received hardly any attention from English-speaking psychologists.

place in children's thinking until age 4. Does that mean that no problem identification takes place before that time? Is no problem solving going on at younger ages?

Demetriou et al. may to some extent have been misled by the focus of their empirical research on metacognition. Study 3 in this *Monograph* focuses on adolescence and young adulthood or, in structuralist Piagetian terms, on formal and postformal thinking. At higher developmental stages, people are often capable of identifying problems consciously—but, even at those levels, consciousness is not required. Indeed, IP theory makes no reference to consciousness when it describes problem solving as search within a problem space or even when "universal subgoaling" switches from one problem space to another during the course of learning (Newell, 1990).

Developmentalists can slice through this Gordian knot by sharply distinguishing between learning and reflective abstraction. Interactivism (Bickhard, 1980b, 1988; Bickhard & Campbell, 1993; Campbell & Bickhard, 1986, 1992b) does exactly that. Under the interactivist conception, learning changes the control structure or the internal functional organization of a system capable of interacting with the environment. In its least-evolved form, learning is a blind variation and selection process; that is, there is no heuristic guidance for what to try next. But, even at this basic level, there is a constructive topology, a space of nearness and farness relations between possible learning trials. What is closer in the topology to what has already been tried is more likely to be tried next.

In more evolved forms of learning, the new variations that are produced come under various sorts of heuristic guidance, and selection criteria develop for avoiding various classes of errors. Changes in the learning process induce changes in the topology of problem types and of possible solutions. What Demetriou et al. explain with acquaintance estimators and task-SSS affiliation estimators are, in interactivist terms, functions of the variation-and-selection learning process and, specifically, of the topology of problem types and solutions. They speak of the "subjective distinctness" and the "subjective equivalence" of mental states, although, again, this way of talking inappropriately suggests the involvement of consciousness. (The very breadth of the SSSs, however, might raise some concerns about undue emphasis on task-SSS matchups, when the space of relevant possible solutions will normally be much more narrowly defined. If I am balancing my checkbook, integration by parts is not a solution procedure that I am likely to come up with. Nor are computer algorithms for drawing ellipses or procedures for inverting matrices, even though all these presumably belong to the quantitative-relational SSS. The *Monograph* makes provision for local "inquiry rules" within the SSSs, but no examples are given.)

How about reflective abstraction? From the interactivist standpoint, reflective abstraction is the process responsible for ascension to the next level of knowing. Interactions between system and environment yield knowledge of the environment, but interactive knowing is irreflexive. In other words, the interactive knowing system may well have properties that would be useful to know, but the knowing system cannot know itself. A differentiated subsystem, however, that can interact with the base-level knowing system in much the same manner as the base-level knowing system interacts with the external environment can know things about the base-level knowing system. If we call the base-level system level 1, knowledge about level 1, made possible by the differentiated subsystem, resides at level 2. Once the two-level system is in place, a strict hierarchy of potential knowing levels is generated. Reflection on knowledge at level 2 is possible at level 3, reflection on knowledge at level 3 is possible at level 4, and so on, unboundedly. The knowing-level hierarchy has two important uses in developmental psychology. First, reflective consciousness is basically knowing level 2 interacting with knowing level 1; if what is known is at a higher level, it could be level 3 interacting with level 2, and so on. Second, in interactivism, the major stages of development correspond to the knowing levels, so reflective abstraction does lead to ascent to a higher stage—because of ascent to a higher knowing level, not the creation of different cognitive structures (Campbell & Bickhard, 1986; Moshman, 1990).

Once reflective abstraction is separated from learning (for Campbell & Bickhard, 1992b, entirely different kinds of developmental constraints are operative in the two cases), it becomes clear that one is more basic in an evolutionary sense than the other. Bickhard (1980b) has argued that learning must have preceded higher-level knowing and reflective abstraction over the course of evolution and that, as a general logical point, unreflective knowing must come before reflective knowing. Moreover, if we have correctly interpreted the shifts around age 4 in children's understanding of false beliefs, in the appearance-reality distinction, and in quite a few other areas as the first instances of level 2 knowing (Bickhard, 1978, 1992; Campbell, 1992), then learning also precedes reflective abstraction during the course of human development.

If these considerations about learning and reflective abstraction are valid, they imply that the hypercognitive-reflecting subsystem ought to be broken up: the truly reflective aspects, like the "personal theory of mind," should be considered entirely distinct from the acquaintance estimators and other problem-identification functions. It is instructive to consider why Demetriou et al. prefer "hypercognition" to "metacognition." They specifically object to "metacognition" on the grounds that "meta-" means "after." As they point out, heuristic problem identification precedes learning how to solve the problem—it could not require prior success in solving the very problem that is being identified. Yes, but only because learning is not reflective abstraction; problem solving does not and cannot in general require consciousness. Some psychologists have contended on the basis of adult phenomenology that knowing is intrinsically reflective (Acredolo, 1992; Blasi & Hoeffel, 1974), a position that would require the hypercognitive system to be present throughout the course of development. The trouble with such claims is at root a logical one. How could knowing about knowing emerge, except out of plain vanilla unreflective knowing (Bickhard, 1992; Campbell & Bickhard, 1986)?

By the same token, genuinely reflective knowledge must be "meta": it must come after what it is about, and it must belong to a higher level of knowing. So knowledge about false beliefs must follow, and belong to a higher level than, the ability to form false beliefs (which is part and parcel of knowing the environment). Knowledge about the self must follow the formation of the self. Demetriou et al. complain that, in Piaget, "the 'grasp of consciousness' . . . is never there when needed because each stage can become the object of consciousness only at subsequent stages. Thus, from the point of view of the utility of consciousness, in Piagetian theory the developing person is condemned to chasing his tail forever" (p. 12). True, if we needed consciousness to identify problems and recognize the relevance of previous solution attempts, then constraints on knowing about knowing would condemn us to Sisyphean labors. But sorting out consciousness from problem identification and learning topologies neutralizes any threat that the irreflexivity of knowing might pose to development. Indeed, interactivism makes the generally Piagetian point that there is egocentrism at every stage of development because there are properties of functioning at that level, for instance, assumptions implicit in one's thinking, that can be known only by ascending to an even higher level. One of Piaget's collaborators, commenting on his later view that knowledge of necessity results from reflective abstraction on procedurally generated possibilities, drew the positive conclusion that "every new construction that makes an implicit necessity explicit at the same time unavoidably generates new implicit necessities. New implicit necessities are always generated faster than they can be made explicit" (Henriques, 1977, p. 263).

Besides, interactive knowing is fallible and error prone, and knowing about knowing has been granted no exemption from these tendencies. Ascent to a higher stage does not guarantee truth; while making new kinds of correct understanding possible, it opens the gates to new kinds of errors (Campbell & Bickhard, 1986). When children begin to make judgments about their own ability to remember, for example, their estimates of how much they will be able to recall are seriously overoptimistic (Kreutzer et al., 1975). There is no way, then, to credit the claim that "an individual's representation of her cognitive structures and functions would be a more or less veridical reflection of structures and functions that can be identified empirically. In other words, *the subjective structure of cognition must correspond to its objective structure"* (p. 24; my emphasis). Taken literally, this means that people can discern the detailed workings of their minds through unaided introspection. Cognitive psychologists could all retire! Considering the on-going controversies about our knowledge of our own minds—some philosophers (e.g., Churchland, 1984) delight in contending that "folk psychology" is a snare and a delusion—the claim is obviously untenable. Nor does our usual rate of success at finding relevant solutions to problems (which is hardly perfect) require veridical knowledge of our own cognitive architecture.

For the first time in neo-Piagetian history, Demetriou et al. have faced the challenges of reflective abstraction. They have also taken on problem identification and of learning topologies. Unfortunately, their hypercognitive-reflecting subsystem tries to do both at once. In consequence, their framework still lacks a "meaning-making executive" (Kuhn, 1983). The problem that Kuhn discerned in IP models was that an executive (defined as the top node in a hierarchy of control) does not interact with and consequently cannot know anything at the lower levels of a knowing-level hierarchy (Campbell & Bickhard, 1986). There is still no hierarchy of knowing levels in the hypercognitive conception; the very substitution of hypercognition for metacognition constitutes a rejection of knowing levels.

In this respect, Demetriou et al. are hardly alone. Karmiloff-Smith's (1986, 1992) three-phase process of representational redescription, one of the most sophisticated treatments of developmental processes currently available, lumps together changes in goals and learning heuristics (matters entirely internal to the learning process) with the emergence of metaknowledge and "conscious access." Changes in the goals and heuristics for learning, however, are of a very different kind than ascension of the levels of knowing (Campbell & Bickhard, 1992b).

Representation

The most basic problem that the *Monograph* touches on is the problem of knowledge or of representation. What does knowledge consist of, how does it emerge, and how is it related to reality?

Piaget's conceptions of cognitive structures and of equilibration were meant first and foremost as answers to epistemological questions. Piaget insisted that knowledge could not be a mere "copy" of reality and that it was knowledge of possible changes instead of actual states; he also believed, however, that cognitive structures were isomorphic to structures in the environment (Bickhard, 1988; Kitchener, 1986). Information-processing theory has devoted a lot less attention to epistemological questions, but virtually everyone who works with IP models would accept the physical symbol system hypothesis (Newell, 1980, 1990). According to the physical symbol system hypothesis, systems that are capable of knowing, learning, and developing perform computations on symbols that denote things in the environment, and denoting is taken to involve causal correspondences of some sort. Moreover, what is known is actual situations, not possible transformations.

The physical symbol system hypothesis considers knowledge to be *encoded:* entities, or structures of entities, in the mind correspond to entities or structures of entities in the world and, by virtue of those correspondences, represent them. Despite his manifold differences with IP, Piaget also endorses a correspondence-based conception; his operatory structures end up as encodings.

The neo-Piagetian refrain seems to be, It was good enough for Piaget, so it's good enough for me. The truth of structuralism has been taken for granted. Up to now, only Halford has dealt with the nature of representation. His conception is based, straightforwardly and strictly, on structural correspondences: representation consists of correspondences between mental events or symbols and environmental events and of correspondences between transformations of mental symbols and transformations of environmental events. Although Halford's conception is distinctive in its reliance on category theory and commutative diagrams, the basic point could not have been put more pellucidly by Fodor (1975) or Wittgenstein (1922/1961). Moreover, in his earlier work, Halford (1982) claimed that symbols and environmental elements could be simultaneously present in short-term store (or working memory) for purposes of comparison; his more recent work (e.g., Halford, 1993) drops this assertion.

The difficulty posed by defining representation in terms of structural correspondence is that no such conception is tenable. To take structural correspondences as constituting representation is (in contemporary terms) to regard knowledge as encoded—but it is impossible for all a system's knowledge to be encoded. In clear cases of encoding relationships, one thing in the environment stands in for another thing. In Morse code, "- - -" stands in for "o." In digital sound recording, strings of 1s and 0s, laid down 44,000 times per second, stand in for a complex acoustic waveform. In order to make use of such stand-in relations, we must already know what is to be encoded. But, precisely for that reason, there must be some kind of nonencoded mental representation. There can be encoding relations within the mind as well. An encoded mental representation Z stands in for another mental representation, say Y. But how does Y represent? It could stand in for another mental representation, X. But at some point the regress must terminate. Suppose that it terminates at X. X, a foundational encoding, does not stand in for any other mental representation—it supposedly represents by correspondence with something in the environment.[7] But, if X does not stand in for another representation, it cannot be an encoding at all. For X to be an encoding, we have to know what X corresponds to when X is supposed to be our only means of knowing that thing. "X represents whatever it is that X represents" is not a coherent definition of an encoding (Bickhard & Campbell, 1989; Campbell & Bickhard, 1986).

Once the incoherence of foundational encodings is recognized, other bases for representation must be sought. Bickhard (1980a, 1980b) has proposed that mental representation is at root *interactive*. Given a goal-directed system that is able to interact with an environment, the internal final states of the system differentiate and implicitly define the type of environment interacted with. For instance, in some environments, after completing the interaction, the system might end up in state A; in other environments, it might end up in state C; and so on. From an interactive standpoint, the system can represent type A and type C environments. Further knowledge of those kinds of environments takes the form of expectations about what can be done in them—for instance, in a type A environment, try strategy S198 and avoid strategy S22. Or, in the formulation to which Demetriou et al. refer: "The final states of an interactive system, thus, contain information—differentiating information or implicit definitional information—about the environment. This information may well be useful for the interactions of other subsystems of the overall system: the internal outcome of one subsystem may serve to differentiate the interactive strategy of another subsystem. Environments of type 'outcome A' may require one subsystem or strategy to achieve a given goal, while environments of type 'outcome B' may require some other subsystem" (Campbell & Bickhard, 1986, p. 37).

Uniquely among neo-Piagetians, Demetriou et al. express an awareness of the problems of encodingism. They claim to have avoided encodingism in their characterization of SSSs. Indeed, they claim to have adopted the conception of representation just quoted: "It is hoped that the reader recognizes in Campbell and Bickhard's systems and subsystems our SSSs and SSS components" (p. 128). Although their move is commendably bold, it cannot go through without further major alterations to their framework. The immediate impediment is one of grain size. If domains are identified in terms of the pattern of learning, the five SSSs are too large to constitute domains. An entire SSS would, in interactivist terms, have to be a vast, complex distributed network of interactive representation; on most occasions, the other systems and strategies to which Bickhard and I referred would reside

---

[7] In Halford's older (1982) model, "environmental elements" are foundational encodings. They are simultaneously in the environment, to be represented by symbols in the mind, and in the mind, constituting symbols that can be compared with other symbols in short-term store.

within the same domain and a fortiori within the same SSS. In a personal communication (April 21, 1993), Demetriou further explicates an SSS as a "multilayered entity" that comprises "core operations" and "conceptual layers"; much more will have to be said about its internal architecture, however, to make good on the endorsement of interactive representation.[8]

Encoding conceptions of knowledge have, in any case, been ingrained in our thinking for over 2,000 years and are hard to get rid of even when the most dogged effort is exerted. Consistently with interactivism, Demetriou et al. seem to believe that all encoded representations are derivative (defined in terms of interactive representations). Symbol systems "lean on the bridges—such as the SSS-specific intuitors—that link the organism with the environment" (p. 129). An intuitor, in turn, is an internal (interactive?) representation of a salient relation. All well and good, but excessive reliance on derivative encodings would be unwise (e.g., speaking and understanding language cannot be adequately explicated as the transmission and reception of derivative encodings—Bickhard, 1980a; Campbell & Bickhard, 1992a).

More seriously, the *Monograph* contains far too many unexplicated references to encoding and to symbols: "Structures . . . constrain the ways in which persons encode, represent, process, and solve problems" (p. 9); "reality . . . consists of elements—be they objects, persons, or events" (p. 9). Granted, it is not the "reality elements" as such that get encoded; rather, it is their properties and relations (many psychologists would say "features"). "The objects of symbolism are the properties of elements and the relations among these properties rather than the elements themselves. Therefore, the same reality element may be encoded in several symbol systems, depending on which of its properties are being considered" (p. 11).

The claim that the subjective structure of cognition must correspond to its objective structure, which drew some attention earlier, also asserts an encoding relation: a structure in the mind corresponds with a structure in the environment (which in this case is not the external environment but the mind at a lower level of knowing; cf. Goldman, 1993). If higher levels merely encode what is known at lower levels, there is no reason to maintain a hierarchy of knowing levels at all. The stand-in relations between representations are transitive, which means that intermediate knowing levels can be eliminated and that the hierarchy of levels undergoes "transitive collapse" (Bickhard & Campbell, 1989).

Encoding is strongly presupposed as well in the conception of capacity

---

[8] Interactivist conceptions of mental architecture were initially based on the theory of finite automata and of Turing machines (Bickhard, 1980b), with subsequent development of the conception of interactive indicators (Bickhard, 1980a), of representational topologies, and of timing as provided by oscillatory processes (Bickhard & Terveen, 1993).

growth that seems indispensable for many neo-Piagetian theories. I am not proposing to enter the continuing debates over the proper measurement of working memory capacity or the course of its supposed expansion during childhood and adolescence, so I will refrain from commenting here on the data of Studies 4 and 5. In any case, constraints based on limited capacity are a legitimate sort of developmental constraint and cannot be ruled out a priori (Campbell & Bickhard, 1992b).

But there is a lingering concern. The usual ways of thinking about working memory capacity encourage encoding-based ways of thinking about representation. Working memory capacity is measured in countable units of some kind: pieces, chunks, atoms. Such units suit encodingism, which conceives of representations as atomic mental objects, but are unacceptable to interactivism. Researchers who study capacity (e.g., Engle, Cantor, & Carullo, 1992; Halford, 1982) hasten to remind us that working memory is not really a fixed set of "slots" that hold "chunks" but is rather a matter of active control processes. Yet, when it comes down to it, the contents of working memory invariably turn out to be countable atoms: symbols to be matched (Newell, 1990) or schemes that have been retrieved by matching (Case, 1985; Halford, 1982; Pascual-Leone, 1970).

Many statements in the *Monograph* suggest that atomic encodings are still being counted: "The processing system is . . . a dynamic field where information is represented (i.e., encoded and kept active)" (p. 25). "The faster a person is as a processor, the more *information units* she will be able to process in a given standard time unit. . . . In turn, the more efficient she is with regard to speed and control of processing, the better she will be at using her storage potential. This is so because the appropriate information units will occupy this potential for the minimum time required to *grasp the concept defined by these units* and to assemble the needed response" (p. 121; my emphasis). The belief in concepts as assemblages of semantic primitives (basic "information units") is an ancient version of encodingism. The challenge before developmentalists who wish to accord a major role in problem solving to working memory, and a major role in development to changes in that capacity, is to rethink capacity in a way that does not require atomic encodings to reside in working memory. Not just the working memory system but its contents will have to be reformulated in process terms.[9]

In sum, up to now, neo-Piagetians have not shown much concern about the nature of knowledge. The only examination of these issues up to now (Halford, 1982, 1993) has continued to affirm knowledge as structural cor-

---

[9] From an interactive standpoint, a process account would involve apperceptive updating of the situation representation (Bickhard, 1980a) and maintenance of a complex pattern of modulated oscillations (Bickhard & Campbell, 1993), but the details of these proposals will have to be presented elsewhere.

respondence. Just as they have broken with horizontal structure and ended the silence about reflective abstraction, Demetriou et al. have made a valiant effort to embrace interactive representation. One of the difficulties of interactivism, however, is that its implications are not easily contained—they ramify everywhere. At present, Demetriou et al.'s framework still harbors many encoding conceptions handed down from IP and from structuralism. To do full justice to their new conception of knowledge, they will have to undertake massive revisions throughout.

The Present Status of Neo-Piagetianism

Neo-Piagetianism has more than a toehold among English-speaking psychologists. And neo-Piagetian theories are supposed to have extracted all the genuine goodness in Piaget and combined that with the best that IP has to offer (Case, 1985). Yet, in recent years, there have been indications that they are not getting the reception that their proponents believe they deserve. Other developmentalists, the complaint goes, pay too much attention to Piaget and too little to neo-Piagetian conceptions: "Theoretical development could be greatly stimulated if less effort were devoted to testing Piaget's theory and more were devoted to testing contemporary theories" (Halford, 1989, p. 351).

I think broader acceptance of neo-Piagetian theories has been limited because anti-Piagetians find them to be too respectful of Piaget whereas Piagetians think that they are not Piagetian enough. The persistent structuralism of neo-Piagetian theories, and their retention of stages, will not endear them to those who believe that Piaget was completely wrong and that his ideas should be expurgated from developmental psychology. On the other hand, those who still consider Piaget's ideas to be relevant and fruitful fault the neo-Piagetians for restricting rather than expanding the Piagetian legacy. Piaget considered himself an epistemologist, not a psychologist, and, for many of his admirers, his greatest virtue was his willingness to confront epistemological questions, yet neo-Piagetian thought has offered nothing new in response to these questions. In addition, there have been persistent concerns not just that some neo-Piagetians are a good deal more empiricist in their research strategies than Piaget was but that they pursue research programs that are unusually confirmatory even according to contemporary norms in psychology (Bickhard, in press).

Psychologists tend to exaggerate the role of data, as opposed to conceptual considerations, in drawing their conclusions, and some predictable overstatements can be found in this *Monograph*. Yet Demetriou et al. have not retreated into empiricism. The great contribution of the present *Monograph* is its willingness to pick up the epistemological questions that other neo-Piagetian researchers have left behind. The nature of knowledge was a crucial question for Piaget; reflective abstraction was a central developmental process; domains were a major issue by implication but were never properly addressed (Feldman, 1980). Demetriou et al., followed more recently by Case (1992), have broken the hold of horizontal structure and begun to take the domain question seriously. They have opened up inquiry into problem identification and reflective abstraction. They have even started to reexamine questions about the nature of knowledge.

If the neo-Piagetians are to reach the position of leadership to which they aspire, they will have to continue what this *Monograph* has started. The questions raised here are not questions just for Demetriou, Efklides, and Platsidou or just for neo-Piagetians; they are questions for all of us in developmental psychology.

References

Acredolo, C. (1992). Commentary [on the age 4 transition]. *Human Development, 35,* 178–181.

Anderson, J. R. (1983). *The architecture of cognition.* Cambridge, MA: Harvard University Press.

Astington, J. W., Harris, P. L., & Olson, D. R. (Eds.). (1988). *Developing theories of mind.* Cambridge: Cambridge University Press.

Bickhard, M. H. (1978). The nature of developmental stages. *Human Development, 21,* 217–233.

Bickhard, M. H. (1980a). *Cognition, convention, and communication.* New York: Praeger.

Bickhard, M. H. (1980b). A model of developmental and psychological processes. *Genetic Psychology Monographs, 102,* 61–116.

Bickhard, M. H. (1988). Piaget on variation and selection models: Structuralism, logical necessity, and interactivism. *Human Development, 31,* 274–312.

Bickhard, M. H. (1991a). *Domains and fields in development.* Unpublished manuscript, Department of Philosophy and Psychology, Lehigh University.

Bickhard, M. H. (1991b). The import of Fodor's anticonstructivist argument. In L. P. Steffe (Ed.), *Epistemological foundations of mathematical experience.* New York: Springer.

Bickhard, M. H. (1992). Commentary [on the age 4 transition]. *Human Development, 35,* 182–192.

Bickhard, M. H. (in press). Staircase? How can we tell? *American Journal of Psychology.*

Bickhard, M. H., & Campbell, R. L. (1989). Interactivism and genetic epistemology. *Archives de Psychologie, 57,* 99–121.

Bickhard, M. H., & Campbell, R. L. (1993). *Topologies of learning and development.* Unpublished manuscript, Departments of Philosophy and Psychology, Lehigh University.

Bickhard, M. H., & Terveen, L. (1993). *The impasse of artificial intelligence and cognitive science—and its solution.* Unpublished manuscript, Departments of Philosophy and Psychology, Lehigh University.

Blasi, A., & Hoeffel, E. C. (1974). Adolescence and formal operations. *Human Development, 17,* 344–363.

Brown, T. (1988). Ships in the night: Piaget and American cognitive science. *Human Development, 31,* 60–64.

Campbell, R. L. (1991). Does class inclusion have mathematical prerequisites? *Cognitive Development, 6,* 169–194.

Campbell, R. L. (1992). A shift in the development of natural-kind categories. *Human Development*, **35**, 156–164.

Campbell, R. L., & Bickhard, M. H. (1986). *Knowing levels and developmental stages.* Basel: Karger.

Campbell, R. L., & Bickhard, M. H. (1987). A deconstruction of Fodor's anticonstructivism. *Human Development*, **30**, 48–59.

Campbell, R. L., & Bickhard, M. H. (1992a). Clearing the ground: Foundational questions once again. *Journal of Pragmatics*, **17**, 557–602.

Campbell, R. L., & Bickhard, M. H. (1992b). Types of constraints on development: An interactivist approach. *Developmental Review*, **12**, 311–338.

Campbell, R. L., Brown, N. R., & DiBello, L. A. (1992). The programmer's burden: Developing expertise in computer programming. In R. R. Hoffman (Ed.), *The psychology of expertise: Cognitive research and empirical AI.* New York: Springer.

Case, R. (1985). *Intellectual development: Birth to adulthood.* Orlando, FL: Academic.

Case, R. (Ed.). (1992). *The mind's staircase.* Hillsdale, NJ: Erlbaum.

Cellérier, G. (1979). Structures cognitives et schèmes d'action [Cognitive structures and action schemes]. *Archives de Psychologie*, **47**, 87–122.

Chapman, M. (1988). *Constructive development: Origins and development of Piaget's thought.* Cambridge: Cambridge University Press.

Churchland, P. M. (1984). *Matter and consciousness: A contemporary introduction to the philosophy of mind.* Cambridge, MA: MIT Press.

Commons, M. L., & Richards, F. A. (1984). A general model of stage theory. In M. L. Commons, F. A. Richards, & C. Armon (Eds.), *Beyond formal operations: Late adolescent and adult cognitive development.* New York: Praeger.

Demetriou, A., & Efklides, A. (1981). The structure of formal operations: The ideal of the whole and the reality of its parts. In J. A. Meacham & N. Santilli (Eds.), *Social development in youth: Structure and content.* Basel: Karger.

de Ribaupierre, A., & Pascual-Leone, J. (1979). Formal operations and *M* power. A neo-Piagetian investigation. In D. Kuhn (Ed.), *Intellectual development beyond childhood.* San Francisco: Jossey-Bass.

Engle, R. W., Cantor, J., & Carullo, J. J. (1992). Individual differences in working memory and comprehension: A test of four hypotheses. *Journal of Experimental Psychology: Learning, Memory, and Cognition*, **18**, 972–992.

Feldman, D. H. (Ed.). (1980). *Beyond universals in cognitive development.* Norwood, NJ: Ablex.

Fischer, K. W. (1980). A theory of cognitive development: The control and construction of hierarchies of skills. *Psychological Review*, **87**, 477–531.

Flavell, J. H. (1971). First discussant's comments: What is memory development the development of? *Human Development*, **14**, 272–278.

Flavell, J. H. (1982). Structures, stages, and sequences in cognitive development. In W. A. Collins (Ed.), *The concept of development.* Hillsdale, NJ: Erlbaum.

Fodor, J. A. (1975). *The language of thought.* New York: Crowell.

Fodor, J. A. (1983). *The modularity of mind: An essay on faculty psychology.* Cambridge, MA: MIT Press.

Gardner, H. (1983). *Frames of mind: The theory of multiple intelligences.* New York: Basic.

Gelman, R., & Baillargeon, R. (1983). A review of some Piagetian concepts. In J. H. Flavell & E. M. Markman (Eds.), P. H. Mussen (Series Ed.), *Handbook of child psychology: Vol. 3. Cognitive development.* New York: Wiley.

Goldman, A. I. (1993). The psychology of folk psychology. *Behavioral and Brain Sciences*, **16**, 15–28.

Gopnik, A. (1993). How we know our minds: The illusion of first-person knowledge of intentionality. *Behavioral and Brain Sciences*, **16**, 1–14.

Halford, G. S. (1982). *The development of thought.* Hillsdale, NJ: Erlbaum.

Halford, G. S. (1989). Reflections on 25 years of Piagetian cognitive developmental psychology, 1963–1988. *Human Development,* **32,** 325–357.

Halford, G. S. (1992). Analogical reasoning and conceptual complexity in cognitive development. *Human Development,* **35,** 193–217.

Halford, G. S. (1993). *Children's understanding: The development of mental models.* Hillsdale, NJ: Erlbaum.

Halford, G. S., Maybery, M. T., Smith, S. B., Bain, J. D., Dickson, J. C., Kelly, M. E., & Stewart, J. E. M. (1992). Acquisition of reasoning: A computational model of strategy development in transitive inference (Tech. Rep. No. CHIPPS-TR-92-1). Brisbane: Centre for Human Information Processing and Problem Solving, Department of Psychology, University of Queensland.

Henriques, G. (1977). La nécessité dans le développement cognitif: Préalable ou achèvement? [Necessity in cognitive development: Prerequisite or consequence?]. *Archives de Psychologie,* **45,** 253–265.

Inhelder, B., Ackermann-Valladão, E., Blanchet, A., Karmiloff-Smith, A., Kilcher-Hagedorn, H., Montangero, J., & Robert, M. (1976). Des structures cognitives aux procédures de découverte [From cognitive structures to discovery procedures]. *Archives de Psychologie,* **44,** 57–72.

Inhelder, B., & Cellérier, G. (Eds.). (1992). *Le cheminement des découvertes de l'enfant* [Children's pathways toward discovery]. Neuchâtel: Delachaux & Niestlé.

Inhelder, B., & de Caprona, D. (1992). Vers le constructivisme psychologique: Structures? procédures? les deux indissociables [Toward psychological constructivism: Structures? procedures? both inseparable]. In B. Inhelder & G. Cellérier (Eds.), *Le cheminement des découvertes de l'enfant: Recherches sur les microgenèses cognitives.* Neuchâtel: Delachaux & Niestlé.

Inhelder, B., & Piaget, J. (1955). *De la logique de l'enfant à la logique de l'adolescent: Essai sur la construction des structures opératoires formelles* [From the child's logic to the adolescent's: The construction of formal operational structures]. Paris: Presses Universitaires de France.

Inhelder, B., Sinclair, H., & Bovet, M. (1974). *Learning and the development of cognition.* Cambridge, MA: Harvard University Press.

Kail, R., & Bisanz, J. (1982). Information processing and cognitive development. In H. W. Reese (Ed.), *Advances in child development and behavior* (Vol. **17**). New York: Academic.

Karmiloff-Smith, A. (1986). From meta-processes to conscious access: Evidence from children's metalinguistic and repair data. *Cognition,* **23,** 95–147.

Karmiloff-Smith, A. (1992). *Beyond modularity: A developmental perspective on cognitive science.* Cambridge, MA: MIT Press.

Keil, F. C. (1990). Constraints on constraints: Surveying the epigenetic landscape. *Cognitive Science,* **14,** 135–168.

Kitchener, R. F. (1986). *Piaget's theory of knowledge: Genetic epistemology and scientific reason.* New Haven, CT: Yale University Press.

Klahr, D., & Wallace, J. G. (1976). *Cognitive development: An information processing view.* Hillsdale, NJ: Erlbaum.

Kreutzer, M. A., Leonard, C., & Flavell, J. H. (1975). An interview study of children's knowledge about memory. *Monographs of the Society for Research in Child Development,* **40**(1, Serial No. 159).

Kuhn, D. (1983). On the dual executive and its significance in the development of developmental psychology. In D. Kuhn & J. A. Meacham (Eds.), *On the development of developmental psychology.* Basel: Karger.

Moshman, D. (1990). The development of metalogical understanding. In W. F. Overton (Ed.), *Reasoning, necessity, and logic: Developmental perspectives*. Hillsdale, NJ: Erlbaum.

Newell, A. (1980). Physical symbol systems. *Cognition, 4,* 135–183.

Newell, A. (1990). *Unified theories of cognition*. Cambridge, MA: Harvard University Press.

Newell, A., & Simon, H. A. (1972). *Human problem solving*. Englewood Cliffs, NJ: Prentice-Hall.

Overton, W. F., & Newman, J. (1982). Cognitive development: A competence-activation/utilization approach. In T. Field, A. Huston, H. C. Quay, L. Troll, & C. Finley (Eds.), *Review of human development*. New York: Wiley.

Pascual-Leone, J. (1970). A mathematical model for the transition rule in Piaget's developmental stages. *Acta Psychologica, 32,* 301–345.

Pascual-Leone, J. (1980). Constructive problems for constructive theories: The current relevance of Piaget's work and a critique of information-processing simulation psychology. In R. Kluwe & H. Spada (Eds.), *Developmental models of thinking*. New York: Academic.

Pascual-Leone, J. (1984). Attention, dialectic, and mental effort: Toward an organismic theory of life stages. In M. L. Commons, F. A. Richards, & C. Armon (Eds.), *Beyond formal operations: Late adolescent and adult cognitive development*. New York: Praeger.

Perner, J. (1991). *Understanding the representational mind*. Cambridge, MA: MIT Press.

Piaget, J. (1972). Intellectual evolution from adolescence to adulthood. *Human Development, 15,* 1–12.

Piaget, J. (1974). *La prise de conscience* [The grasp of consciousness]. Paris: Presses Universitaires de France.

Piaget, J. (1977). *Recherches sur l'abstraction réfléchissante* [Studies in reflecting abstraction]. Paris: Presses Universitaires de France.

Piaget, J. (1980). *Les formes élémentaires de la dialectique* [Elementary forms of dialectic]. Paris: Gallimard.

Piaget, J. (1985). *The equilibration of cognitive structures: The central problem of intellectual development*. Chicago: University of Chicago Press. (Original work published 1975)

Piaget, J. (1987a). *Possibility and necessity: Vol. 1. The role of possibility in cognitive development*. Minneapolis: University of Minnesota Press. (Original work published 1981)

Piaget, J. (1987b). *Possibility and necessity: Vol. 2. The role of necessity in cognitive development*. Minneapolis: University of Minnesota Press. (Original work published 1983)

Piaget, J., & Henriques, G. (1978). *Recherches sur la généralisation* [Studies in generalization]. Paris: Presses Universitaires de France.

Piaget, J., & Szeminska, A. (1941). *La genèse du nombre chez l'enfant* [The origins of number in children]. Neuchâtel: Delachaux & Niestlé.

Richie, D. M. (1984, June). *On the determination of psychological domains in development*. Paper presented at the annual symposium of the Jean Piaget Society, Philadelphia.

Siegler, R. S., & Jenkins, E. (1989). *How children discover new strategies*. Hillsdale, NJ: Erlbaum.

Turiel, E., & Davidson, P. (1986). Heterogeneity, inconsistency and asynchrony in the development of cognitive structures. In I. Levin (Ed.), *Stage and structure*. Norwood, NJ: Ablex.

Wellman, H. M. (1990). *The child's theory of mind*. Cambridge, MA: MIT Press.

Winograd, T., & Flores, F. (1986). *Understanding computers and cognition*. Norwood, NJ: Ablex.

Wittgenstein, L. (1961). *Tractatus logico-philosophicus*. New York: Humanities Press. (Original work published 1922)

META-PIAGETIAN SOLUTIONS TO EPISTEMOLOGICAL PROBLEMS

Andreas Demetriou, Anastasia Efklides, and Maria Platsidou

Campbell's Commentary has been insightful and, to our satisfaction, provocative. Happily, he directed the discussion to the hot and long-standing issues of our field. Discussion about issues of this kind not unnaturally generates misunderstandings and disagreements, but it may also initiate new ways of looking at the problems, which may lead to better solutions than those we have at present. Thus, in the following pages, we will try to clarify our position on the issues raised by Campbell so as to help remove the misunderstandings and put the disagreements on a basis that would lead to their resolution.

In his Commentary, Campbell focused his analysis on the problems of (*a*) domains, (*b*) reflective abstraction and hypercognition, and (*c*) representation. We will organize our Reply around the same issues.

Domains

Regarding domains, Campbell has raised three important issues: (*a*) What is a domain? (*b*) How are the domains to be identified? (*c*) What happens to domains as they develop?

What Is a Domain?

According to Campbell, the approach to this question that has prevailed in the field of cognitive development since Piaget is an "external one." That is, a field of knowledge, like mathematics or categorization, is theoretically defined by the observer according to a given set of criteria, and then any-thing that satisfies these criteria is considered part of the domain. Campbell does not favor this approach. In his own words, "The perspective that ought to prevail in developmental psychology is an *internal* one, the perspective of the developing organism. Just because an external observer regards cer-tain facts, problems, and phenomena as belonging to the same *field*, it by no means follows that the learner treats these facts, problems, and phenom-ena as belonging to the same *domain*" (p. 173).

We fully endorse this statement, and we are puzzled that Campbell's penetrating eye overlooked the fact that one of our criteria for specifying domains is the principle of subjective equivalence-distinctness. This princi-ple does bring the developing person onto the stage and gives him or her a primary role in the decision process that specifies what does or does not go with what. Indeed, one of the studies presented in this *Monograph* (Study 3), as well as many other studies conducted in our laboratory (Demetriou & Efklides, 1988; Demetriou, Makris, & Adecoya, 1992; Demetriou, Platsidou, Sirmali, & Spanoudis, in preparation; Gonida, 1993), took the perspective of the developing person in order to specify whether the subjective structure of mind bears any resemblance to its objective structure. All these studies indicated clearly that the subjective structure of mind does reflect its objec-tive structure to a considerable extent. To our knowledge, no other labora-tory or theorist has so explicitly adopted this approach.

Campbell also points out that the assumption about big domains, like our SSSs or Gardner's (1983) intelligences, may be incompatible with the fact that skills in very narrowly defined fields of expertise, like procedural programming, do not transfer to other very similar fields, like object-oriented programming. According to Campbell, "Such a mosaic of tiny do-mains cannot be reconciled with the broadly based approach unless domains have some kind of hierarchical or network organization" (p. 176). But this is precisely our definition of domains. It is clearly stated in the discussion that "the mind is conceived by us as a network of relations connecting the intellectual units into systems that are functional vis-à-vis the demands of specific environments" (p. 127). The units may range from as basic a level as a single mental act specific to categorization, quantification, causation, etc. to as global a level as a personal theory for good and bad people, family expenditures relative to the family's yearly income, the role that desires and beliefs play in the causation of human behavior, etc. Thus, our SSSs are very broad attraction systems that, once activated by environmental or internal stimuli, orient the person how to connect with this or that domain of the world. In other words, these systems are dynamic multilayered and multidi-mensional entities that involve very general, ever-present core operators, subfield operators, and processing skills as well as the products of their past operations. These products are conceptions and misconceptions, beliefs and

misbeliefs, ideas and ideals, about the world with which the person is interacting. That is, we view our SSSs as the means through which people construct foundational theories about the physical, the biological, the psychological, and the social world (see Wellman & Gelman, 1992). Specifically,
each of these theories is seen as the product of the combined functioning
of more than one SSS. Thus, although transfer is more easily attainable
within rather than across subfields (like those already specified in the *Monograph* for each of the five SSSs), it is never automatic. To be attained, it
requires the individual to work out how the core and the subfield-specific
operators and skills, together with the foundational theories to which the
SSS is related etc., will be adapted to the new situation. This requires time
and effort, and it would probably be impossible if there were no systems,
like our SSSs, to provide pathways to this adaptation.

How Are the Domains to Be Identified?

Campbell points out in his Commentary that, although the methods
that we employed in the, *Monograph* may be able to show that two sets of
abilities, like those required to design an experiment and those required to
specify a proportional relation, do not belong to the same domain, they are
not able to show what else goes in each of the domains. We are in full
agreement with this comment. In fact, the primary aim of the studies presented in the *Monograph* was to show that the domains and the principles
specified by the theory are indeed distinct from each other and that they
do operate as organizational forces of mind; it was not our aim to map in
detail what is included in each of the domains. This has been done in a
series of other studies, either published (see Demetriou, Efklides, Papadaki,
Papantoniou, & Economou, 1993; Demetriou, Platsidou, Efklides, Metallidou, & Shayer, 1991) or still in progress (Demetriou & Efklides, in preparation; Efklides, 1991; Langford, Demetriou, Efklides, & Kordas, 1993).

In any case, however, we fully agree with Campbell that we need to
use converging evidence generated by different methods before we come
to final decisions about the boundaries between subdomains, main domains
like our SSSs, or even broader domains like Gardner's (1983) intelligences
or Turiel and Davidson's (1985) realms and specify their relations. The
psychometric-like methods that we adopted in this *Monograph* are no more
than starting methods. To use an analogy from astronomy, these methods
function like a global telescope, which may show that, very far out in space,
there are signs of unknown galaxies. Astronomy has been very successful
in developing maps of the universe on the basis of information generated
by its own global telescopes because to be global does not imply that the
information provided is false. However, in order to know the galaxies better, we need other methods that would enable us first to verify that they do

exist and then to zoom in on them in order to see the stars, the planets, and the satellites they comprise.

To return from space to mind, we would be happy if cross-cultural studies would verify the presence of the various SSSs and their components in different cultures. It needs to be mentioned here that our studies in this regard have been very encouraging. Specifically, a study by Demetriou et al. (1992) has shown that three of the SSSs, namely, the causal-experimental, the quantitative-relational, and the spatial-imaginal, are structured in the same way in both Greece and Nigeria and conceived as such by the thinking subjects themselves. Other studies (Demetriou, Pachaury, & Metallidou, 1993) have shown that the componential composition of one SSS, the quantitative-relational, is the same in India as in Greece, although there are differences between cultures in the relative strength of the different components. We would also be happy if we were able to test the theory on very young infants. This would show whether, as we would predict, the same SSSs obtain before the advent of language and formal education. Computer simulation studies would provide a hard test of the computational specificity of each of the SSSs. Finally, neuropsychological studies, like those recently published by Thacher (1992), would indicate whether the SSSs are hard wired or, in Pylyshyn's (1984) terms, present only at the level of functional architecture.

We do not agree with Campbell, however, that we "have not progressed beyond a priori distinctions based on familiar and plausible ways of dividing up fields of knowledge" (p. 175). We would argue that we offer a theory of domain delimitation (the system of organizational principles) and a theory of domains (the five SSSs and their composition) that go beyond earlier theories in at least two respects. First, although it is about structure, the theory places emphasis on process (see the principle of computational specificity) and representation (see the principle of symbolic bias). Thus, it enables one to focus on the dynamic-procedural aspects of structures. No one, ourselves included, has even attempted to pinpoint and model the procedural and representational differences of the domains. Admittedly, earlier research and theorizing has recognized and dealt with one or another of the domains specified by our theory. However, their aim was to construct not a theory of domains but a theory that would demonstrate that the domains are apparent only as they reduce to the same underlying grand structure (see the analysis of V-models in the introduction to this *Monograph* and elsewhere and in Demetriou & Efklides, 1988). True, some psychometric theories of intelligence, like Thurstone's (1938) theory of primary mental abilities, Cattell's (1971) theory of fluid and crystallized intelligence, or Vernon's (1979) hierarchical theory, have gone further than cognitive developmental theories in identifying domains and levels in the organization of intellect. However, for reasons that cannot be discussed here because of

space limitations, these theories confounded the domain-general components of intelligence either with its really specialized domains (Thurstone,
e.g., placed memory and arithmetic or spatial abilities on the same organizational level) or with the various culturally defined manifestations of the
different domains. In any case, these theories were devoid of developmental
or processing concerns. Thus, they have had no story to tell about what
develops, when, how, and why it develops, how it functions now and then,
and how development propagates from unit to unit. We offer our theory
as a start of the journey in this labyrinth, and we are pleased to mention
that, ironically, Campbell (personal communication, June 4, 1993) himself
admitted that, were he to model different domains, he would have to model
object representation, space and time, mathematical knowledge, and categorization—that is, by and large, our domains.

What Happens to Domains as They Develop?

To move to Campbell's third question, we are tempted to make a strong
and—to the satisfaction of our Popperian colleagues—falsifiable statement.
Our domains do not change with development. They are always there as a response to the structure of the world. Certainly, the functioning of their core
operations becomes more skillful and refined, and new operations may be
generated in each as a result of development. Moreover, new relations may
be established both *within* and *across* SSSs, and, of course, the products of
their functioning do become increasingly richer, old products get forgotten
or abolished, etc. The mapping of the process has barely started.

Reflective Abstraction and Hypercognition

Campbell developed his analysis of our hypercognitive system in the
framework of the theory of knowing levels that he has proposed with Bickhard (Campbell & Bickhard, 1986). This theory is built on the assumption
that knowing is basically irreflexive. That is, a knowing system cannot know
itself unless a part of this system can be differentiated and broken away
from the mother system so as to be raised to a higher level. This new level
can then interact with (and reflect on) and thus know the lower-level system.
Campbell and Bickhard ascribe this differentiating function to Piagetian
reflective abstraction. Thus, in their theory, the knowing that characterizes
a given level L can become known only at the subsequent level $L + 1$;
according to Campbell, "genuinely reflective knowledge must be 'meta': it
must come after what it is about, and it must belong to a higher level of
knowing" (p. 131). In the theory presented in this *Monograph*, the assumption is made "that self-understanding and -management come before, or

concurrently with, cognition as well" (p. 21). Hence, our preference for the term "hypercognition" over the term "metacognition." According to Campbell, "the very substitution of hypercognition for metacognition constitutes a rejection of knowing levels" (p. 182) because, in his theory, the knowing levels must be clearly distinct from each other. In so doing, he claims, we remain, like other neo-Piagetians, without a meaning-making executive because knowing implies hierarchically differentiated levels.

We readily accept that there is a difference here between our theory and the knowing-levels model of Campbell and Bickhard. Specifically, Campbell and Bickhard's model is actually a V-model. That is, it describes development as a series of four major knowing levels that basically coincide with Piaget's major stages plus at least one postformal stage. Thus, this model, as the genuine V-model that it is, does not need to invoke a system of self-understanding and -management to guide problem-solving behavior because the single knowing system available at any given level will be activated and applied to the input. Consciousness will come as a by-product of the movement to the next level, which comes about via nonconscious differentiation of a subsystem from the present system. In other words, Campbell insists on viewing only one of the sides of awareness: that is, that awareness about a given activity, process, or function of a given level L must by definition come after this activity, process, or function has been executed; it must come at level L + something. However, Campbell underestimates the possibility that, once attained, awareness of any level may contribute retroactively to the reorganization of both the level L, the level L + something, and it may also proactively affect the formation of the subsequent levels.

In our theory, self-guidance is needed because cognition is by definition multistructural and multidimensional. Furthermore, levels are not of the Piagetian or neo-Piagetian variety—that is, global and long lasting. They may be very specific (i.e., related to the state of an SSS-specific component) and very short in duration. We have argued in the *Monograph* and elsewhere (Demetriou et al., 1991; Demetriou et al., 1993) that development is basically continuous because it is the result of an unceasing interplay between mental units having slightly diverging functional efficiencies. Thus, in our theory, as in Campbell's formulation, level 1 may become known only at level 2, and this may be knowable at level 3. However, levels 1, 2, and 3 may all be attainable over a period of days, if not hours, not over long phases of our life. Therefore, in our theory, there may be a continuous interplay between cognitions and metacognitions because metacognitions may just be transient states of mind and feelings generated by other, albeit associated, states of mind, feelings, etc. That is, in our theory, self-monitoring and self-guidance are not identified with explicit awareness as in Campbell's model. There are many levels of mental experiences of which the individual is aware both

197

prior to and after reflective awareness. The basic questions to be answered are how awareness is formed at different age levels and how the levels of awareness interact with cognition and hypercognition itself.

Of course, Campbell does offer a solution to the problem of process selection. This is the clear distinction between learning, which makes the selection, and reflective abstraction, which generates awareness. In his view, successive learning trials generate "a constructive topology, a space of near-ness and farness relations between possible learning trials. What is closer in the topology to what has already been tried is more likely to be tried next" (p. 179). We do accept this formulation. In fact, four of our organizational principles (i.e., domain specificity, computational specificity, symbolic bias, and developmental variation) aim to explicate the forces that constrain how an initially blind variation and selection process results in a stable and law-abiding constructive topology that is more or less the same across persons and environments. According to our theory, the loci and subloci in this topology are our SSSs and SSS-specific components. However, the construc-tion of this topology generates experiences about how to relate to the differ-ent aspects of the environment that must somehow be useful to and usable by the individual more or less at the time they are acquired and not many years later, that is, when the person will get into the Piagetian formal opera-tional stage, as Piaget (1974) clearly stated and Campbell seems to accept. That is, as formulated in our principle of subjective distinctness and equiva-lence, a product of interactive learning is learning about intelligence, the mind, and the self. Were this learning to wait for many years to become usable by the person, interactive learning would actually be blind and, there-fore, not really interactive: it would simply be a copying process. We assume that Campbell would not like to see interactivism drifting toward empiricism via supposedly interactive processes!

Representation

According to Campbell, all previous theories of cognition in general and cognitive development in particular, Piaget's theory included, fell into the trap of encodingism. That is, they regarded knowledge as involving structures of mental entities and transformations that somehow correspond to organizations of real entities and transformations that exist in the envi-ronment. The knowledge structures acquire and preserve their meaning through a series of encodings that define the meaning of mental entities and transformations in reference to other mental entities and transforma-tions that have a well-specified meaning for the subject and that therefore can be used as codes. The problem with this interpretation of knowledge is that it leads to infinite regress, for reasons analyzed in the *Monograph* and in Campbell's Commentary. Therefore, the argument goes, any theory that succumbs to encodingism is, by definition, a deficient model of knowledge and representation. Thus, an alternative approach is needed. Campbell adopts Bickhard's view "that mental representation is at root *interactive*. Given a goal-directed system that is able to interact with an environment, the internal final states of the system differentiate and implicitly define the type of environment interacted with" (p. 184). That is, differentiable and thus recognizable knowledge resides in the patterns of interaction qua interaction with the different domains of the environment.

Campbell recognizes that our theory adopts a minimally interactive interpretation of representation so that it does not succumb to encodingism. On the other hand, however, he believes that our interpretation of representation is not interactive enough and that it therefore needs further development in this direction. In his view, three reasons are responsible for this state of affairs. First, the encodingism conception of knowledge is very old and strong and thus so much ingrained in our thought that it is difficult for one to resist thinking in its terms. Second, our SSSs are too large to constitute domains that would direct the knowledge-abstracting interactions. Third, our assumption about the operation of processing constraints on cognitive functioning and development directs the analysis of representations to countable units that are somehow encoded and related to each other, and thus it biases the modeling of cognitive processes to an encoding approach. We will respond briefly to each of the "accusations."

Whatever progress has been made in our understanding of cognitive organization, functioning, and development has resulted from approaches that interpreted knowledge as systems of encodings. This is not without serious justification. The interpretation of knowledge as involving systems of variably related encodings has the unique advantage that it permits an analytic approach to the structures of knowledge. In our view, this is precisely the characteristic of this approach that opened the way for the scientific study of knowledge structures. Neither Piaget nor Newell and Simon would have been able to go as far as they went without adopting such an approach *at the time they started.* Thus, we do not think that we have to feel guilty for not entirely breaking away from a tradition that proved so fruitful and fertile. The question is whether there is now insufficient harvest to be had from this old tradition, indicating that it is time to work for the creation of a new tradition. We believe that the time seems ripe for such a movement. Interactivism as defined in the discussion of the *Monograph*, in Campbell's Commentary, and elsewhere (see the references in the Commentary) is a good start. But we still have to bear clearly in mind that, at some phase in the process of defining interactive structures, we will need to see how they are interrelated, interchanged, and interdefined either in the same mind or by different minds that need to communicate with each other, such as the mind of a teacher and the mind of a student or a human mind and an artificial mind. In that case, an encodingism approach seems unavoidable, at least as a method of analysis. This will be all the more necessary as we move from a plain change in epistemological orientation to the use of new methods in the study of the organization and development of conceptual networks, such as the connectionist methods recently used by Halford (1993). In other words, we will need to study encoding processes and the interaction of mental codes even after throwing encodingism away.

The complaint that our SSSs are too large to constitute domains is not actually relevant. We did not propose our SSSs because we liked them. They originated as descriptions, and subsequently (together with the principles) they were intended as explanations of empirically observed patterns of co-variation that could not be accounted for by any other of the extant models of cognitive organization. Thus, if our field is to make any progress in the understanding of the structure of mind, it would have to take our SSSs as something to be better mapped and understood rather than as something to like or dislike. More important still, our SSSs must *not* be considered as the only unit of analysis. They are, as has already been mentioned and as Campbell would like them to be, "vast complex distributed networks." Thus, the unit of analysis can be either lower or higher than an SSS, depending on the researcher's focus. In any case, anything in any SSS, however complex or abstract it finally becomes, leans on an intuitor, that is, on a genuine interactive construct, rich with meaning, that at a given moment in time bridged the person with a given, very specific—at that moment—pattern of properties and relations in a given environment. Thus, the task of the interactivists and the encodingists alike is to understand how these intuitors get differentiated, intertwined, and, to return to Piaget, sometimes reciprocally assimilated to form dynamic fields of mind, that is, units like our SSS-specific components and the SSSs themselves.

Campbell recognizes that cognitive functioning and development may be constrained by the operation of a processing system such as the system proposed by other neo-Piagetians and ourselves. His objection is that further progress depends on a more dynamic definition of working memory that would enable us to understand how situations are represented qua situations, that is, as interactive networks rather than as single units. This is so because "memory is not a storage bin but an arrangement of reconstructive processes" (personal communication, June 4, 1993). We would of course have no objection to a more dynamic definition of the window to self-monitoring and awareness. However, we have to bear in mind that this construct proved useful in our attempt to understand why humans fail on certain cognitive tasks and succeed on others precisely because it itself could be quantified in some way and thus subsequently used as a measure of task complexity and, by implication, as a measure of cognitive complexity. Therefore, even if defined as an arrangement of reconstructive processes, we would still need to find a yardstick for measuring the complexity of arrangements of this kind and the load that they pose on the system. We need to have this yardstick because understanding the human processing system in general and the storage system in particular is no more than a means to the end of understanding how meaning is made at the level of real-life situations. Therefore, even if Campbell were able to offer us this yardstick, and we believe that he is, we have to remember that he is offering us a more inclusive unit of analysis that can still somehow be decomposed into the smaller units we want to abandon. Of course, such a more inclusive unit may be indispensable if we are going to understand why two problems that are made to involve the same number of working memory units but that belong to two different SSSs, other factors being constant, do not pose the same load on the thinker. It might be the case that, as arrangements à la Campbell, these units do not consume the available resources in the same way. This is made all the more probable by evidence indicating that there may be more than one kind of short-term storage or even processing systems (see Baddeley, 1991) that specialize in the representation of information coming from different sensory modalities, such as the visual and the auditory. An exciting prospect in this regard is to test how and in what proportions each of the SSSs makes use of the different storage systems that may exist and how the relations between the different SSSs and the storage systems change with development.

But this is already another story, and we will give our version of it very soon. We would be delighted if Campbell would offer us his own version too. But we have to bear in mind that these stories will be *meta*-Piagetian rather than *neo*-Piagetian. That is, our new stories will assert that knowledge and development are considerably different from what the giant was ready or willing to envisage.

References

Baddeley, A. (1991). *Working memory*. Oxford: Oxford University Press.
Campbell, R. L., & Bickhard, M. H. (1986). *Knowing levels and developmental stages*. Basel: Karger.
Cattell, R. B. (1971). *Abilities: Their structure, growth, and action*. Boston: Houghton Mifflin.
Demetriou, A., & Efklides, A. (1988). Experiential structuralism and neo-Piagetian theories: Toward an integrated model. In A. Demetriou (Ed.), *The neo-Piagetian theories of cognitive development: Toward an integration*. Amsterdam: North-Holland.
Demetriou, A., & Efklides, A. (in preparation). Networks of relations within and between specialised structural systems during cognitive development.
Demetriou, A., Efklides, A., Papadaki, M., Papantoniou, G., & Economou, A. (1993). Structure and development of causal-experimental thought: From early adolescence to youth. *Developmental Psychology*, **29**, 480–497.
Demetriou, A., Makris, N., & Adecoya, J. (1992, July). *Metacognitive awareness about the*

structure of mind in Greece and Nigeria. Paper presented at the twenty-fifth International Congress of Psychology, Brussels.

Demetriou, A., Pachaury, A., & Metallidou, Y. (1993). *Universals and specificities in the structure and development of quantitative-relational thought: A cross-cultural study in Greece and India.* Manuscript submitted for publication.

Demetriou, A., Platsidou, M., Efklides, A., Metallidou, Y., & Shayer, M. (1991). The development of quantitative-relational abilities from childhood to adolescence: Structure, scaling, and individual differences. *Learning and Instruction: The Journal of the European Association for Research in Learning and Instruction,* **1,** 19–43.

Demetriou, A., Platsidou, M., Sirmali, K., & Spanoudis, G. (in preparation). *Networks of relations between dimensions of processing capacity, specialised structural systems, and hypercognition: A longitudinal study.*

Efklides, A. (1991, August). *Cognitive and metacognitive aspects of propositional reasoning abilities.* Paper presented at the fourth European Conference for Research on Learning and Instruction, Turku, Finland.

Gardner, H. (1983). *Frames of mind: The theory of multiple intelligences.* New York: Basic.

Gonida, S. E. (1993, May). *Cognitive and metacognitive dimensions of deductive and inductive thought.* Paper presented at the fourth Hellenic Conference for Psychological Research, Thessaloniki.

Halford, G. S. (1993). *Children's understanding: The development of mental models.* Hillsdale, NJ: Erlbaum.

Langford, P., Demetriou, A., Efklides, A., & Kordas, D. (1993, May). *Dimensions of reasoning with hypothetical propositions and their relations with the SSSs of experiential structuralism.* Paper presented at the fourth Hellenic Conference for Psychological Research, Thessaloniki.

Piaget, J. (1974). *The grasp of consciousness: Action and concept in the young child.* Cambridge, MA: Harvard University Press.

Pylyshyn, Z. (1984). *Computation and cognition.* Cambridge, MA: Bradford/MIT Press.

Thacher, R. W. (1992). Cyclic cortical reorganization during early childhood. *Brain and Cognition,* **20,** 24–50.

Thurstone, L. L. (1938). Primary mental abilities. *Psychometric Monographs,* No. 1. Chicago: University of Chicago Press.

Turiel, E., & Davidson, P. (1985). Heterogeneity, inconsistency, and asynchrony in the development of cognitive structures. In I. Levin (Ed.), *Stage and structure: Reopening the debate.* Norwood, NJ: Ablex.

Vernon, P. E. (1979). *Intelligence: Heredity and environment.* San Francisco: Freeman.

Wellman, H. M., & Gelman, S. A. (1992). Cognitive development: Foundational theories of core domains. *Annual Review of Psychology,* **43,** 337–375.

CONTRIBUTORS

Andreas Demetriou (Ph.D. 1983, Aristotelian University of Thessaloniki, Greece) is acting professor of psychology in the Department of Psychology, Aristotelian University of Thessaloniki, and currently the editor of *Psychology: The Journal of the Hellenic Psychological Society.* His research focuses on cognitive development throughout the life span. He has published or edited several books and monographs, including *The Neo-Piagetian Theories of Cognitive Development Go to School: Implications and Applications for Education* (1992).

Anastasia Efklides (Ph.D. 1983, Aristotelian University of Thessaloniki, Greece) is acting professor of psychology in the Department of Psychology, Aristotelian University of Thessaloniki. Her research interests are related to cognitive development, reasoning, metacognition, comprehension of mathematical notions, and the interaction of motivational and cognitive factors in performance. She has published or edited a number of books, including *Cognitive Psychology* (in Greek).

Maria Platsidou is a Ph.D. candidate in the Department of Psychology, Aristotelian University of Thessaloniki. Her research interests are related to developmental psychology, especially cognitive development, from childhood to adolescence.

Robert L. Campbell (Ph.D. 1986, University of Texas at Austin) is an assistant professor of psychology at Clemson University in Clemson, South Carolina. From 1985 to 1991, he was a research staff member at the IBM Thomas J. Watson Research Center in Hawthorne, New York. His research interests include the philosophy of psychology, cognitive and developmental theory, mathematical development in children, moral development, and the acquisition of expertise by adults. He is currently translating a chapter from Piaget's *Études sociologiques.*

STATEMENT OF EDITORIAL POLICY

The *Monographs* series is intended as an outlet for major reports of developmental research that generate authoritative new findings and use these to foster a fresh and/or better-integrated perspective on some conceptually significant issue or controversy. Submissions from programmatic research projects are particularly welcome; these may consist of individually or group-authored reports of findings from some single large-scale investigation or of a sequence of experiments centering on some particular question. Multiauthored sets of independent studies that center on the same underlying question can also be appropriate; a critical requirement in such instances is that the various authors address common issues and that the contribution arising from the set as a whole be both unique and substantial. In essence, irrespective of how it may be framed, any work that contributes significant data and/or extends developmental thinking will be taken under editorial consideration.

Submissions should contain a minimum of 80 manuscript pages (including tables and references); the upper limit of 150–175 pages is much more flexible (please submit four copies; a copy of every submission and associated correspondence is deposited eventually in the archives of the SRCD). Neither membership in the Society for Research in Child Development nor affiliation with the academic discipline of psychology are relevant; the significance of the work in extending developmental theory and in contributing new empirical information is by far the most crucial consideration. Because the aim of the series is not only to advance knowledge on specialized topics but also to enhance cross-fertilization among disciplines or subfields, it is important that the links between the specific issues under study and larger questions relating to developmental processes emerge as clearly to the general reader as to specialists on the given topic.

Potential authors who may be unsure whether the manuscript they are planning would make an appropriate submission are invited to draft an outline of what they propose and send it to the Editor for assessment.

This mechanism, as well as a more detailed description of all editorial policies, evaluation processes, and format requirements, is given in the "Guidelines for the Preparation of *Monographs* Submissions," which can be obtained by writing to the Editor designate, Rachel K. Clifton, Department of Psychology, University of Massachusetts, Amherst, MA 01003.